GETTING A JOB AFTER

50

GETTING A JOB AFTER 50

JOHN S. MORGAN

LIBERTY HOUSE®

LIBERTY HOUSE books are published by LIBERTY HOUSE, a division of TAB BOOKS Inc. Its trademark, consisting of the words "LIBERTY HOUSE" and the portrayal of Benjamin Franklin, is registered in the United States Patent and Trademark Office.

First Edition
First Printing

© 1990 by TAB BOOKS Inc.
Printed in the United States of America

Library of Congress Cataloging-in-Publication Data

Morgan, John Smith, 1921-
  Getting a job after 50.
  Bibliography: p.
  1. Age and employment—United States. 2. Job
hunting—United States. I. Title. II. Title: Getting
a job after fifty.
  HD6280.M58 1987
  650.1'4'024056
  ISBN 0-89433-311-9

87-25804
CIP

TAB BOOKS Inc. offers software for sale
For information and a catalog, please contact:

TAB Software Department
Blue Ridge Summit, PA 17294-0850

Questions regarding the content of this book
should be addressed to:

Reader Inquiry Branch
TAB BOOKS Inc.
Blue Ridge Summit, PA 17294-0214

Cover photograph by Susan Riley, Harrisonburg, Virginia.

CONTENTS

1

Tomorrow, Life and Work Begin at 50

You know them—for example, Jack. At 69, he operates a tiny silver-replating shop in suburban Pittsburgh "to keep busy." Until he sold out in his sixty-fifth year, he ran a successful metal-refinishing business in the city. He now bitterly regrets that decision.

Consider George. He took early retirement from a publisher of a national magazine. "With my savings, pension and a supplement for the Social Security I will begin getting at age 62, I have no financial worries." Yet he developed concerns of another kind. At 59, he finally admitted to himself that he had become an alcoholic. He joined Alcoholics Anonymous, but then contracted diabetes. By the time he regained psychological and medical stability, he was 61. He won back the stability by going to work part-time for a suburban weekly in Connecticut.

Helena joined the ranks of the underemployed, too. At the insistence of her retired husband who's six years older than she, she retired early at 62 from her vice-presidency at a bank. A year later, she opened an antique shop. "It at least passes the time and is clearing out my house."

America faces a new phenomenon—an estimated 18 million seniors (50 or older) who are underemployed or unemployed. They want work or more work, but can't find it. This is a tragic waste which society and the economy cannot afford, which distresses the victims, and which is largely unnecessary.

At least half of the 18 million consists of underemployed seniors, according to the Andrus Gerontology Center of the University of Southern California, which made the estimate in 1984.

Louis Harris & Associates polled middle managers at 600 corporations for *Business Week* in mid-1986. Among the questions asked was: When a company lays off or buys out salaried employees, which group of workers do you think has the most trouble adjusting? Seventy-eight percent believed those in their 50s or older suffered the most; 17 percent answered those in their 40s. The remaining 5 percent were not sure or picked those in their 30s.

A study directed by Margaret Ensminger at the Johns Hopkins School of Public Health of 360 senior men and women culled from the Baltimore unemployment rolls compared them with a group of working seniors. Most studies of the psychiatric effects of joblessness show that it affects women more negatively than men. This study indicates it troubles both sexes about the same, and suggests that one impact of unemployment is on family relationships.

Unemployed men in the study were more likely to live alone and less likely to be married than employed men. Among the unemployed of both sexes, those who were married were more likely to go back to work than those unmarried, but jobless women were less likely to return to work than men.

You *Can* Find a Satisfactory Job

As an underemployed or unemployed senior, you can get work that satisfies you. Finding the right job may not be as easy as when you were younger, but it also may be easier than you think.

Robert O. Snelling, Sr., who heads the nationwide employment agency of Snelling & Snelling, says, "We are in the midst of an opportunity explosion the like of which mankind has never before seen. Get with it . . . There is a job in the United States today for everybody who really wants to work. Yes, and a 'future'."

The task of finding a job when you're 50 or older is different than when you were younger, although there are similarities of course. Often, the major difference is a changing psychological outlook, which Henry Adams calls "the Indian Summer of life." In his *The Education of Henry Adams*, he says it "should become sunny and a little sad, like the season and infinite in wealth and depth of tone—but never hustled."

That's the ideal, of course. Too frequently, unemployed and underemployed seniors find themselves hustled. They are more than a little sad and do not consider themselves wealthy. Above all, they have done a little tentative job-probing and are shocked at the differences they find in jobhunting now and a quarter-century ago.

Among the many differences they must learn to cope with are overcoming the stigma of failure that unnecessarily plagues many seniors, sidestepping biases against age, and offsetting the disadvantage of time. We will deal with these in reverse order.

Offsetting Time

Some employers suffer from a mindset concerning lifetime employment. They let the wish father the thought. They *hope* the people they hire will stay with them for many years because hiring the right new person is almost as traumatic for the hirer as for the hiree. Such employers suffer from the delusion that the younger the person they hire, the longer he or she will stay with them.

A lifelong job in the U.S. is no longer common. The average American holds eight different jobs in his or her lifetime. To hold even more is not unheard of. If a person works 40 years overall, he or she will have labored on average just five years for one employer. If you're job-hunting at 50, you can offer the prospect of working 15 years for the new employer, triple the average tenure.

The essence of successful job-seeking for seniors is to ignore time by presenting yourself as a solution to a problem—to make the employer want you as much as, or more than, you want the employer.

Nobody claims such a tactic is easy, so the rest of this book delves into techniques for spotting problems and devising solutions for them that involve your expertise. "Expertise" is the operative word. It's the main asset that you have to sell. Most of you possess more varied and deeper expertise than you suspect. Time works to your advantage with expertise by allowing you the opportunity to develop it. How to analyze and market your own experience-honed abilities also awaits deeper discussion later.

Side-stepping Prejudice

So pernicious are the biases against age that we'll devote Chapter 5 to how to deal with the problem. Now, we can say that prejudice against age in hiring is as severe as against minorities and women.

The bias against seniority in the U.S. has historical support. In the early nineteenth century, Henry David Thoreau, Ralph Waldo Emerson, Herman Melville, Walt Whitman, Thomas Jefferson and the historian Francis Parkman extolled youth and denigrated age.

Don't count much on laws against such attitudes. Rely on yourself to think so creatively and to act so vigorously that your age becomes irrelevant in the mind of the potential employer. Keep in mind that Thoreau, the most outspoken in his praise of youth, died at the age of 45.

The Stigma of Failure

Before we can cope successfully with prejudice and time, we need to deal with the stigma of failure that devastates so many unemployed and underemployed seniors.

"Outplacement" is the currently popular euphemism for placing people out. In plain English, this too frequently means kicking seniors out, but helping them with a dash of compassion to look for another job. Unfortunately, outplacement often helps the conscience of the former employer more than it aids the person who is let go. Outplacement, early retirement, quitting—too often they mean "fired," and that word carries a heavier load of guilt than most of us can shoulder.

Says George Bowers who heads a search firm of that name and who deals with scores of job-seeking seniors every year, "The biggest problem the older jobless people have is loss of confidence. It affects their attitudes, image-projection and mental acuity—often to dramatic degrees. When they get let out by companies such as Eastman Kodak, AT&T, DuPont or Rockwell, it's as though the Rockies were crumbling. Their world and self-perception crumbles, too."

Until a senior who suffers from such a loss in confidence recovers his equilibrium, the odds are strongly against his finding a new job. So, the first step in recovery is to realize that you are more a victim of your times than of your own shortcomings. As in other abnormal eras such as the Great Depression, forces outside of you tend to direct your fate. In finding a new job, you must realize this, both for your own psychological stability and for the strategies you employ in your search.

Getting fired isn't the career blemish it used to be, says Lee-Hecht & Associates, an outplacement firm. Amid the rush of mergers, "white-collar layoffs have been so widespread, we're seeing a positive change in corporate attitudes toward the executive who is unemployed."

Although America is the first nation to face the phenomenon of widespread senior unemployment and underemployment, Western Europe and Japan will soon follow because the same conditions that caused this development here exist there, too. Of the many factors that contribute to the problem, three stand out:

1. An Economy That Is Being Restructured

The nation is restructuring from smokestack to service and other forms of employment, resulting in a fallout of more seniors who, many employers mistakenly think, do not fit into new patterns as well as younger members of the workforce. We shall see later that older employees may fit *better* than younger people into many of the newer jobs, but the fallacious perception persists to the detriment of seniors.

While employers don't like to discuss it publicly, they usually reduce their immediate payroll costs when they let seniors go because most of them command higher compensation than the people who replace them. Yet, this is in an accounting rather than a real sense. Under most accounting procedures, a pension is not a current cost because it already has been accrued and paid for and permitted as a business expense against income taxes. If the expense of the pension and the compensation of the person who replaces the pensioner were added, the total cost in nearly every case would far exceed the compensation of the original job-holder.

The effects of restructuring and accounting quirks can be seen in some dramatic figures. In 1935, the Depression year when Social Security began, 11 people were in the workforce for every one on Social Security (then only at age 65, but now permitted at 62 on a reduced basis). The ratio is 3.5:1 now and will drop to 2.5:1 in the next decade if eligibility rules remain unchanged.

Partly because of this, the American economy is under extreme pressure to produce the goods and services needed to support itself. We are importing steadily increasing quantities of steel, automobiles and a myriad of other goods because we have partly passed such products by as a result of our high wages that enable lower-paying countries to outcompete with us.

We are changing, in the words of Peter Drucker, from muscle workers to knowledge workers. In this transition, seniors are bearing the brunt of the pains of change. Today's unemployment and underemployment differ significantly from that during the 1930s. Then, joblessness hit younger production people the hardest because the demand for the products they made didn't exist. Now the demand does exist, but it's supplied increasingly from overseas or by robots and other forms of automation that don't require as many people as formerly. There and in the offices where computers and other technological marvels make many white-collar people obsolete, seniors are the first to go.

This happens partly because some employers believe (mistakenly) that seniors can't cope with the technology and partly because of an ironic example of compassion. Since many seniors do get a (reduced) pension if they retire at 55 or even earlier in the case of military and other government employees, the employers think seniors won't "suffer" as younger people would if let go. How wrong they are!

2. The Population Ages

In 1883, Prince Otto von Bismarck set 65 as the age when a person would become eligible in Germany for a social security pension. He had consulted with industrialists in his empire and was told that 65 was supportable for their private pension plans. So, that became the magic age in his country. It was adopted by the 12 private pension plans that existed in the United States by 1900, including American Express Company's (the first) and B&O Railroad's (the second). The age was adopted for the Social Security system when it went into effect in 1935. It is now inextricably woven into our social fabric, despite the fact that it is obsolete by more than a century.

By the year 2030, aging trends will have produced a U.S. population with the highest percentage of older persons in recorded history. However, an average American today of 75 is probably equal in physical stamina and mental acuity to a person of some 60 years a century or less ago. This is due to improvements in medicine, public health, diet, and a consciousness of the importance of physical fitness which have dramatically increased longevity. When historians look back at the accomplishments of our era, longevity may outweigh all others. That's exciting, but disturbing, too, for those of us who happen to be 50 or older now. The double-edged sword cuts us more sharply than younger people because many of us seniors have not yet learned how best to use the priceless gift of a longer life. That often includes the seniors who could employ us.

The expectation of life at birth for the total population in the U.S. reached an all-time high of 74.5 years in 1982, according to life tables prepared by the Metropolitan Life Insurance Company. Both males and females shared in this record. Life expectancy for newborn males rose to 70.7 years while the expectation of life at birth for newborn females increased to 78.2 years.

Demographers knew that women outlive men but ignored the fact when Social Security came into being in 1935 because the number of women in the workforce was negligible. Now, about half of our workforce is female, but their greater longevity is still not factored into the workings of most public or private pension plans.

Women's greater longevity and participation in the workforce make both male and female seniors' efforts to find satisfactory work more complex. Once, a senior male had to compete chiefly with younger males; now, he must compete with both men and women of nearly all ages. Once, a senior female didn't even work at a paying job; now, she must compete with men and women of all ages and the double bias against her sex *and* age.

3. Earlier Retirement

More and more employers are using the early retirement provisions in their pension plans. Almost every time you pick up a newspaper, you see examples. DuPont, USX (U.S. Steel), Rockwell International and Time are cases among many private employers who do this. President Reagan has attempted to do the same in federal employment. Proud of its no-layoff policy, even the Hewlett-Packard Company offered early retirement enticements to 1,800 in mid-1986.

The first burst in early retirement came during the inflation-recession spells of the late 1970s when employers began making older workers lucrative offers to ease them out to make the books appear that they had cut labor costs. By the 1990s, when the aging baby-boomer generation begins pressuring for senior corporate jobs, the urgency will swell so much that early retirees of 50 will become increasingly common. This belief is held by many gerontologists, including William Crown of the Policy Center on Aging at Brandeis University.

Employers are doing more than encouraging early retirement. They are recognizing the economies of contracting out work to experienced hands at what amounts to bargain rates. First Chicago Corporation, a bank holding company, increasingly contracts with senior professionals for property-management, architectural and design work that its staff once handled. William Crandall runs a company called The Corporate Staff that provides employers with senior people competent to fill managerial or professional slots on a short-term basis. His clients pay up to the hourly equivalent of $100,000 a year for this executive help. He recruits his "associates" from among the estimated 500,000 executives who have been displaced in corporate America from 1982 to 1987. J.R. Hipple, executive director of Operation Able, a Boston group that helps seniors find jobs, says that employers will increasingly provide options that are not full-time, such as temporary work and projects. This is a logical outgrowth of the already-established trend whereby organizations provide "temps" in narrower fields such as secretarial, accounting, and nursing.

Of those who return to the labor force, about half will stay in the same field, says Linda George, Professor of Sociology at Duke University. The other half of the returning seniors will try something completely different—teachers becoming real estate agents, executives running charter cruises, lawyers developing low-cost housing, managers turning their hobbies into successful businesses such as furniture repairing or guided fishing junkets.

Dual-worker families continue to surge, growing in number by 570,000 through the first three-quarters of 1985 to 22.4 million, reports the Labor

Department. Although this development cushions the impact of unemployment on a senior, it raises complications, too. The unemployed spouse feels psychologically disadvantaged. That's why Helena's husband nagged her until she took early retirement from the bank. Although she eventually opened an antique shop, Helena was still underemployed.

To encourage quick departures, private employers often sugar-coat the early-retirement package by calculating retirement benefits as though the retiree had reached age 65 or some age older than the actual chronological span. If the potential retiree is under 62, an additional benefit may be a supplement until he or she reaches 62 and is eligible for the Social Security benefit due at that age.

Employers who implement early retirement plans tacitly admit to staffing mistakes. The euphemistic explanation of Time's chief executive officer, J. Richard Munro, is typical. In announcing staff cuts, he said, "Habits that inflict unnecessary expense need to be broken." He added that the company needs "significant dollar cutting" and "not penny pinching." He explained that the company is finding it harder to impose price increases at present and anticipates "a strong possibility of a less buoyant economy" in 1986 and beyond.

So widespread now is early retirement that 52-year-old Merrell Clark spends his time considering the subject. In a one-man crusade to increase the employment of seniors, he has helped develop and fund hundreds of job programs throughout the country—from "heart" work (nonpaying), such as mentoring troubled children, to "hand" work (paying), such as learning to sell computer software or Australian-made giftware.

Clark, president of Elderworks, a Scarsdale, New York-based think tank and foundation he established in 1978, says, "It's ridiculous that we live in a society where some of our most able people are encouraged to sit in their hammocks and watch TV. I am impressed by the unused capacity of highly skilled, retired people who have the flexibility, the freedom, and generally the affluence to make a wide range of choices about what to do with their free time, who have a great deal of experience and wisdom to offer any employer."

On the other side of the continent, Mike Parker fosters senior entrepreneurship from his headquarters in Glendale, California. His New Career Opportunities, Inc. has helped launch about 200 new small businesses in southern California since 1976 ranging from word processing services to custom jewelry manufacture to specialized food manufacture. His organization is not for profit; it is funded by grants from foundations, companies and others interested in entrepreneurship. The Small Business Administration named him its Senior Entrepreneur Advocate for 1982. For 24 years he was involved with Junior Achievement, the program that fosters the concepts of capitalism among high school students. "I transferred some of the JA basics to start my brand of Senior Achievement," he says. In expanding his concept beyond southern California, he now offers a course in starting a small business to people of any age.

Even the new law that prohibits forced retirement until 70 of all but top officials has caused earlier, not later, retirements, at least thus far. This paradox results because employers might have felt they could live with an employee of 63 whom they considered below standard, knowing they could rid themselves of him or her in two years when the individual reached 65 and could be forced to retire. However, they cannot live with the situation seven years until that person is 70. So, they eliminate the job or apply subtle or not-so-subtle pressures to "persuade" the employee to voluntarily retire early.

The Big Wake-Up

Unions have had little or no effect on curbing early retirement. Indeed, until recently they have been encouraging it. Now, some are beginning to try to slow down this trend, without measurable results to date.

Some private employers—Polaroid, Arco, Mutual of Omaha, McDonald's, IBM, Banker's Life, Grumman and other companies—see the dangers. They have had no effect either on curbing the momentum. The majority of their peers still use early retirement like a scythe. Most government units at all levels remain in the post-World War II mindset when they were trying to encourage earlier retirements in their own forces and in the private sector.

The transitions in our economy, the growing age of our workforce, the unbridled trends toward earlier retirement, and the increasing number of women working converge to give a strange picture of age-sex group percentages in our labor force from 1950 to 1980:

AGE GROUP & SEX	1950	1955	1960	1965	1970	1975	1980
Males, 55-64	86.9	87.9	86.8	84.6	83.0	75.8	72.3
Males, 65+	45.8	39.6	33.1	27.9	26.8	21.7	19.1
Females, 44-64	27.0	32.5	37.2	41.1	43.0	41.0	41.5
Females, 65+	9.7	10.6	10.8	10.0	9.7	8.3	8.1

Note that the percentages slide down in nearly every age category and for both sexes as we get closer to the present.

Even if we'd like to stay retired in our fifties or early sixties, inflation means that fewer and fewer of us can afford to.

Yet, take heart. We *can* get a job. Skills, not age, are the main factor in hiring decisions, according to a study by Right Associates, a nationwide outplacement firm that tracked 125 unemployed white-collar workers in the Northeast. "Our figures show that the job market values people for their skills and recognizes that older workers, on the average, have the more valuable skills," says Larry Evans, a partner at Right.

Bob Snelling of Snelling & Snelling adds, "If you must retire, do it early and often."

Nearly half of all people who retire don't want to, at least not at the time they are "persuaded" to do so.

A Louis Harris survey reveals that 37 percent of those pensioners interviewed in 1981 retired unwillingly because of a mandatory retirement age, health or disability rule. In the Harris report, 62 percent of those interviewed retired willingly, but 7 percent of those later regretted the move. According to a composite of several studies, nearly half of all who are retired say they don't particularly like it. A more recent Harris poll reveals that 70 percent of preretirees hope to work after retirement.

They sense the demographic changes beginning to reshape the world of work. By the year 2000, we face a labor shortage, predict Nobel Prize winner Wassily Leontief and Faye Duchin of the Institute for Economic Analysis at New York University. Although automation will eliminate nearly 2 million semiskilled jobs by then, they believe, a similar number of positions will be created to make the necessary capital goods embodying the new technologies. What's more, the shortage could grow to crisis proportions by 2010, resulting from slowing growth in both the population and the labor force. We see it already in farm work (hence, the Mexicans flowing into the Southwest) and various high-tech areas such as computer engineering (hence, the high salaries in those fields).

In the past, we solved our labor shortages by immigration, the movement of rural populations to the cities or the flood of women into the workforce. Increasing immigration may solve the upcoming shortages for entry-level positions, but it will do little or nothing to alleviate short-falls in more skilled positions which seniors are more likely to fill.

The population shift to the cities has ended; a minor reversal trend is now occurring. We have practically exhausted the possibility of more working women who will make up 46 percent of the workforce by 1995, up from 40 percent in 1975.

So, the best bet to relieve the coming shortage lies with seniors. Tomorrow, life and work will begin at 50.

PART I

How To Prepare for a New Job After 50

It makes no sense to start a trip without a map. Job hunting at any time is a journey that requires at least that. At age 50 or older, it's a voyage that demands maps and compasses. The six chapters in this part tell how to prepare for an expedition of discovery, especially of yourself.

Partly in response to demographic shifts, Americans increasingly view retirement as a time to launch new initiatives in the workplace. A recent Harris poll found that more than 70 per cent of preretirees hope to work after the normal time of retirement.

For many it's a matter of preference. For some it's a financial necessity. But all are part of a trend that is expected to revolutionize employment patterns in this country by the end of the century.

2

It's Easier Than You Think

The septuagenarian Harlan Sanders could look back upon a moderately successful life. If he were financially prudent, he could live comfortably for the rest of his days, regaling friends and relatives with stories of his adventures, mostly as a salesman.

Many of those friends and relatives thought him anything but prudent, even crazy, when at 72 he threw all his resources of capital, intelligence, emotion and expertise into a fast-food enterprise selling fried chicken. Restyling his beard and mustache into a vandyke, cultivating an even deeper Southern accent and wearing white suits *all* the time, he parlayed his mother's recipes into the Kentucky Fried Chicken franchises you can see today in every town and city in the United States and abroad. A grateful state even made his military title quasi-legitimate by bestowing its colonelcy upon him.

Before his death, he said, "Easy to start over at 72? No, but it was easier than I thought it might be. Fun, too."

You are one of 60 million Americans 50 or older, one-fourth of the population, and 30 percent of the 60 million want more satisfactory work.

Can the government help? What about the 28 national associations who cater to the interests of seniors? Can groups such as Success Over Sixty or Forty Plus do anything for you? Where are your friends and family in your time of crisis?

They are all ready to assist. The aid is always well-meaning and sometimes even useful. Yet it cannot be useful until *you* first do your part.

Whether your dismissal is a stuning surprise, half-expected or even fully anticipated, the reality of being "at liberty," as theater people call it, is a shock. The common first reaction is to go away "to regain your perspective." Another is to get your resume written for you and to embark on a furious round of job interviews arranged by friends and family. A third characteristic response, especially for the underemployed, is to do nothing.

None of these answers is right. The fact of your unemployment or underemployment results partly from the times in which we live, but it may also stem partly from gaps in your self-knowledge.

"People set adrift from the corporate world most often suffer from such gaps," says George Bowers. "They think they manage employees well or are good at administration. In reality, their former corporate employer did all or a large part of their personnel management or administration for them. They have grown so used to the assistance that they honestly don't realize they can't do it or can't do it well. But the corporate employer knows it, and that's why the person was let go, not another who had better skills."

Those adrift from large corporations often have another blank in understanding themselves. They think they want to start a small company. "Success is unlikely," believe Bowers and most other outplacement specialists. The reason: By the time a person has worked for a corporation most of his or her adult life, the corporate mold is formed. However, some seniors do start profitable small ventures. Chapter 9 reports on how they succeed.

A third type of senior who typically suffers from poor self-knowledge is one who loses a top-level job. This paradox results because such people often have unbalanced skills. Their great sales abilities push them into marketing vice-presidencies. Only then do their subpar managerial talents surface. They won't accept demotion back to the ranks where they belong, so they are out. Or the accounting whiz flounders as vice-president of finance because she never quite understands how bankers think and react. She sincerely believes that male chauvinist peers politicked to get her kicked.

A fourth common gap in self-knowledge involves the failure to admit or even recognize personality defects. Many an abuser of alcohol or drugs thinks his or her habit is "recreational," but the employer doesn't who sees the records of absenteeism and errors. A less dramatic flaw in character involves recklessness or its opposite, undue caution. Seniors may suffer more from the latter than the former, but it eventually catches up with them either way because they most likely blame their employers for undue caution or recklessness, not for the mirror image of what *they* do.

So, as an unemployed or underemployed senior, you must first get to know yourself. How? By conscientiously following a course of self-instruction, a five-step process that we call Program RENEW:

- *R*estoring self-confidence
- *E*xpanding creativity

- *N*arrowing goals
- *E*nlarging contacts
- *W*elcoming change

R: Restore Your Self-Confidence

Being let go is a psychological shock. Whether expected or unexpected, it results in some feeling of rejection. That, in turn, erodes most seniors' self-confidence.

Here's how to start repairing such erosion. First, consider these statistics about your age group:

- People 50 and up account for more than half-a-trillion dollars in annual personal income and nearly 30 percent of all consumer expenditures. The 50-plus group accounts for half of all discretionary buying power in the U.S.—double that of people under 35.
- Some 80 percent of all money in savings and loan institutions is controlled by people 50 and up (some two-thirds of whom are women).
- About a third of all personal income in the U.S. is earned by seniors.
- Per capita expenditures for travel are highest in the 55 to 64 age group.
- Households headed by seniors account for more than 30 percent of all expenditures on food and liquor, more than 40 percent of every dollar spent in beauty parlors, and more than one-fourth of all money spent on cosmetics.
- Companies such as Amtrak, Greyhound, Eastern Airlines, McDonald's, Pepsi, General Foods, Colgate Palmolive, Proctor & Gamble, and even youth-conscious Levi Strauss and baby-conscious Gerber Products are concocting new strategies to capture seniors whom they correctly see as the growth market of the late 1980s and 1990s.

Okay, you may say, that's the general situation for seniors, but I'm special case and in trouble. Of course you're a special case, but your trou ble may not be as bad as you think.

One key to your attitudes about yourself is your appearance and healt! Other books go into that, such as *Growing Old, Staying Young* by Chri topher Hallowell. Heed their suggestions and lose that weight, tint tl gray hair, dress a little younger.

This volume will confine itself to less tangible deficiencies. To learn these, answer the following:

1) Compared to 10 years ago, I like myself
  __more
  __less
  __about the same.

2) Compared to younger peers, I am
  __more
  __less
  __equally
productive or effective.

3) Because of my age,
  __more
  __less
  __the same
should be demanded of me.

4) Now, I feel I'm
  __more
  __less
forgetful than I was 10 years ago.

5) Today, sex is
  __more
  __less
important than it once was.

Next, answer yes or no to register agreement or disagreement with the following statements:

6) There are new worlds left for me to conquer. _____

7) I can adapt to changing conditions even though they're changing fast. _____

8) I can develop and carry out ambitious plans. _____

9) I think of myself basically as energetic as ever. _____

10) I am as good and decent a person now as I used to be. _____

11) I am as concerned as ever about what's going on around me. _____

12) I am still self-controlled and slow to anger. _____

13) I sleep a little less than I did a decade ago. _____

14) I read more than formerly. _____

15) I still consider myself a creative person. _____

If you answered *less* to any of the first five questions and *no* to any of the *yes-no* statements, you need to improve your attitude(s) in the problem areas.

For example, if you like yourself less than a decade ago, ask yourself why. Write down the negatives that you suspect have caused this decline. If it's your appearance, we've already discussed what you can do. If you're morose and depressed, try to *act* enthusiastic, even if you don't feel that way at the start. Amazingly, you will probably find yourself enthusiastic before long.

If you are less productive than younger people, change that at once with the sustained energy you think you have. Also, more and not less should be demanded of you because of your age. As to forgetfulness, remind yourself that you have more to remember than younger people simply because you have lived longer. As to sex, use it or lose it.

In questions 6 through 12, you can control the positive sides of these. As to sleeping, you should need less now than a decade ago. If you are taking more sleep, try to get along on less. Sleep is partly a matter of habit.

In regard to reading, plot a series of books, magazines and newspapers that you will read over the next three months. You can't reach your reading destination without a map.

In regard to creativity, guard against complacency. *Nobody is ever creative enough.*

E: Expand Your Creativity

Although creativity is widely, not narrowly, distributed among human beings, most of us only partly utilize it.

To determine your own creativity quotient, answer these questions:

1) Can you get enthusiastic about problems outside your specialized area?

2) Do you feel excited and challenged in solving major or minor problems in many areas?

3) When a problem at first seems uninteresting, do you persist with it, anticipating that it will become interesting?

4) Do you meet standards of creativity set by yourself and others whom you respect?

5) Do you seldom assume limitations in what you do?

6) Do you recognize weakening persistence and set the problem aside temporarily, to return to it another day?

7) Do you resist "blocking" a project, even though you think it trivial and distracting from problems more to your taste?

8) Do you occasionally accept illogical thoughts from your subconscious mind, recognizing that they can help creativity?

9) Do you carry a notebook in which to record ideas?

10) Do you seek many ideas, not settling for a few?

11) Can you simplify and organize your impressions?

If you honestly answered *yes* to 8 of the 11 questions, your creativity level is high.

Creative people need tenacity of purpose and a stubborn resistance to discouragement. They need to accept a partnership of their subconscious and conscious minds. They need initiative, curiosity, and the ability to simplify the myriad impressions that descend on them. Above all, they need a firm belief in the validity of their ideas.

Creative people often suffer from fragile self-confidence, perhaps because they recognize their ability and fear they won't realize their potential. That's why unemployment or underemployment shatters self-confidence—and therefore the creativity—of the highly creative seniors more than those less gifted.

Put your failures in proper perspective; creative people generally experience more failures than those who are less creative because they try more things and take more chances. In times of unemployment or underemployment, show courage, if only to restore your creativity.

Here are suggestions on how to expand your creativity.

Visualize in wordless images. Let your subconscious mind anesthetize your conscious and restore the innocence of vision. Practice thinking in terms of pictures, not words. Children may be more creative than adults because they can do this naturally. Temporarily, try to recapture your childlike innocence. The absent-minded professor is a stock figure of fun, but if you know one, he or she may be the most creative person you ever met. It's the ability to forget what's "commonly known." Thomas Edison carried the art of forgetting to such extremes that on one occasion, when he was standing in line to pay taxes at New York City Hall, he forgot his name when the clerk called it.

Shift the emphasis. Your subconscious mind does this more easily than your conscious mind, but you can spur the subconscious along such lines by deliberately giving your conscious mind practice in shifting emphasis. The subconscious will follow. For practice, think of your problem of finding a more satisfactory job. Ideally, what do you want to do? Dream a little at this stage. Your subconscious may come up with some surprising ideas. Colonel Sanders' chicken franchises proved to be a far cry from his prior experience in conventional businesses, which included a stint at running a restaurant for a time.

Use analogy. Again, practicing with the conscious mind helps exercise the skill of the subconscious. Look for analogies. Is there an analogy between what you want to do and what historical figures have done? Suppose you love board games. Charles B. Darrow invented the popular board game, Monopoly, in 1930 after the Great Depression left him unemployed as a heating engineer. In 1935, he sold the game to Parker Brothers, Inc. Today, it is still popular in 12 languages throughout the free world. What analogies with Darrow can you see for yourself?

Impersonate. Put yourself in another's place. Imagine how you would act as Darrow. Impersonation is one of the most common routes to creativity; it happens frequently in dreams. Colonel Sanders may have put himself in his mother's place and imagined what she would do—parlay her fried chicken into a dish that could be enjoyed by a far larger circle than her family and friends.

Symbolize and concretize. In Darrow's economic distress in 1930, he thought of wealth and symbolized his dream in the concrete form of his game. In dreams, we commonly symbolize. Thinking in symbols becomes a way of creating by imagining in uncommon patterns. The trick is to transform the symbols into specific or material things that will help us get valid ideas or transform abstractions into concrete terms. Colonel Sanders has written that he symbolized an infinity of picnic tables piled with his mother's fried chicken. How to create at least partial infinity? With franchises, of course.

N: Narrow Your Goals

Darrow narrowed his goals from vague yearnings for economic ease into a specific, focused objective of his game. You must do something comparable. Start by evaluating your strengths and weaknesses:

- Define your real interests in life. Do this by analyzing your present or most recent work and all your former jobs; list the things you like and dislike about specific jobs.

- Assess your special skills and abilities. Do this by reviewing all your educational experiences; list areas in which you consistently received high marks and recall commendations from teachers. This exercise is to identify aptitudes, not to give you an ego trip, even if you need one!

• Analyze your work history and look for those things you are particularly proud of and the skills you brought to those projects.

• Next, list all activities that no longer challenge you. For each, make at least three suggestions on how they could be made more challenging. Choose the most practical.

In this exercise, concentrate on the important; the trivial will usually look after itself. Today, trivia is put on a pedestal as something great. Trivial Pursuit is a best-selling game. Professors intone, "Trivia is American folklore." Books on trivia abound. Trivia may be amusing, interesting and entertaining, but it is not important. Don't let it throw you off the track of preparing yourself for a more satisfactory job.

E: Enlarge Your Number of Contacts

A preoccupation with minutiae goes with a tendency to narrow social and business contacts for the unemployed or underemployed senior. The psychological impulse to turn inward and to rely on the safety of unimportant matters probably accounts for this. While you must make your goals narrower and more specific, you must also broaden your contacts with people in every way you can. We've said it before, we'll say it now, and we'll say it again: Job hunting is a numbers game; the more contacts you have, the better your chances of eventually connecting. Colonel Sanders approached 2,008 people about his idea for marketing chicken before he finally sold it on his 2,009th contact.

To widen your contacts, investigate organizations such as The Success Over Sixty Institute. If you want further information about attending its seminars, organizing and becoming a member of a local chapter, or receiving its newsletter, write to President Albert M. Myers, The Success Over Sixty Institute, Box 3095, Aspen, CO 81611.

Forty Plus is another group to look into. It's loosely organized by people of age 40 and older to assist each other in finding employment. It operates as a nonprofit employment agency for its members. Unlike a regular employment agency, it directs its efforts toward finding jobs for its members, not toward finding candidates for jobs. The exact organization and operational methods vary from group to group because each is completely independent; initiation fees and dues vary. There are clubs in New York, Washington, Boston, Chicago, Los Angeles and elsewhere. Check your phone book for one in your area.

Forty Plus's greatest value lies in the psychological and emotional benefits that it confers, not greatly dissimilar from those of Alcoholics Anonymous. Helpful is the discovery that the circumstances that cost you your job are not unique. However, membership does not guarantee that you will find a job. About one-third of the members find them through the organization; another third find jobs on their own, but cite Forty Plus's help in putting them on the right track. Nevertheless, some of its members who have been unemployed for a long time can depress you unduly. Use this contact with discretion.

In many major cities and areas, nonprofit organizations exist such as Chicago's Operation Able or the Los Angeles Council on Careers for Older Americans which attempt to coordinate and focus the many public and private efforts to help seniors find jobs. Coordination is imperative. In Los Angeles County alone, for example, at least 45 public and private agencies provide job-finding assistance of some degree to seniors.

The federal government may "help" even more than at present if Congress passes a bill entered in 1986 by Rep. Silvio Conte (R., MA). His measure would offer a targeted-jobs tax credit to employers who hire people over 55. Such credits already go for hiring certain handicapped persons, disadvantaged youth and war veterans.

You may prefer a less organized form of support through friendship with congenial folk unemployed and underemployed with whom you can exchange experiences and tips. A way to meet them is through the foregoing organizations or even at your state unemployment office. This may be the most important benefit you derive from a visit to the establishment. Unfortunately, the average state unemployment office is more interested in finding jobs for younger clients.

Another way to contact the senior unemployed or underemployed is through your local chapter of the American Association of Retired Persons or the 27 other national organizations devoted to the interests of seniors. AARP is the largest by far.

Of course, keep green your relations with old friends, relatives and your immediate family. Divorce is not uncommon when a senior loses a job. The best way to forestall such an outcome is to make your spouse your partner in your job hunting. You will need a confidante in this enterprise. What better one than your own spouse?

W: Welcome Change

So much of life is changing, and changing so fast, that you must learn to take change into account as a permanent factor in the workplace. Even more dramatic changes appear likely in the future. Those who deal with change most effectively will fare the best in their careers.

Changes interact with other changes. A change that is primarily technological may force profound, but largely unforeseen, organizational shifts. A relatively minor change in the method of doing things—in selling, for example—may result in disturbing changes for people far removed from the selling profession. Be alert to the phenomenon of interacting changes, especially those involving technology, methods, organization and people, the four most common types in the working world.

Technology

Many established companies have missed the boat with new technologies because they were unwilling to make changes. For instance, at least two major firms knew about, but failed to pursue, xerography. Xerox Inc. saw the potential and created a corporation that now employs more than 100,000 people—technology interacting with people.

Methods

Changes in job design are common examples of shifts in methods that result in changes for people. The elder Henry Ford invented nothing, but his changes in assembly methods ushered in mass production.

Organizations

The failure to see—and welcome—change in the organization is the most frequent explanation of why seniors are stunned by severance. In your next job, know how to spot the need for it in your new organization, how to judge when it isn't necessary, and what you want the change to accomplish.

People

Probably the most complex of all change are those that occur in people themselves. People generate changes in technology, methods, and organizations, but "people change" is more complicated. It occurs on at least two levels—in social mores and in psychological mutations due to age, changes in environment, or other factors.

Welcoming change effectively requires more than technique and strategy. It calls for a new kind of thinking. Change needs to be included as an element in planning for a more satisfactory job, as a factor in all decision-making, and as a pervading force in all other aspects of finding a better position.

One small example: A change we see, but probably don't notice, every day of our lives are those little black bars somewhere on the label of practically every packaged item we buy in the supermarket. It's a bar code that enables the checkout clerk to record its price automatically, the store management to keep track of inventory and sales trends, and the manufacturer to trace the time and place of production. The relatively new technology of automatic identification has subtly changed methods of doing much business, the organization for accomplishing it, and the nature of work—and, hence, people.

With your RENEWed confidence, you're going after more than a job. You're going after the best job you ever had in your life.

3

The Differences By Age and Sex

"Age and skill will overcome youth and treachery." That statement hangs mounted and framed on the office wall of a retiree counselor practicing in Pittsburgh. The city has had more than its share of retirements—early and otherwise—because of the contraction of the steel industry, the disappearance of Gulf Oil in a merger, and staff reductions among many of its nonsteel household names such as Rockwell International, Alcoa, Westinghouse and others.

"I had that put up," says the counselor, "to reassure my clients. I modified it from what a woman shocked me by exclaiming, 'I guess even my age and treachery aren't enough to overcome the skills of those bright young things.' She was so wrong! Older people have tremendous skills they don't market properly. And the youth are treacherous in the sense that they push and push and push from below until they push the older folks out."

You probably accepted the first job you were offered after answering an intriguing help wanted ad or hearing a recruiter make the position sound promising. Although you will have to accept the following statement on faith for the moment, believe us when we say: At age 50 or older, you won't need to, and probably shouldn't, accept the first offer made to you.

Albert Einstein in his twenties would have produced a resume that could only have landed him a job as a meter reader in Pittsburgh's Water Department. Indeed, he took the equivalent, a junior examinership in the Swiss Patent Office. It gave him so much boredom and free time that he maintained his sanity only through abstract speculation. From this period grew his theories by which he changed physics more than any man since Isaac Newton. By age 50, Einstein took his pick of job offers from all over the world.

At 50 or older, you won't read a single help wanted ad aimed at your age bracket, and not only because age stipulations are illegal. In the clas-

25

sifieds, the euphemism for maturity is a reference to experience. The ads that seek someone with it want a 40-year-old with 30 years of experience. Nor is a headhunter likely to tap you. Most executive search firms seek people under 50. When you're older, they will come after you only if you have an outstanding reputation and are already employed in a good position. This book does not address them. They don't need our help.

You need our help because you want a better job and because finding one is much different than finding your first or even your second or third.

Yes, negatives do exist where you're seeking a new position at 50 or older. We discussed them in the first two chapters—the stigma of failure, biases, time, etc.—but now we can get into the positives which far outweigh the negatives.

Of course, none of you are Albert Einstein, but age does give you marketable advantages over junior job-seekers. You have so much more going for you now than when you landed your first job that you should feel buoyant and optimistic, not loaded with stage fright and the sense of inadequacy you suffered in the early days of your first job. Even when you compare yourself to other seniors holding secure jobs, you have an advantage. You can change your life far more than they can.

Let's see how you can do this.

The Positives for Jobless Seniors

A cartoon in *The Wall Street Journal* showed a personnel man saying to an applicant, "Actually, we're looking for somebody who will be eternally grateful for the job." The employer should be eternally grateful to *you* for accepting the job. You can be grateful, also, but don't overdo it. Gratitude doesn't go far or last long in jobhunting.

Among the many advantages most senior jobhunters hold over their juniors, these stand out: Unique experience, multidimensional abilities, self-knowledge and risk knowledge.

Unique Experience

A 25-year-old may have first said, "Experience is the one thing you have plenty of when you're too old to get the job." Yet, we're talking here in the sense of Aldous Huxley who said, "Experience is not what happens to a man; it is what a man does with what happens to him."

Because you are unemployed at 50 or older, you have undergone an experience no junior can know. This should be a singular advantage, even if you may not think so at first. It should teach you humility, a rare quality among juniors. It should teach you the determination never to be in such a predicament again, a firmness of purpose not given to many juniors. It should teach you a special wariness embodied in an observation by Richard Armour:

> *Of late I appear*
> *To have reached that stage*
> *When people look old*
> *Who are only my age.*

In other words, remember to maintain enthusiasm, optimism and energy. These qualities signal your psychological age far more than appearance. Youth never has monopolized them and you can cultivate them. Act enthusiastic, optimistic and energetic even if you don't always feel that way. As good actors will testify, "When you act it, you'll soon be it."

Ed's first job after graduating from college was with a new company that had a license to sell in the United States a French-developed machine that made rolls and pastries for commercial bakeries. All went well for a short time. The four bachelors who had bought the license treated him well. However, it gradually dawned on Ed that he was the only heterosexual among the five males in the firm. It had dawned on the four homosexuals even earlier that he did not share their sexual preference. By mutual agreement, he left the company within six months.

By the time he was 50, that and other experiences served Ed well because he made them work for him to land the best job of his life designing and equipping restaurants. It created a synergy for him that rekindled his enthusiasm, optimism and energy.

If you make such experiences work for you, your senior campaign against joblessness should teach you that "youth is a quality, not a matter of circumstances," in the words of Frank Lloyd Wright when he was old in years and young in spirit. The adversity of unemployment at any age is a trial of principle. Success over it at 25 is a victory; at 50, it's a conquest.

Multidimensional Abilities

A senior is far more likely than a junior to have acquired multidimensional abilities, some of them merely because of greater exposure to various experiences, some of them because of career shifts along the way.

Charlie, a successful teacher of psychology, got lured into the personnel department of a major corporation because of higher compensation. He topped out at 50 as head of the company's recruiting effort. Hard times dictated the "temporary" abandonment of significant recruitment; the chief recruiter was out. Yet, Charlie had an option of returning to teaching, not likely for a junior.

Janet, a senior employee communicator, returned to public relations—where she started a quarter of a century earlier—when the employer cancelled the employee magazine in an economy move. Younger people on the staff had no such background and consequently no such option.

Self-knowledge

Most, but not all, seniors know themselves better than when they were half their present age. Yet panic and outward or inner pressures, such as might develop after job severance, can blind even the most mature individuals to an objective self-appraisal.

To be sure you're still on the track, it's wise for jobless seniors to perform these three exercises:

1) Write at least 10 answers to the question, Who am I? Obviously, you might be a business or professional person, but think further. For example, *I'm a manager, I'm more of a doer than a dreamer.* Let your thoughts wander and include both good and bad traits. Don't read meaning into the answers, just gather information.

2) List things you do well, specific tasks that have brought praise and/or personal satisfaction. These may be simple, even relatively unimportant, but list them if you remember them with pleasure. Then list things done unsuccessfully and/or with little or no pleasure.

3) With free choice and none of the usual limiting factors, what would you most like to do? These can be of long or short duration, important or unimportant, vocational or avocational.

When you have completed this review, share it with at least one other person, perhaps your spouse. Don't discuss it from the standpoint of right or wrong. Look at it descriptively. Does the other person agree with your self-appraisal? Disagree? Why?

When you have reached a mutual agreement about yourself with the other person, check it with the analysis done years ago. You've never done one before? Shame! You can only hope that your junior competitors in the job market don't similarly analyze themselves. Otherwise, you face a more formidable struggle.

Yet, let's hope for the best. When the new or renewed perceptions about yourself become settled and you can look at them objectively, begin to use the insights to make decisions about your future.

Risk Knowledge

A myth persists that juniors seek risks while seniors seek the status quo. Not true. Examples abound of seniors making a sensational success of risky ventures—from Colonel Sanders with Kentucky Fried Chicken to Helen Hooven Santmyer and her best-selling novel, . . .*And Ladies of the Club,* published when she was long past age 65. Although the opposite isn't true either, what is true is that seniors have a greater knowledge about when to take sensible risks. Seniors also usually have greater financial resources than juniors and can better afford to take risks.

More seniors than juniors know to ask themselves questions such as these when considering the risk of a new job or career or business:

1) Do I feel the urge and confidence to change?
2) What do I want to be or do in 5 years? Ten? Fifteen?
3) Is risk necessary for me to reach my life goals?
4) If I take this risk, what do I stand to gain? Lose?
5) Will my experience work well for me in this new job, career or business?
6) Have I researched the new venture adequately?
7) Have I researched alternatives?
8) How will my risk-taking affect my family and friends?
9) Will I have more control over my life if I take this risk?
10) Who can help me in taking this risk? Family? Friends?

William James, the American psychologist and philosopher, wrote in *The Will To Believe,* "It is only by risking our persons from one hour to another that we live at all. And often enough, our faith beforehand in an uncertified result is the only thing that makes the result come true."

Prescriptions for the Underemployed

The underemployed senior faces more subtle problems than his jobless counterpart. The worst is deciding what ails him or her. Sometimes, it just seems to be boredom and apathy. Should you go jobhunting only because of that, to which most people are subject now and then?

To determine how drastic your remedies should be, take these steps:

- For at least a week, keep a record of when you feel most energetic, when fatigue catches up with you, when you feel sharpest mentally, and the periods in the days when you are psychologically up or down.

- Guard against weariness because it can seem like boredom. Temporarily set aside tasks that begin to weary you, or work on them only until you reach a convenient stopping point.

- Find good ways to rest. You don't have to be idle to relax. Turn to another task, change your pace, get up and walk to the water cooler.

- Avoid misusing your eyes. Your office or workplace should have uniform illumination. Your eyes must adjust both to your work and to nearby walls and windows. Monitor the intensity of your light. Several studies show that efficiency improves with greater light intensity (up to the glare point).

- Avoid clothing that is too tight or a chair, desk or workbench at the wrong height. These may cause nagging aches and pains that distract you from working efficiently.

- Maintain your general level of health and have a regular medical checkup.

If these simple adjustments don't relieve your general sense of malaise, ask yourself the earlier questions about risk, plus these additional ones:

1) Are you changing and growing in your current job?

2) Is your natural curiosity being tested and challenged?

3) Do you sense that your creativity is waning?

4) Are you encouraged to communicate your opinions, ideas and feelings to coworkers and superiors alike?

5) Are you as committed to your work as you were ten years ago? Five years ago?

6) Does your work provide you some imaginative stimulus, some not impossible ideal to shape vague hope and transform it into effective desire? You need this to carry you on without disgust through the dull routines which are so large a part of life.

All of these supplemental questions deal with growth, creativity and commitment. If your present job does not offer at least three, you are underemployed. It's time to move on.

Yet, too many never do, which is another subtle problem not faced by unemployed seniors. The typical underemployed hesitate to cut the umbilical cord to a job even when it is boring and stifling. However, no decision in a matter this important may be worse than a wrong decision.

Here's how to come to a determination about your present job situation that may lead to action:

- Diagnose your circumstances to define basic problems and parameters, to clarify your objectives, and to identify a solution.
- Study the facts to isolate the key factors affecting your decision. A shorthand way to do this is to list all the pluses and minuses that you and your friends can think of concerning the decision.
- Develop alternative courses of action. Perhaps neither the status quo nor a career change are right for you. Think of others.
- Evaluate each alternative to determine which best meets your specific needs.
- Pray a little.

Ross, a 60-year-old bank vice-president, went through these exercises which convinced him that he had to do more with his life. Instead of quitting the bank, he chose an alternative course of action. In partnership with his wife, the couple started a retail shop they called Package Deal. It specialized in uniquely packing gift and novelty items which it also sold. Before and early in their marriage, his wife had been a buyer for a major chain of department stores, so knew the retail end of the business. As a banker, Ross was familiar with the financial demands upon retailing. She ran the day-to-day operation; he handled the accounting and financial end. The store was making money three months after it opened. Within a year, the couple opened a second outlet.

The underemployed seniors' major advantage over juniors is that they usually have both the time and financial resources to pursue two careers at once. Until his death at age 84, Fred Waring, who studied electrical engineering at Penn State University, was both a musician and an inventor. His best-known musical enterprise was the Pennsylvanians; his best-known invention, the Waring Blender.

The Job You Should Want

Whether you're unemployed or underemployed, you should give thought during your self-appraisal stage about the job you seek next, even though you are not yet ready to actively look for it. It would be far different from your first position (we speak here about its general qualities, not its technical specifics).

First, you should select your new job on the basis of interest and stimulation. If it looks like it might bore you quickly, you will have gained nothing. This is the chief reason why we suggest the job should be different; at your present stage in life, the last thing you want is boring work. Next, the job should offer serviceability. How well would the new job serve you, your family and your interests? Then, you should consider the job's size. Does it offer you room in which to grow and create? Can you define its parameters to a reasonable degree? Next, the question of dependability looms large. Will your peers prove reliable and supportive? Will the job last? Finally, does the job offer fair compensation?

Everybody, regardless of age, should ask such questions from time to time. Alas, few do until necessity forces this inquisition.

Only in the matter of compensation is there apparent similarity between the needs for your job at 25 and your next one at 50 or older. Then and now, you want as much pay and benefits as possible. Or do you *now*? Not necessarily. For example, your previous employer's health insurance may still be in effect for you as an early retiree. You don't need more. This might be traded for something else, or your early retirement pension from your former employer may mean a somewhat lower salary from your new employer in exchange for something else—for example, a deferred salary arrangement after you retire the next time.

How do you get answers on serviceability and the other factors? By asking both the person offering you the job and employees, if you can find them, and other people familiar with the employer. Visit your library to check out the employer in *Moody's* and other references. Search for articles about the employer in back issues of your local newspapers and magazines, and check with users of its products or services. Consult a local business directory.

Above all, learn as much as possible about the specifics of what the employer expects from you. At first, you will likely receive little beyond generalities. Strange as it seems, many employers don't know precisely what they want in an employee. We'll delve deeper into this phenomenon later as a big opportunity for you to create your own job, but now we remind you about it in your preliminary self-appraisal. You also will need to keep probing, a course you probably never took as a junior, even if you had thought of it, for fear of offending. If your questions offend now, that employer is not for you.

This author once refused a job to write an executive's biography because the subject could not answer a preliminary biographical questionnaire. He excused himself by saying, "This is not necessary now. We'll get into it when we agree to go ahead with the project." However, it *was* necessary to test how cooperative the subject would be.

Should you not have done all the research and asked all the questions before accepting your previous jobs, as well as your next job? Of course, but the odds are that you did not. You might not have thought to research or ask the questions, or you might have thought the questions presumptuous, or you might have been diffident—and it was not as important to do this earlier as it is now. Then, you sought a starting or self-developmental position; now, you want a finishing job that you can relish and enjoy during the Indian Summer of your life. It will help make the following days richer and more rewarding.

For Women, All of the Above—And More

Upon graduation from college, Dolores could cite five superlatives on her resume. She was the first woman in 62 years to receive a degree from Montana Tech. She was first academically in her class. She was the only female among 33 graduating seniors. At 35, she was the oldest senior and had taken the longest to win her degree because she had supported herself and an invalid mother while doing so. Finally, she was the first woman in the institution's history to win a degree in metallurgy.

She had no trouble finding a job with a major defense contractor in 1965. She had much trouble taking early retirement in 1986 because her employer lost the defense contract on which she was working. At 56, she had served her one employer loyally and well for 21 years. She wanted to find a job with another defense contractor doing metallurgical work, but no opportunity was available.

Senior women seeking better jobs must take into account all of the foregoing differences between getting the first job and the next—plus additional factors. Your skills are usually less salable than those of Dolores. Yet, even she couldn't easily find suitable work. Generally, you can't tap the wide job markets open to men because women usually entered the workforce when fewer types of work were open to your sex. There aren't many Doloreses around, especially over 50; consequently, your experience is more limited. You must deal both with prejudices against age *and* women.

Helena, the antique shop proprietor we met in the first chapter, dealt with the first two problems by entering a field where her sex already is preeminent. "It may be a cop-out," she says, "but I think it only makes sense to aim for fields that seek women." Among these, she counts merchandising, education, medical and financial services, advertising, publishing, law and journalism as the most welcoming. Females today outnumber males five to two in the nation's journalism schools. Currently, almost as many women as men are enrolled in our law schools. The number of female candidates for MBA degrees has jumped more than 100 percent in the last decade.

While that holds promise for senior women of the future, what about those who happen to be 50 or older now and want better jobs? Education is the major answer here, too, which helps explain why women outnumber men in adult education by four or five to one.

In combatting prejudice, females have honed their skills to fight it since they entered the job market. They should transfer what they've learned to combat bias against age, too.

More senior women than senior men who seek new technical, supervisory or managerial jobs are either single or divorced, another handicap.

Helena's advice is simple: "Be more skilled than your male counterparts. Work harder. Work smarter."

Dolores and Helena never heard of each other, but Dolores intuitively followed her counsel. She finally asked herself why she had to work for someone else. Why not work for herself? She had the expertise and reputation to set up as a metallurgical consultant. Within two years, her annual income exceeded that of her last 12 months with the defense contractor.

Now she asks herself, "Why didn't I do this five years sooner?"

What About Minorities?

The prescriptions for women also apply to senior minorities who want better jobs.

The big influx of blacks and other minorities into management, supervisory and technical jobs in industry began in the 1960s. The early-retirement syndrome now reaches them, too. Furthermore, John L. Jones, director of corporate resources for Xerox Corporation and a black, points to other frustrations—an "invisible ceiling that blacks, and women as well, hit as they move up the corporate ladder, regardless of their achievements, motivation, preparation and training." The "invisible ceiling" explains why minorities start a disproportionate number of new businesses, nearly 20 percent, compared with 11.2 percent of blacks in the total U.S. population.

A 1985 survey of the nation's 1,000 largest companies by Korn/Ferry International found only four black top executives, one more than the executive search firm found in 1979. Companies acknowledge that black executives are rare. Yet they also believe that many blacks, particularly MBAs in such high profile areas as finance and marketing, are now poised to break into upper management ranks. "It's just a function of time," says Robert Belden, a Southwestern Bell Corporation manager for affirmative action. "We see continuing growth at the middle-management level and within a very few years we'll see dramatic change."

Jerry O. Williams, the black president and chief operating officer of AM International Inc., says he had to prove himself above and beyond his white peers while hopscotching around prejudiced bosses. He was successful and is now one of the highest-ranking blacks among the country's largest publicly held companies, in line to become the first black chief executive. His advice to any minority member hunting for a better job: "You need a very good wife who can support you or a tire to kick in the kitchen to get the frustration out. You need perseverance, some canny and some divine guidance."

The skill involved in overcoming the advantages of youth primarily relies on wisdom. As Bergen Evans said, "Wisdom is meaningless until your own experience has given it meaning . . . and there is wisdom in the selection of wisdom."

4

The Handwriting on the Wall

Grow old along with me!
The best is yet to be,
The last of life, for which the first was made.
Our times are in his hand.

Few seniors who find themselves unemployed or underemployed are likely to believe Robert Browning's words in "Rabbi Ben Ezra." They are more likely to believe the message implicit from our government and from our employers. When we go on Social Security, or get Social Security "equivalents" before age 62 and/or an early retirement pension from our employer, we get a much different signal. It is, "We no longer need seniors like you," or, "You are getting too old to work for us," or even, "You are useless."

That's one kind of handwriting on the wall. Another kind involves euphemisms. At age 59, this author went around saying too long that he "took early retirement" from one employer as though the choice was his. At age 62 he even believed for a couple of weeks the announcement from another employer that he "left to pursue other interests." Everybody but him read the real message, "John Morgan was fired."

What John Should Read

Anyone else in this author's situation should become expert in reading another kind of handwriting on the wall, the message that he will soon lose a job. Morgan's first firing came as a stunning surprise. He expected his second, but it still left him with feelings of inadequacy and depression. If he had read the second message more perceptively, he would have escaped even the negative emotions.

37

"Reading" really involves understanding. The corporations forcing early retirements all do it in the name of efficiency and compassion. They have discovered their pension plans enable them to cut staff at the older- and higher-paid end of their workforce. Eureka!

Of course, an economic slump in an industry or region sends the most obvious and grimmest signal. Between 1981 and 1982, the 20 largest Pittsburgh industrial companies cut their workforces by an average of 16 percent. The author was employed by one of them, knew all about the recession, but still remained convinced it wouldn't affect him. It did.

The "it can't happen here" syndrome even extends to the refusal to acknowledge that practically every public and private employer has an informal list of people who will go during the next cutback. Every manager would deny it, but he or she has such a list if only in the back of the mind. Unfortunately, the majority of those on it are over 50.

Many corporations hired these now "unnecessary" people during the go-go days of the 1950s and 1960s. They stockpiled people just as they did commodities. Furthermore, the corporate system encourages empire- building because managerial salaries depend, in part, on the number of people supervised. Managers even exist who deliberately overhire in good times to have heads to cut off during the next round of personnel reductions.

What's more, businesses may be poor forecasters in predicting their labor force. *Dun's Business Month*[1] admitted that some of the participants in its annual survey of expected employment growth were "naive" in 1984 and 1983. The Center for International Research on Economic Tendency Surveys did a special analysis for those years and found that many companies in the sampling of firms of all sizes made a low-risk—or naive—forecast that assumes employment in the following year will be approximately what it is currently.

As a result, the study shows that their forecasts are way off base. Of the companies in the sampling that predicted in the previous year no charge in their 1983 workforce, only 35.5 percent were correct within 1 percent, 25.4 percent were off by 1 to 25 percent, while an astounding 37.3 percent were wide of the mark by more than 25 percent. The same companies did only slightly better the following year in predicting how many people they would be employing in 1984: 41 percent were correct within 1 percent, 23 percent were off 1 to 25 percent, while 33.6 percent missed by more than 25 percent.

[1] Reprinted with permission *Business Month Magazine*, October 1985. Copyright 1985 by Business Magazine Corporation, 38 Commercial Wharf, Boston, MA 02110.

Such forecasting errors are not restricted to smaller companies, but are prevalent across the board.

Since, over the years, the aggregate employment forecasts have been a good indicator of the situation in the economy as a whole, the errors of the individual companies would seem to cancel each other out. However, the errors made on the upside by companies eventually translate into layoffs and early retirements.

Whether caused by a recession, a forecasting error, or the corporate penchant to overhire in good times, manpower stockpiles result, and you need to sense when you are in one. The fact you don't have enough meaningful work to do constitutes handwriting on the wall that you have landed in a stockpile and may be among the first to go in the next cutback. "Meaningful" is the operative word because work of some sort expands to engage even members of a stockpile.

They do projects, studies and surveys whose findings go into written reports to gather dust in obscure file rooms. They count inventory twice a quarter, they repaint walls every quarter, they call on prospects who don't spend a dollar a decade with the company. They get "volunteered" for Red Cross and United Way drives. They serve on committees to promote the metric system in the U.S. and other hopeless causes. When all else fails, they join task forces to improve productivity in the company. That's the last straw, because an honest task force has little choice but to report, "We must go."

Of course, the signs that you are in a stockpile or at hazard to be assigned to it are sometimes more subtle. One common faint indicator occurs when you find yourself working for younger and younger bosses. When he or she is 10 or more years younger than you, watch out. The author's boss was seven years younger than he at the time of his first discharge, 14 years his junior at his second.

A "youth kick" widely prevalent throughout your company is a decidedly bad sign even if you still have a meaningful assignment. So are chronically eroding profits. A merger is terrible news. There are three great lies in the world: "The check is in the mail;" "I'll still respect you in the morning;" and "Everything will be the same after the merger."

If your company is the junior partner in the merger, it's a disaster because most of the surviving company's employees get first consideration in the case of overlaps. When Chevron took over Gulf, their combined employment of about 80,000 skidded by almost 15 percent by the end of 1985, nearly all of it from the Gulf side. For example, at Gulf's former operating center in Houston, the workforce dropped from 5,750 to 3,000, with significant numbers in the remaining group transferred into it from other Chevron units. Gulf's former corporate headquarters in Pittsburgh, once employing 1,500 people, dropped to zero.

In a merger or takeover, top people face the greatest risk because there's never room for two vice-presidents of human resources. Yet the trauma goes even deeper than that. Every corporate merger involves differing cultures. For example, when Mellon Bank executives from Pittsburgh met in Florida with Girard Bank officials from Philadelphia to plan the consolidation of the institutions, the Mellon people brought their golf clubs, and those from Girard had tennis rackets. Little socialization followed. In the next two years, 65 Girard officers at vice-president or higher levels departed.

Surveys by Leslie Associates Inc. of top executives at companies that had been taken over showed that 20 percent of them sought other positions within one year in 1981, but 47 percent did so in 1984. Some 52 percent left within three years in the 1981 survey and an estimated 75 percent planned to do so in the 1984 check.

The rise in leveraged buyouts and takeovers motivated by a chance to buy undervalued assets has also led to deep cost-cutting. "The company's assets and franchise are primary, and the people are secondary," says Windle Priem, a managing director at Korn/Ferry International, the New York executive-search firm.

Adds Alfred Rappaport, a professor at the J.L. Kellog Graduate School of Business at Northwestern University, "Cash flow is king." In leveraged buyouts, he says, managers buying the company often want to profit by ultimately selling the company or going public again. "That means operating with leaner staffs," he says. After Chicago inventor William Farley acquired Northwest Industries Inc. in a leveraged buyout in 1985, for example, he eliminated all but about 25 of the 125 corporate staff members.

One reason more executives are leaving these days lies in the fact that the stigma of severance is no longer as deep as formerly. "Corporate nomads are becoming more common," says Robert Kamerschen, who was an executive vice-president at Norton Simon Inc. before Esmark Inc. acquired it. Beatrice Companies acquired Esmark, and then Kohlberg, Kravis, Roberts & Co. led an investors' group to buy Beatrice, again traumatic for top people in the organizational maze.

Top executives aren't the only ones at risk. Middle managers are often the last to know their employer faces bankruptcy. If they hold a reasonably responsible position with the company, they'll be tarred with the same brush, even if unjustly. If they are among the top people, they may go out on a rail. Re-employment prospects are then bleaker, but not hopeless.

The Fifties: The Dangerous Age

This is the dangerous decade, particularly for people in management and administration. Mistakes of the past catch up with them. That long-festering feud with a peer comes to a head, and they find themselves out, not the rival. The effects of marketing mistakes made five years ago still bother their employers and plague them.

Suddenly, their divorces are held against them, although they occurred three years ago. Or their diabetes, from which they suffered since their teens and which was never a secret, inexplicably becomes an issue. Even mild improprieties—from expense account finagling of 20 years ago to a sex discrimination charge that was dropped—get dredged up.

When a person reaches his or her fifties, a kind of accounting takes place, often by management osmosis. Usually there's no specific meeting held to consider the case, just a consensus by the boss and perhaps a couple of his confidantes. If they have problems of a performance or personal nature, this is the time a boss becomes tempted to use early retirement provisions in the pension plan to ease someone out, especially if the manager is experiencing pressure to cut costs.

Normally, the people who lose out because of cumulative strikes against them are square or oval pegs in round holes who have bumbled along for years. They have never erred spectacularly on the job; they have never scored sensationally, either. Sometimes, they were hailed when they were hired as geniuses who could solve some specific problem. They never did. The embarrassment for all concerned was so acute, especially when the individual didn't quit, that he or she spent a long time, perhaps years, in some obscure job.

A person in his or her fifties caught in this situation first notices it when no raise is granted or year-end bonus paid. No promotions come. An actual demotion may occur, disguised as a lateral transfer. When the individual finally complains, the axe falls.

Would it be wiser never to complain? Some don't and manage to hang on for a while longer, growing steadily more frustrated and unhappy. The situation can even cause mental and physical illness. A better course is to move on when it's clear there's no future left with the organization. Even if the individual doesn't find a new job immediately, he or she will be happier than in the former no-win circumstances.

Special Case for Long-Time Jobholders

Regardless of age, a person who has held the same job, especially in management, for about 10 years or longer faces special problems. During that decade, he or she has unavoidably made at least a few enemies, and they have not forgotten the real or imagined grievance—the slight, the failure to give credit, the unjustified acceptance of credit, or whatever else upsets them, even if the long-time jobholder genuinely cannot remember ever giving offense.

If enough people hold enough such grievances, the cumulative effect makes the target individual less effective. His or her productivity declines, decisions don't get implemented smoothly or errors slip through that formerly would have been caught by subordinates or peers. "Old John (or Jane) has lost a half-step," decides the boss.

The same accounting by osmosis takes place for the long-term jobholder as for the person in his or her fifties. This is why wise and perceptive people frequently move on if they have spent enough time in the same job. If they are not bored themselves, their peers and subordinates may be bored and piqued with them.

Special Case for Women

The foregoing examples of handwriting on the wall apply to women, too, but with a twist. Up until recently, there has been such a chronic shortage of clerical help that many females slated for the stockpile could, if they wished, accept meaningful office work. However, more and more don't want it as they have moved up the ladder to administrative and supervisory positions.

Furthermore, the boom in clerical employment is waning. Soon, the handwriting on the wall will be completely unisexual. That will at least please the feminists among us.

Another factor favorably affects women—generally, their compensation is below that of men. While an unjust state of affairs, it works to females' advantage in layoffs and forced retirements. Since the employer will usually "save" less in letting females go than males, the men normally depart before the women.

Special Case for Minorities

Again, many of the factors applying to women also hold for minorities, men and women. Minorities may win some benefit here from the Equal Opportunity laws, but they too should consider moving on when the handwriting on the wall unmistakably signals, "Watch out."

Special Case for the Underemployed

The underemployed—male and female—must pay especially close attention to the handwriting on the wall because they will be among the first to go. Some underemployed think no one but themselves knows their secret. It's more likely that every other employee knows—and perhaps resents—it.

Still other underemployed persons have been in that state so long they have forgotten what it's like to work at full capacity. Invariably, severance comes to them as a stunning surprise.

The large majority of the underemployed know they are not performing at their optimum potential, chafe about it, and want an improvement in their circumstances. They should see the handwriting as a reprieve to begin living fully again doing something else.

When a Negative Is a Positive

Employee attitudes toward their jobs, their bosses, their employers and business in general are changing. In this topsy-turvy era, signals that used to sound negative may actually be positive. Over 50 studies during the past 20 years involving more than 500,000 workers show people are less satisfied with work today than at any time in the past. The temper of the times may make a person see negatives where they don't really exist. Here are examples:

- If the employer fails to withdraw all operations from the Union of South Africa, or puts on a drive to improve profits, or bids on Department of Defense contracts, these actions or lack of action are not aimed at the individual.

- Similarly, a new boss less agreeable than the former one is not normally appointed as an affront to any individual. Don't take it personally.

- A lateral transfer may be an accolade, not an insult. Increasingly, employers make such moves to develop promising people.

- Pay freezes are much more common now than as recently as five years ago because of the urgency of competition, especially from abroad. Such actions are general, not specific, even though they still hurt.

- To stay healthy, every employer must add younger people into the workforce; most new people, naturally, will be younger than 50.

This constitutes a threat to seniors only when nearly *all* recent managerial appointments are Young Turks.

Therefore, the signals to pay attention to are those aimed at the senior individual, not those for all employees. Use common sense. One more bit of advice: Ignore signs that are illegible, such as the one-time disagreement with the boss, or a pay raise lower than hoped for, or a rare disagreeable assignment.

When Retirement Palls

In her monumental study of seniors, *The Coming of Age*, Simone de Beauvoir said, "Work almost always has a double aspect: it is a bondage, a wearisome drudgery; but it is also a source of interest, a steadying element, a factor that helps to integrate the worker with society."

The depression of the 1930s left many of us in our late 50s or older with a mindset that retirement means loafing, fishing, travel and one long vacation. Perhaps growing older means more loafing, fishing, travel and vacation, but any of those pursuits can pall.

Retirement Is Like Sex—Okay Until You Get Too Much

A study made in 1973 of people who had retired in 1969 attempted to learn if they would return to work if the opportunity presented itself. About half said no; of the other half who said yes (799), 359 were physically able to work and 440 proved unemployable usually for health reasons, even though they said they wanted to work. Of those who could work, 70 percent were blue collar and 30 percent white collar. A similar study made in 1983 of people who retired in 1979 showed significant changes. About one-third said they would not return to work. Of the two-thirds who said they would return part-time or full-time, about 70 percent were physically able to do so. About 60 percent of those had held blue collar jobs and 40 percent white collar jobs.

Dr. Alex Comfort is best known as the author of *The Joy of Sex*, but in his less well-known book, *A Good Age*, the gerontologist wrote, "What the retired need . . . isn't leisure, it's occupation . . . Two weeks is about the ideal length of time to retire." He's not the only one holding that view. George Bernard Shaw wrote, "A perpetual holiday is a good working definition of hell." When asked why he performed professionally after he reached the age of 80, cellist Pablo Casals answered, "To retire is the beginning of death." Ernest Hemingway stated, "Retirement is the ugliest word in the language."

All insurance and pension ads depict retirees as a happy couple doing something recreational. Never a picture of a single person. Never scenes showing anybody coping with boredom, illness or just routine exasperations that go on whether you're retired or not—taking out the garbage, fighting traffic, trying to make ends meet. Few retirement counselors can help; they perpetuate the myth that retirement is right, normal, happy and affordable. Often, it is none of these. The misreading of the financial signals is probably the most common reason for returning to work.

Also, bankruptcies leave retirees with reduced or no pension benefits, forcing them back to work. Since the government formed the Pension Benefit Guaranty Corporation (PBGC) in 1974, it has taken over 1,345 plans of companies which have sought protection under bankruptcy laws. When it must assume obligations, it pays a monthly maximum of only $1,857.95 and doesn't insure monthly supplements often offered to induce early retirements. In mid-1987, financial collapse threatened it because of the rash of bankruptcies, especially in steel where one-fifth of the U.S. industry has filed for bankruptcy law protection since 1982. A PBGC failure would imperil the retirement income of 40 million Americans because it insures plans covering about one of every three workers in the U.S. Many private pension plans are sorely underfunded. The U.S. Department of Labor which oversees PBGC estimates that nearly 10,000 of the 110,000 plans insured by the agency have a shortfall of $45 billion.

Other companies—for example, Colt Industries Inc., Allis-Chalmers Corporation, and Bethlehem Steel Corporation—have shed or reduced retiree programs on grounds of financial hardship without seeking bankruptcy protection, compounding the jeopardy for many retirees.

Many new retirees are like an appliance with the plug pulled out—deactivated. The factors which brought them successful careers—experience, judgment, and a network of career friends and acquaintances—are of much less value in retirement.

Some retirements occur without taking into account the spouse's situation. Even if she (or he) doesn't work, retirement may disrupt the other's life, too.

When a man (or woman) retires, another phenomenon surfaces—self-freedom. All our working lives, we know we are being watched and assessed. This is usually benign, but it's still there, and we know it from the peformance appraisal forms if from nothing else. When we retire, one of two things usually happens. First, we are so in the habit of getting approval that we still seek it, thus annoying our spouses. Conversely, we may for a time become somewhat selfish, more opinionated, and more careless in dress, language and behavior.

The new retiree also becomes bereft of his or her sense of time and accomplishment, always present when working. So, many retirees impose a sense of time upon themselves. They will bank on Monday, do yard work on Tuesday, shop on Wednesday, perform household chores on Thursday, and have lunch with the boys (or girls) on Friday. The sense of accomplishment arises from having done all these things on schedule. Yet, it's artificial, if not actually embarrassing when the boys (or girls) cancel the lunch on Friday for a second time in the month.

Therefore, it's possible to underestimate what retirement will do for you, and you may wish you had a job again.

What To Do When the Signs Are Bad

When the indicators are unmistakeable that you must change your status of work or retirement, don't panic. Be grateful for the blessing that you at last know where you stand. No more nagging uncertainties, no more hanging on in a situation you know is not right for you.

We devote the rest of this book to advise you on what to do next, but for the moment, write or rewrite your resume, rebuild your network of contacts, and put out feelers.

When Henry Ford II fired him, Lee Iacocca reports in his autobiography that he could not believe it. Yet, when he regained his equilibrium, he saw that the handwriting had been written in large letters. He simply didn't want to read it. Although painful, his severance jet-propelled his career. Staying on at Ford Motor Company, as he once expected, would also have been prestigious, but it would not have given him the fame and recognition he has now.

This author can attest to the same experience, although on a more modest scale. John Morgan writes full time now, as he has always dreamed of doing. As Christopher Morley said, "There is only one success—to be able to spend your life in your own way."

5

The Ins and Outs of Age Discrimination

Pack up your troubles
In your old kit bag
And smile, smile, smile.
What's the use of worryin' —
It never was worthwhile.

So go lines in the World War I song.

Such insouciance may be appropriate in wartime, but not in seniors' battles to stay effectively employed.

Age discrimination laws give many people 50 and older a false sense of security. Here are a few case histories of people who discovered how false their security was:

- "I felt if I'm skilled, I could go anywhere and find a job," remembers 57-year-old Raymond Arnista who worked for 38 years without a layoff as a machinist at Torrington Company near Hartford, CT. After his plant closed, he won a transfer to another Torrington facility by relinquishing seniority rights. In a year, he was out there, too. "When I went looking for a job, I didn't realize the reason I wasn't getting one was my age." In desperation, he had to elect for early retirement and a reduced pension. He didn't view himself as retired, however. He took training as an electronics technician and eventually found work in that field.

- Ogden Food Services Corporation employed Irving Chern for 32 years as a concession manager, then let him go at age 61. He was replaced by a 25-year-old. He eventually found similar work with a competing company, but this ended when he was 63. He retained a lawyer to pursue an age-bias suit against Ogden and has held various part-time, temporary positions in food concession work while hunting for a full-time management job. "When people let you go when you're in your sixties," he worries, "they're practically ringing the death knell for you."

● Mark Lorah lost his job as a supervisor of slag processing in 1982 after steel cutbacks led to the closing of a plant in Allentown, PA. Fifty-six years old and untrained in any other field, he was rejected for jobs ranging from bank guard to building maintenance. He enrolled in a 15-week floor-covering course organized by Dislocated Workers Program, a federally-funded effort designed to train and find jobs for the large number of unemployed in the Lehigh Valley. At the end of his training, Lorah had four job offers. Although all gave starting pay far below the $21,000 he made in slag processing, he chose one of these jobs.

Does ADEA Help?

The Age Discrimination in Employment Act was first passed in 1967 and has been amended several times since. It has probably generated more work for lawyers than anyone else. Most of the litigation comes from three provisions. The first is BFOQ, which excuses the employer from the law if a job has a "bona fide occupational qualification" that the laid-off employee doesn't possess, or RFOA when a laid-off employee is not offered another job because of "reasonable factors other than age." The second exception recognizes seniority systems as "not a subterfuge to evade" the act. This one makes possible collective bargaining agreements that set a mandatory retirement age below 65. The third exemption protects employers who "for good cause" might discharge a worker. Insubordination, for instance, constitutes "good cause."

Although ADEA says all but top people can work until they're 70, employers use those exceptions and other strategies to circumvent the provisions and ease people out before (sometimes long before) that age. As we have seen, they usually do it with early-retirement incentives. The employer can also eliminate the job in some cases and leave the employee, regardless of age, with little recourse.

In a recent survey, Charles D. Spencer & Associates of Chicago found that 80 percent of 13,744 retirements from 105 employers were before 65. The firm tried to learn what proportion of the early retirements were voluntary, but had to give up because of "invalid data." You can bet the data was invalid because employers were reluctant to give any. Also, most employees hated to admit they were forced out.

The following are just a few among many companies who made the mass layoffs (of seniors for the most part) in 1985 and found ADEA no hindrance at all: AT&T, Ford Motor, Union Carbide, CBS, ABC/Capital Communications, Eastern Airlines, TWA. The list can go on and on. The message: ADEA might save your job, but don't count on it. Even if you sue and win, the likelihood is that the personnel grapevine will quickly label you litigious, a worse tag than incompetent.

Even in the 13 states (including California and New York) that have banned forced retirement policies, the effect may have been to increase, not decrease, severances. The legislation has spurred a dramatic rise in *voluntary* separation plans, often called quick-quit incentives. Some involve payments of 50 to 200 percent of annual salaries. Hewitt Associates in Lincolnshire, IL, has identified 74 such plans throughout the U.S. Since 1981, according to a Hewitt survey, some 24,000 employees quit jobs under such plans. Only 48 of the companies said they would offer separation incentives in 1986, but, says Hewitt's Jerry Y. Carnegie, the actual number is likely to be much higher and will probably top the previous year's figure. "Employees might leave without incentives and save the company money, so companies like to keep it quiet," he says.

He believes companies worked harder than ever in 1986 to get more workers, especially seniors, to quit. "Older workers are the ones companies want to get rid of. They have the highest pay and the most expensive benefits."

We need not feel sorry for employees equipped with golden parachutes, the agreements that guarantee cash settlements to top executives whom mergers force overboard. Nevertheless, we should note that the number of such arrangements soars despite lingering tax questions. Towers, Perrin, Forster & Crosby, a consultant firm headquartered in Philadelphia and New York, says 35 of the nation's top 100 industrial companies offered such settlements in 1986. The total was up from 21 in 1985 and only two in 1981.

Life Begins at 50—If Biases Don't Get You

Our public and private pension systems discriminate against seniors who want to keep working. The most ironic twist of all lies in the fact that ADEA's 70 age limit has probably lost more jobs for seniors than the provision ever saved.

Prejudices against age are as pervasive, pernicious and cruel as against minorities. There's a widespread conspiracy to ignore aging, hide it, and even denigrate it like alcoholism or herpes. This comes as the greatest shock to a white Anglo-Saxon male; relatively, he enjoyed king-of-the-hill status all his life. Others—minorities, women—have faced biases most of their lives and may take this new roadblock in stride, but even they need to be aware of what faces them as they move into this age group.

Two factors unique in western society have made seniors particularly vulnerable. One is the decline of the family. In other societies, the family would have supported them with a network of kinship. This has dramatically weakened, especially in America. The second is the rate of technological change which makes people's skills obsolete in a much shorter time than formerly. An electronics expert is no longer expert in five years if he hasn't kept up with the changes crowding into his specialty. A doctor can quickly become obsolescent if he doesn't keep up with the developments in medicine. These factors, together with demographic considerations, have probably worsened the biases against seniors.

Here are some common prejudices against seniors and rebuttals:

Fancy: Employees over 50 are less productive than those who are younger.

Fact: "Employees in their late fifties and sixties are, by far, more conscientious and hard working than younger workers," according to a study conducted by Robert Half International. Overall, work productivity does not decline as a function of age. The difference in productivity between younger and older workers is generally less than the differences within the ranks of younger workers or any one age group. Age-related productivity studies by the Bureau of Business Management at the University of Illinois, Bankers Trust and Casualty Company, Texas Refining Corporation, and the U.S. Department of Labor confirm this.

At the heart of the misconception about productivity is probably an attempt to explain this nation's sluggish output per manhour. The fallacious reasoning goes this way: "We have more older people in our workforce who are, of course, less productive. Therefore, our productivity has worsened." Indeed, our productivity has declined. After growing at a compound annual rate of 2.3 percent from 1947 through 1973, output per worker grew by only 0.3 percent annually during the next decade. Many people muddily attribute this to the rising age of the workforce, not realizing or admitting that productivity declines result from a complex of high taxes, other lowered financial incentives, a transition in our economy from smokestack to lighter industries that's not yet completed, and a host of other factors, none related to aging in the population.

Fortunately, this myth may be fading. A study by Yankelovich, Skelly and White Inc. for the American Association of Retired Persons reveals that "on the productivity issues . . . older workers receive the highest rating." A study of 400 companies in all size groups showed that 88 percent rated attendance/punctuality as essential to productivity; 86 percent rated seniors as excellent in this category. Also, 88 percent of the companies surveyed rated commitment to quality as essential; 82 percent scored older workers as excellent. Finally, 74 percent of the companies considered a solid performance record as essential to productivity; 71 percent found seniors excellent performers.

Fancy: Older workers get sick more than younger ones.

Fact: Workers between 17 and 44 call in sick an average of 3.7 days annually. Those 45 and older do so only 3.1 days yearly, according to the American Council of Life Insurance.

Age alone is a poor predictor of health, says the Andrus Gerontology Center. Some people do suffer rapid decreases in health with age, while others experience little or no decline.

For the average person, the five senses decline in acuity with age. However, change in vision and hearing are the most important and can be corrected by glasses and hearing aids.

Occupation probably has the most severe adverse impact on an individual's health. The Department of Labor's seven-year study of white male workers aged 45 through 59 showed that 13 out of every 100 manual and less skilled workers were unable to work or had died by the study's end, compared to only 3 out of every 100 professional and technical workers. The steady increase in the number of service jobs and a decrease in heavy labor jobs will contribute to a larger proportion of people in their fifties and older being able to work longer.

Fancy: Turnover is higher among older employees than younger ones.

Fact: The opposite is true. Turnover among senior women is 88 percent less than among younger women, according to a study by Nine-to-Five, an association of office workers. Employers generally can count on seniors being more stable than younger workers.

Fancy: Young managers are more competent than older bosses.

Fact: If so, employers generally don't believe it. The age of candidates being recruited for top positions has increased steadily over the past 10 to 15 years, according to a study by the Andrus Gerontology Center.

Fancy: Older managers are less capable of making decisions and evaluating information than younger managers.

Fact: Utterly false. A study conducted in 1975 for the Andrus Center found that older managers are more capable of evaluating available information when making decisions than are younger managers because of their greater experience. Older managers, however, take longer to reach a decision and are less willing than younger managers to take risks, probably because experience has taught them the danger of some risks.

Fancy: Intelligence declines with age.

Fact: Age appears irrelevant. Most important in evaluating intellectual functioning are an individual's perception set, attention span, motivation, and fund of knowledge. Dr. Jerry Avorn of the Harvard Medical School says that most aspects of intelligence that may be lost with age are, at most, "a nuisance." Crucial areas of human intelligence do not decline with age among people who are generally healthy, gerontologists agree.

One key mental faculty called "crystallized intelligence" continues to rise over the life span of healthy, active people. This unfortunately-named factor refers to a person's ability to use an accumulated body of general information to make judgments and solve problems. Such intelligence comes into play in dealing with problems for which there are no clear answers, but only better or worse options. Dr. John Horn, a University of Denver psychologist who specializes in crystallized intelligence, says it continues to increase throughout life, although in old age the incremental gains grow smaller. People in their fifties and older who stay mentally active, socially involved and possess flexible personalities have a greater store of "world knowledge"—information acquired both from formal education and day-to-day experience. They also have, according to Avorn, "a rich, evocative fluency; they can say the same thing in five different ways."

Research shows that, for most people, IQ declines little with age. Generational differences in IQ have been found, however. These are due to differences in education, media exposure and nutrition.

Motivation strongly influences intellectual functioning. Some seniors believe the fallacy that the mind inevitably atrophies with age. They then tragically behave in ways which reinforce negative stereotypes. Typically, they exaggerate bad characteristics they have shown all their lives. If you hesitate to ask the time of a person of 40 because he'll reply with the evolution of the clock, you would never ask that same individual at 80 because he'll respond with a discourse on the role of sequential relations in the history of man.

Be assured: If age takes a few marbles away from you they aren't all that important.

Fancy: Older people have poorer memories than younger ones.

Fact: It's more correct to say that seniors have more to remember than their juniors. They only *seem* to forget more.

Phenomenal differences in memory functioning occur among individuals of any age. Some factors which affect memory functioning are poor health, depression, emotional upsets and poor nutrition. In the absence of these factors, age-related declines in memory are slight and minimally affect job performance.

Fancy: You can't teach an old dog new tricks.

Fact: Maybe not, but we're talking about people, not dogs. Supervisors who nourish this bias often give older workers less chance to learn new job skills, contributing to make this another self-fulfilling prejudice. Here are facts to rebut this fancy:

● People who were capable of learning at a younger age, and who continue to use their intellectual abilities, maintain their ability to learn in later life. A study of Dr. Eleanor Simon, a professor of psychology at California State University in Carson, showed no significant difference in the grade point averages of those over 50 compared to younger students. She compared 16 students between ages 18 and 25 with 16 between 49 and 72.

● Once recruited and registered for training, older men are more likely than younger ones to complete their training. Furthermore, once trained, seniors are likely to remain with their employers longer than are younger trainees.

● In some cases, it may take a senior longer than a junior to learn new skills or knowledge required for a job. Yet, research also shows that the over-50s tend to remember it longer.

Fancy: Older people are more accident-prone.

Fact: The accident record of seniors is better than for juniors. This is true even when older workers have no more experience on the job than younger employees. Juniors are more likely to accept foolish risks than seniors. Seniors, on the other hand, remove themselves from unsafe circumstances and thus avoid situations where accidents are likely to occur.

Seniors function more effectively and have the fewest accidents in a work setting where both the task and pace are not rigidly structured.

Over-50s generally have different types of accidents than the under-50s. Seniors are more likely than juniors to fall or to be hit by flying objects. Seniors are less likely to be caught in a machine or to be injured in starting a machine than are juniors.

Seniors avoid accidents by using judgment based on experience. They are less able to avoid accidents which call for quick, evasive actions.

Fancy: The over-50s demand special treatment and facilities.

Fact: Holders of this bias confuse seniors with the handicapped. This age group, statistically, has only a slightly higher proportion of the handicapped than other age groups, largely attributable to arthritis. Seniors, per se, are *not* handicapped.

Fancy: The older worker costs more to employ than the younger one. The doctrine of cost-effectiveness has assumed almost religious proportions in the current business/social climate; hence, this is the most pervasive myth of all.

Fact: "This view is not substantiated by survey data," says Yankelovich, Skelly and White (YSW). Its study points out that health insurance costs less for a 55-year-old employee than for a 30-year-old with two dependents. The generally higher pay for "older workers is justified when you consider their value to the company," believe 90 percent of 400 companies surveyed by YSW.

Fancy: People 50 and older often lack ambition. The YSW study suggests this is the second most pervasive myth in industry, especially with companies employing 1,000 or more.

Fact: Seniors may be more ambitious than juniors because time may be running out in achieving long-held objectives.

Fancy: Most seniors are less inclined to work than juniors.

Fact: The same rebuttal holds for this one as for the fallacy about ambition. Statistics don't support this one either. The Andrus Center, for example, estimates that a *minimum* of 8 million people over 65 want to continue working.

Overcoming Prejudice

Those biases are elements of the environment in aging. You must take them into account and overcome them in your jobhunting campaign. Rail against them, but it won't help. Ignore them at your peril. Here are ways of coping:

1) Adopt the mental attitude that aging is nothing more than being around longer, with the resulting greater experience. Any audience tends to mirror what you project. Project the right image.

2) Consider jobhunting as a change from one activity to another, having nothing to do with your age.

3) Make your jobhunting age-neutral. Never refer to your age yourself; if others, particularly potential employers, do so, reply

in terms of experience rather than age (more on this in the next section).

4) Use "firing" and all its synonyms and euphemisms as sparingly as possible in your vocabulary. Instead, use "career change," "new direction," "new mode," and so on.

5) Remember that aging is a fact of life for you and everyone else. Program yourself for it as a natural event. In bees, a change in social role is programmed with the passage of time. So should it also be with people. We progress from being children to being parents, and then to being grandparents. Unique to our culture is the roleless status assigned to so many seniors.

6) Make jobhunting and/or career-changing the role for yourself. Avoid limbo.

7) Join an organization representing seniors, preferably one representing jobhunting seniors. The American Association of Retired Persons has a new Worker Equity Department. Its director, David Gamse, says, "When the baby boom peaks out, older workers are going to be an important factor in the workforce." AARP believes, "Americans increasingly view retirement as a time to launch new initiatives in the work place." With more than 22 million members, AARP is the largest senior organization around. Founded in 1958 by Dr. Ethel Andrus, she wrote, "We . . . feel a need to have a function in society, to have a respected place in the eyes of others, to be doing something that is interesting and significant in our own eyes, to have a national voice." The University of Southern California's Andrus Gerontology Center is named after her.

The Crusade Against Prejudice

AARP often plays a crusading role on behalf of the over-50s (its cutoff age for membership), especially concerning state and federal legislation. Unfortunately, it and every other advocate of America's fastest growing population segment have failed to correct some of the insidious tax code and Social Security provisions against senior citizens, although not from lack of trying.

These provisions could force people *not* to work. Consider this frustrating news: If you are between 65 and 70, you could pocket as little as $2,000 for working in a job all year that pays $20,000. Take into account commuting costs and other job-related expenses, and you could actually lose money by working.

Paul Westbrook of Buck Consultants, New York, prepared the tables
below for *Money*. They appeared in its "1985 Money Guide—Planning
Now for Your Successful Retirement". They show how much two people—one 66, the other 71—can add to after-tax income with post-re-
tirement jobs in 1984. (1984 was selected to minimize complications
caused by changes in the tax law. The ages 66 and 71 were used to reflect
a full year's Social Security payment past 65 and 70.)

Assume that both people are single and collect the maximum Social Security benefits ($8,808 in 1984 for the 66-year-old and $9,120 for the
71-year-old; the latter is higher largely because of annual cost-of-living
increases). Both have pensions paying $17,000 a year and investment in-
comes of $15,500. Until he reaches 70, the 66-year-old will lose 50 cents
in Social Security benefits for every dollar he earns above $6,690 a year.
(Although the threshold became $7,320 in 1985, the final financial re-
sults stayed about the same.) Both will pay FICA (Federal Insurance Contributions Act, the tax for Social Security) 6.7 percent on their earnings.
Income tax figures assume tax and local levies totaling 19 percent of the
federal tax rate and reflect a new penalty—up to half of Social Security
benefits may be subject to federal income tax.

Although the penalties decrease at 70, even then you're likely to retain
less than half of your earnings at best. The changes in Social Security
and taxes that went into effect in 1985-86 make the penalties even more
severe.

How does this disappearing act occur? First, your Social Security check
shrinks in proportion to growth in your job earnings above $6,960 (in
1984). Next, because of tax legislation effective in 1984, your salary may
boost your taxable income sufficiently to make as much as half of your
Social Security benefits subject to federal income tax, and your job earnings may push you into a higher tax bracket. Also, you'll keep on paying
FICA tax on your earnings.

An effective strategy—beyond illegally not reporting all your income
—to counteract the prejudices shown against the over-65s by our law-
makers is not to collect Social Security benefits regardless of how much
you earn on the side. If you hold off until 70 on getting Social Security
checks you will receive 3 percent more, plus cost-of-living allowances for
every year that you postponed benefits after 65. (The increase is 1 percent
for those who are now 68 or older.) If you begin receiving Social Security
checks and then decide to defer benefits, however, you forfeit that 3 percent annual bonus.

A crusade is needed to get these laws changed. They constitute one
more barrier and bias against seniors.

AT AGE 66

Post-retirement job income	$6,960	$10,000	$15,000	$20,000	$30,000	$40,000
Reduction in Social Security benefits	-	$1,520	$4,020	$6,520	$8,808	$8,808
FICA tax due	$466	$670	$1,005	$1,340	$2,010	$2,533
Federal, state and local income taxes	$2,819	$4,520	$6,780	$10,000	$15,000	$22,840
Net gain (% of earnings retained)	$3,675 (53%)	$3,290 (33%)	$3,195 (21%)	$2,140 (11%)	$4,182 (14%)	$5,819 (15%)

AT AGE 71

Post-retirement job income	$6,960	$10,000	$15,000	$20,000	$30,000	$40,000
Reduction in Social Security benefits	-	-	-	-	-	-
FICA tax due	$466	$670	$1,005	$1,340	$2,010	$2,533
Federal, state and local income taxes	$3,146	$4,520	$7,500	$10,000	$17,130	$22,840
Net gain (% of earnings retained)	$3,348 (48%)	$4,810 (48%)	$6,495 (43%)	$8,660 (43%)	$10,860 (36%)	$14,627 (37%)

Is Everyone Prejudiced Against Seniors?

Sometimes it almost seems so. Yet, take encouragement from what these wise people have said about our stage in life:

Samuel Johnson—"As a man advances in life he gets what is better than admiration—judgment to estimate things at their own value."

Aeschylus—"It is always in season for old men to learn."

Pablo Picasso—"Now that I have arrived at a great age, I might as well be twenty."

Bernard Baruch—"To me, old age is always fifteen years older than I am."

Oliver Wendell Holmes—"To be seventy years young is sometimes far more cheerful and hopeful than to be forty years old."

Henri Frederic Amiel—"To know how to grow old is the master work of wisdom, and one of the most difficult chapters in the great art of living."

Anne Bradstreet—"Youth is the time of getting, middle age of improving and old age of spending; a negligent youth is usually attended by an ignorant middle age and both by an empty old age."

6

When the Axe Falls

When Jim got fired, he didn't tell his family for a month.

When Ed had to take early retirement, he hired a "professional" to write his résumé, got friends to line up job interviews, and launched into a whirlwind of jobhunting activity.

When Sally lost her job, she left on a six-week vacation.

Jim should have brought in his family to support him at once. He could have learned from his wife, for example, that his loner tendencies and his overweening pride may have contributed to his dismissal.

Ed's whirlwind bred discouragement, not true self-knowledge.

On her vacation, Sally never let herself think seriously and objectively about herself.

What Shall We Do With the Rest of Our Lives?

When the axe falls, that's the first question we should ask ourselves, even before we ask what new job or career we should seek. We suggest a methodology to discover the answer and to avoid the usual pitfall that afflicts seniors—excessive reliance on solving the problem at hand as quickly as possible, with little regard for the history that led up to it or the future consequences of actions taken.

First, list the key elements of the immediate situation, namely those *known, unclear* and *presumed*. This simple procedure puts attention on the situation itself instead of on the question, what to do? That's kept at bay for a while.

Then, identify any past situations of friends or relatives that appear analogous and quickly note the *likenesses* and also the *differences* that can block the use of potentially misleading analogies. Before defining the desired objective, examine the history of the issue. First, ask: What's the story?, and note significant changes in the story so far. Next, ask the journalists' questions—who, what, where, when, how and why? Finally,

place yourself in the situation. At this point, the answer to what to do
emerges, sometimes almost automatically, but always more clearly than
if we had not gone through the exercise.

Case Study of Jim

When Jim was fired, the known element of his situation was that he
was out of a job. The unclear element was why. The presumed factor was
that he had to find new work. After he stopped sulking and told his wife
of his severance, he reluctantly agreed with her that his high-handed actions may have led to his dismissal. As a former vice-president of human
resources, he had won the enmity of both unionized and nonunionized
employees by unilaterally imposing changes in work rules.

Coached by his wife to try the foregoing methodology, he saw an analogous situation with his own father, but he quickly ceased thinking along
that line. His father committed suicide in 1938 following four years of
unemployment or gross underemployment. A more satisfactory analogy
lay in the circumstances of his stepfather whom his mother later married.
When he lost his job as a traffic manager during the Great Depression, he
used his own and borrowed resources to buy a used truck which he at first
drove himself. Eventually, he developed a thriving trucking business.

Could Jim go into business for himself? The journalists' questions led
to depressing answers at first. Consultants on human resources function
mostly on a national or regional basis out of major cities, nor did he particularly relish their style of high-pressure life and constant travel. He and
his wife wished to remain in their small city in northeastern Ohio.

After much study and discussion, which included agreement that he
was too young (57) to retire, they hit upon a possible solution. His town
couldn't support an employers' association, but it did boast a thriving
Chamber of Commerce. He persuaded it to sponsor him to organize a section that would offer members counseling on human resources matters.
The venture flourished, attracting new smaller-business employers as
members and generating enthusiastic responses from the current ones
without formal human resources departments. Jim thus created a new job
for himself. By distancing himself from his members' employees, he also
avoided his old nemesis of jousts with the employees themselves.

Case Study of Ed

Ed had no trouble with the first part of the methodology. He lost his job
as a shift foreman because his employer went bankrupt. There was no

doubt he needed a new job. He was determined that all four of his children would get college educations; his two youngest, twin boys, were freshmen at a state university, his second, a daughter, still hadn't found a satisfactory job as a teacher, and his oldest son was in his final year at law school.

He needed a job that would pay at least as much as his former position did. Although all four of his youngsters did part-time work, they couldn't support themselves fully, and his daughter was discovering that jobhunting was nearly a full-time task in itself.

Ed's family convinced him that his true goal in life was to find a job he enjoyed with a stable employer, not to get a position that paid the most money. After a brush-up course, his wife could return to secretarial work. The twins applied for and obtained student loans. The law school son did the same. The potential teacher gave up her apartment temporarily and moved back with her parents.

Relieved of his immediate financial stress, Ed looked around at his friends, particularly Art, another shift foreman with their now-defunct employer. Art had returned to an hourly position as a machinist, with eventual prospects of earning nearly as much as formerly. Ed took refresher courses and returned to his first love, tool-and-diemaking, where he quickly found a job. It, plus his early-retirement pension, eventually gave him an income slightly higher than he earned as a foreman.

Case Study of Sally

Sally had a different problem. She lost her executive secretarial job after her boss of 30 years retired. When the company could not offer her a comparable position, she chose early retirement, making her decision more in a huff than after calm consideration, even though her employer would have kept her on at lower-status work until the proper job opened up. The truth was that no other executive wanted her, and she knew it, at least subconsciously.

Over the years, she had soured. She had kept house for her semi-invalid, cantankerous father, worked at her job and never married. Although her father's death relieved her of financial and emotional strain, she found retirement left her profoundly dissatisfied. She hadn't much enjoyed her vacation. At 62, she had reduced Social Security benefits, a modest pension from her former employer and income from her inheritance, plus the house that her father left her. She had no financial problems, just emotional ones.

A Job Advisory service in Pittsburgh encouraged her to apply the methodology first to retirement generally, not to her specific case. Here is what she found from reading and from interviews with retirement counselors:

Although we can afford retirement, we should still do something that gives meaning and purpose to our lives. Many Americans accept this fallacious reasoning about retirement:
1) That we are owed it.
2) That the nation's employers can afford it.
3) That society can afford it.
4) That we can afford it.

The first three assumptions are false. The fourth may be untrue for an increasing number of us.

Assumption Number 1

The first assumption is erroneous because even Social Security was never intended to fully support anyone's retirement. It was developed as a safety net to help people in their senior years when they might not have as high an income or be earning as much as when younger. Private pensions had the same goal. Over time, these purposes became perverted into a concept held by too many of us that "the world owes me a living after 65 or even younger."

The whole concept of mass retirement is scarcely a century old. The phrase in its present meaning did not appear in Noah Webster's great dictionary of 1841. Mass retirement resulted from the Industrial Age, and there was not much "mass" about it until the mid-1950s when Social Security was extended to virtually all Americans.

Assumption Number 2

We know something is wrong with the second assumption when news surfaces so frequently about a private pension plan going broke or reducing retirees' payments. Even with ERISA (Employee Retirement Income Security Administration) and the government's Pension Benefit Guaranty Corporation established by legislation in 1974, the failures continue.

Assumption Number 3

The Social Security system suffers periodic crises that rival The Perils of Pauline. Despite repeated fixes, another will come, perhaps as early as 1989. The troubles continue because Social Security is still largely based on the demographics that prevailed at its establishment in 1935 when the average life expectancy of the American male was about 55 years. It's 70.7 years now. In 1935, those who did survive to 65 and qualified for Social Security pensions could then expect to enjoy them for only two more years. Males who reach 65 today can anticipate living another 14.5 years. When a man reaches 70, he can expect another 12 years.

The foregoing figures alone show why the third assumption—that society can afford it—is false. The steadily narrowing ratio of active workers vs. people on Social Security also should convince us. If eligibility rules are not changed even more than they have been, the ratio will be 2.5:1 in the next decade, untenable both economically and politically. This ratio, to be supported, would mean that younger people would have to fork over 25 percent of their earnings so that people could stay on Social Security. Impossible.

Assumption Number 4

The fourth assumption is the most treacherous of all, perhaps fatally so for the person who chooses to do nothing. A loafing retirement is bad medically and psychologically. Every successful retired-person has taken on responsibility for someone or something outside himself.

Anyhow, inflation and demographic changes are making fewer Americans able to afford full retirement.

Revolution in Aging Attitudes

As a step toward developing an answer to what we should do with the rest of our lives, Sally studied what has happened to attitudes toward aging in the last two centuries. From about 1770 to 1820, a revolution in age relations began in the United States and spread throughout the western world, culminating most dramatically in the American and French revolutions.

An Englishman, Dr. Richard Gem, was a particularly vehement proponent of youth. Thomas Jefferson wholeheartedly adopted his views and wrote, "It is reasonable we should drop off and make room for another growth. When we have lived our generation out, we should not wish to encroach upon another."

Changes in word meanings illustrate changes in values. In the late eighteenth century, "novelty," "innovation" and "modern" were pejoratives. By about 1820 they became praise words. A "graybeard" in Shakespeare's day meant an honorable old age; it has come to mean a comic oldster. "Old guard" in Napoleon's and Wellington's time meant elite veteran troops; it has come to mean reactionary, corrupt and aged politicians or other power groups.

The opposite phenomenon exists, too. To "grandfather" in the eighteenth century meant to flatter with excessive veneration, a meaning now lost. Similarly, many words in the seventeenth and early eighteenth centuries that expressed contempt for youngsters—youngling, skipper, upstart—have either dropped out of use or no longer have the pejorative meaning of two centuries ago.

Encouraged, if not actually egged on by Jefferson, writers of the early nineteenth century took up the cudgels for youth. At the arrogant age of 30, Henry Thoreau wrote, "Age is no better, hardly so well, qualified for an instructor as youth for it has not profited so much as it has lost. One may almost doubt if the wisest man has learned anything of absolute value by living. Practically, the old have no very important advice to give the young, their experience has been so partial, and their lives have been such miserable failures . . . they are only less young than they were." Thoreau invented a corrosive creed in the Walden Woods, and we still suffer from some of its hangover today.

Why this transformation that erupted at the turn of the nineteenth century? The basic reason was demographic change as typified by growth in the median age in America from 16 in 1790, 1800 and 1810 to 16.5 by 1820. That seems a slight change, but had profound significance. The population experienced a demographic shift, with more people in their early twenties feeling their oats and, furthermore, having the political and economic power to make themselves felt. Combining with this, especially in America, was a strong egalitarian feeling. The area, unlike Europe, had no radical differences in wealth and seemingly unlimited land and opportunities. So, why should age carry some special caveat?

Thus, the pendulum swung to a cult of youth that grew steadily in strength from 1770, culminating in such idiocies of the 1960s as, "Never trust anyone over 30."

Yet, the pendulum is starting to swing closer to the attitude prevalent before about 1770. The demographic changes becoming evident in the 1970s lie at the base of the shifts, just as they did in the metamorphosis of about 200 years ago.

Good News for Seniors?

In her studies of retirement, Sally decided the demographic shifts now making themselves felt generally mean good news for seniors.

Today, however, just as two centuries ago, we find groups in our population who don't or won't recognize the watershed period in which we live. It's clear that the youth rebellion we endured during the 1960s was a wave at the past, not at the future. The youth of 20 years ago may have sensed, subliminally or otherwise, that the long ascendency they held in the social psyche was ending. They had a last fling.

Many politicians, employers and union leaders are only now waking up to this demographic trend. Beginning shortly after World War II, they began instituting mandatory retirement rules into their pension plans, contributing to the early retirement phenomenon we see today. Of course, Congress contributed to early retirement trends by modifications to the Social Security system that permit reduced payments beginning at 62. Many private plans trailed along, or offered even more liberal inducements at earlier ages. (They weren't completely crazy. Immediately after World War II, much of the population feared—unwarrantedly, as it turned out—that the nation's employers couldn't absorb the influx of returning veterans.)

A few of the vestigial fears linger on, especially among some politicians, managers, union officials, and job counsellors. These people are decades out of date. We must take such people into account when deciding what to do with the rest of our lives.

We should look with care at the paternalistic efforts of employers and others who give well-meaning but often inappropriate advice to early retirees on starting a small business, writing a résumé, jobhunting and interviewing. Much of it is bad advice at worst or irrelevant at best. Furthermore, it's too soon to get into this. It turned Sally off when she took early retirement, for reasons that grew clearer to her only after she had studied the whole issue of retirement. The company's advice on retirement was to adopt a hobby, join a group of senior citizens, and get a physical examination. She did the last, which showed her physically sound, but she never had a hobby in her life and wasn't going to start one now. She never had been a joiner, and spending much time with people her own age or older didn't intrigue her.

We should also scrutinize the advice of job counselors, both public and private. At this transitional stage, it's too early to get into specific job and career suggestions. Sally almost left in the middle of her first interview with Job Advisory because all it originally advised was to return to secretarial work. Then, she realized she no longer wanted that. She wanted something different.

We should rely, ultimately, only on our own instincts in answering the question of what to do with the rest of our lives. At this point, we should consider, without the usual constraints of time and money, what we would most like to do in the years ahead. If we listen to the nay-sayers, we'll land in trouble. Ralph Waldo Emerson provides a case in point. He listened to his friend Thoreau on age, and at 63 wrote his ominously titled "Terminus":

> It is time to be old,
> To take in sail:—
> The god of bounds,
> Who set to seas a shore,
> Came to me in his fatal rounds,
> And said: "No more!
> No farther shoot
> Thy broad ambitious branches, and thy root.
> Fancy departs; no more invent;
> Contract thy firmament
> To compass of a tent."

Although Emerson lived in good health to the age of 79 and continued writing, he did indeed narrow his firmament. He deliberately slowed down. .

Sally rejected full retirement. She took a volunteer position with Job Advisory, specializing in counseling people considering retirement.

When the Axe Should Fall

For their own good, the axe should fall on underemployed and stockpiled employees. They are people in the wrong job, in the wrong field, or working at far below their capabilities. About 80 percent of all employees may be underemployed, according to research, including that by the California State University at Fullerton after a 16-year study of 350,000 job applicants.

How did so many of us get into such a fix? By ignoring or being ignorant of the methodology outlined earlier in this chapter.

How can we determine if we are underemployed? By going through the process and by heeding the signs detailed in the previous chapter.

Now, here are 15 chief elements that a good job should offer:

1) A sense of security. This doesn't mean tenure necessarily. It means a sense of inner security—that we are doing the right thing.
2) Opportunity for advancement.
3) Convenient location. That is, convenient for *us*.
4) Pleasant working environment.
5) Appreciation from boss, customers or others.
6) A minimum of office politics, although some is inevitable.
7) Equal rights without regard to age.
8) Respect for individual opinions.
9) Reliability.
10) Progressive management.
11) Efficiency.
12) Identification with the whole—the feeling that what we do figures importantly in the overall operation.
13) Acceptable social standing.
14) Chance for a satisfactory personal life.
15) Suitable financial rewards.

When we reach 50, we should appraise our present job and career on the basis of these criteria. We should stay put if the answer is positive on 11 or more. We should consider moving if the answer is positive on eight to ten, but not necessarily do so. If we can answer positively on only seven or less, we are in trouble.

What can we do about it? Hunt for another job. The minority of underemployed seniors do this. Those with gumption tackle it. Those who get forced out do it. Perhaps they are the luckiest of the lot; they have no choice. Both Jim and Ed now admit that getting let go was the most fortunate thing that ever happened to them.

Many companies that have recently gone through a merger or other restructuring even offer jobhunting advice to their early retirees. We should appraise such advice with care *after* we have gone through the methodology on our own. A clue to the motives behind such counsel comes from the manager of a plant that was closing: "It makes people feel you care about them." We want commitment less tepid than that. The only sure way of getting it is from within ourselves.

The Good Actors

We do not wish to leave the impression that all employers discriminate against seniors. Many go out of their way to help. Among the many who do, these stand out:

● The Travelers, Hartford, CT, issued 800 invitations to an "Un-Retirement Party" with information on how respondents could rejoin the insurance and financial services organization. It found jobs for more than 300. Harold Johnson, The Travelers' senior vice-president of personnel administration, said, "Everyone benefits when companies rehire retirees or retain a worker beyond normal retirement dates."

● Grumman Aerospace in Los Angeles has a training program for people of any age. Nearly 60 percent of those participating in a retraining program to develop systems engineers are over 40.

● Sterile Design Inc. in Tampa, FL, has four-hour shifts for seniors who want it in a plant which packages medical and hospital supplies.

● Aerospace Corp., Los Angeles, has a "casual employee" category whereby people who work less than 20 hours a week or 1,000 hours a year can continue to receive their monthly pension benefits in addition to their earnings.

The Final Piece of Advice

When an interviewer asked Nelson Algren, the novelist and short story writer, for his advice on how to succeed, he replied, "Never play cards with a man called *Doc*. Never eat in a place called *Mom's*. Never sleep with a woman whose troubles are worse than your own."

In other words, the best piece of advice is to rely first on your own common sense.

7

Redirect Your Career

"Work is the refuge of people who have nothing better to do." Oscar Wilde worked hard to polish that aphorism, as he did to make most of his others shine.

Actually, he demonstrated considerable productivity during his 46-year life, publishing 15 volumes of plays, poetry, stories, letters, and an autobiography. He also often redirected his career, moving from satiric plays to tragedy, from lyric poetry to ballads, from fairy stories to fantasies in prose. Besides excelling as a writer, he enjoyed success as a lecturer. Some have said that the common denominator of his life was performance, both on stage and off.

Wilde might not agree, but there's nothing sacred about any career, whether it's writing or bricklaying. What's sacred is the individual and his or her survival as a happy, productive person.

Career-Changing

Formerly, a job change was considered okay provided it didn't happen too often, but even one was judged a sign of instability. That's no longer true. Indeed, working Americans change their jobs and sometimes their careers eight times during a lifetime, on average.

Career-changing has long been more common than many people think. A teacher who becomes a school principal, a salesman who becomes a sales manager, a machinist who becomes a foreman, a line engineer who becomes engineering vice-president—all have changed careers if not employers.

When a senior wants a new job, he or she will probably have to redirect or change careers. Why?

Hear Peter Drucker, the author, consultant and teacher, on the subject. "The real career crisis is the extension of the working-life span. In the time of our grandparents, man's working life was over at 45. By then,

69

few people were physically or mentally capable of working. It was a rural civilization and the pre-industrial farmer was either worn out or had been killed by an accident by age 45. The Chinese or Irish who built our railroads had a five-year working life. Within five years they were gone—by liquor, or syphilis, or accident, or hard work.

"Now suddenly you have people reaching the age of 65 in the prime of physical and mental health. This is due partly to the movement of people from the farm to the city—accidents occur on the farm with about ten times the frequency of that in the most dangerous industrial employment —and partly to scientific management taking the toil out of labor . . .

"I am absolutely convinced that one of the greatest needs is the systematic creation of second careers. At 45, after having been a market research man, or a professor of English or psychology, or an officer in the armed services for 20 years, a man is spent. At least he thinks so. But he is mentally, biologically and physically sound. His kids are grown up and the mortgage is paid off and he has plenty to contribute to society . . .

"The older professions are best suited to become second careers. Middle age is really the best time to switch to being the lawyer, the teacher, the priest, the doctor and the social worker. Twenty years from now, we'll have few young men in these fields."

Systematic studies of the lives of men listed in *Who's Who* for the years 1934-35, 1950-51, 1974-75, and 1984-85 disclose that for each year the overall frequency of career-changing among the people listed remained at approximately 40 percent. It's not stretching the data too much to suggest that this is a characteristic of many successful persons.

Most people who thrive after career changes have had enough financial resources in the form of savings, inheritance, investments, equity in a home, or the income of a working spouse to absorb the financial risks that most career changes likely will involve. A majority probably end up with a reduced level of income as a result of their change, although many return to previous incomes or go even higher within three to five years. Nevertheless, a financial cushion is almost essential.

Case Studies of Four Career Changers

Dwayne nursed a steel foundry back to precarious economic health. One way he did it was to win the cooperation of his United Steelworker local, not for pay cuts but for improved productivity. Fortunately, Dwayne and the president of the local shared a deep interest in religion. They began a series of prayer meetings with employees on company time.

The gatherings included discussions about practical motivational and productivity matters, akin to the topics that surface during Quality Circle meetings in Japan and America where workers meet regularly to talk about ways to improve efficiency.

Unfortunately, the owners of the foundry did not do their part by investing in capital equipment, one of the suggestions that grew out of the prayer meetings. Instead, the owners closed the foundry because it wasn't profitable enough.

Dwayne was out of a job, but he had found a new and far more rewarding career as a leader of a religious revival in business and industry.

Loretta had a musical career that was emotionally but not economically satisfying. She was paid to sing in two different church choirs; she appeared in regional musical productions; she gave voice lessons. Yet, as time went on, her theatrical assignments dwindled and her interest waned in her other musical activities.

Influenced by her husband, a lawyer, she decided to change to law. He financed her successful law school studies and took her into his firm when she passed her bar exams.

Martha has had four different careers at age 58. She started as a high school English teacher, but left that field when the first of her four children was born. When her youngest was 12, she decided to become a hypnotist, or hypno-consultant as practitioners prefer to call themselves. She took training and practiced for seven years. While she found it rewarding to help people overcome sleep and other disorders, stop smoking and lose weight, she could not persuade enough surgeons to entrust their patients to her to undergo surgery without anesthetics, her major interest.

When her husband died, she needed more income. She took a calculated risk, invested her slim capital in a medical education, and emerged as a nurse specializing in anesthetics. If the doctor permits it and the patient is a good subject, she still practices hypnotism. Otherwise, she performs as an anesthetist's assistant. She also continues her medically-related hypnotism in relieving disorders concerning sleep, speech, obesity, alcoholism, and drug dependence. To her delight, she has discovered that all her careers as a teacher, mother, hypnotist and nurse mutually support one another and she now finds herself in great demand.

Bill was the band director in a high school in Westchester County outside New York City. When he lost his hearing, he had to give up that career. He and his wife had long been enthusiastic gardeners and amateur authorities on wine. They decided to combine the two interests. They moved to western Oregon, bought a vineyard there and grew grapes for wineries.

The common denominators in all four cases are these:

1) Each had a financial cushion. Dwayne took early retirement and a pension and was eligible for reduced Social Security benefits at 62. Loretta's husband supported her during her transition. Martha inherited enough from her deceased husband to finance her education in nursing. Bill and his wife supported themselves through his disability pensions (from Teachers Insurance and Annuity Association and Social Security), from profits on the sale of their Westchester property, and from savings until their Oregon vineyard began to yield an income.

2) A thread of commonality goes through all their careers. Dwayne's religious vocation had begun as a teenager. Loretta had acquired an interest in law by osmosis from her husband. Martha's instincts for helping extended throughout all four careers. The hobbies of Bill and his wife became combined in their new vocation.

3) An event or series of events precipitated all career changes. All but Loretta had to change, largely for economic reasons. Even Loretta had to change if she wanted to stay active, aside from housewifely duties.

4) Competitive pressures demanded new careers. Dwayne's steel foundry couldn't compete. Loretta's musical skills were not good enough to keep her in the first rank of a singing career. Martha's hypnotism couldn't compete with anesthetics; in effect, she combined the two. Due to his hearing disability, Bill couldn't compete with others not similarly impaired.

5) The four were surprised at the amount of self-promotion they needed to do to succeed in their new careers. Dwayne wrote a moderately successful book telling his story. Loretta had to overcome skepticism about a singer turning lawyer. Fortunately, her theatrical experience served her well as a trial attorney. Martha continued her lectures on hypnotism to promote her new career. With his disability, Bill encountered problems with self-promotion, but surmounted them with a 10-minute video extolling his grapes. The novelty intrigued the proprietors of wineries. They learned the wisdom of W.S. Gilbert's lines from *Ruddigore*:

> *If you wish in the world to advance,*
> *Your merits you're bound to enhance,*
> *You must stir it and stump it,*
> *And blow your own trumpet,*
> *Or, trust me, you haven't a chance.*

The author asked 100 seniors (81 men and 19 women) who had changed their careers to rate each of the following motivations for making the shift:

Motivation	Important	Unimportant
Chance for greater achievement	55	45
Better salary	11	89
More meaningful work	74	26
More congenial colleagues	26	74
Greater responsibility	24	76
More time with family	26	74
Better fit of values and work	73	27
Time for recreation and hobbies	22	78
Live in better locality	18	82
Less hectic pace	27	73
Greater security	13	87
Felt pressure to leave	18	82
Laid off or terminated	36	64
Health reasons	13	87

Note the three that the 100 seniors rated important 50 or more times—more meaningful work, better fit of values and work, and chance for greater achievement. Also, ponder the fact that the seniors rated the following as unimportant 50 or more times—salary, more congenial colleagues, greater responsibility, more time with family, time for recreation and hobbies, live in a better locality, less hectic pace, greater security, pressure to leave, layoff and health reasons. These 100 seniors are not unstable citizens.

For the most part, the 100 left large bureaucratic, usually profit-making organizations and jobs in which they were dealing with data and objects. They entered smaller organizations, businesses of their own, or professions where they would enjoy more personal autonomy, such as law or teaching in colleges. Their new occupations tended to be ones in which they were more involved with helping other people. They took new positions that allowed them to be able to see some specific value or results from their work.

The motivational ratings showed no particular tilts according to sex. However, for new careers, many of the men chose areas that were less traditionally masculine than their former fields—education, nursing, social work, and generally helping kinds of professions. Women, on the other hand, veered more toward traditionally masculine positions—management and supervision. In one case, a lady changed from selling real estate to selling new and used mobile homes "because it made me sick to see so many people getting ripped off in the used mobile home market."

Most of the 100 decided early not to look for something else in the same field. The time between when they first thought of leaving their old jobs and the time they actually left ranged from one hour (in layoff cases) to more than five years. The average appears to be about three years.

Most confined their discussions to within their families, many just with their spouses. Very few consulted with business associates, even outside their own organization. A large majority were satisfied with the outcome of their change. Of course, the 18 who felt pressure to leave and the 36 who were laid off or terminated were not pleased with the way the change came about. Only 11 of the 100 took retraining or more education to facilitate their career changes.

Planning a Change in Careers

Failure to plan will almost certainly be fatal. An ingredient in the planning should be time. Most of the 100 thought the change took too long. Yet, there's no way to predict how long you will need. There's also no point in saying you must not take too long, or do the task quickly. At this moment, we can say the following about time: The choice now may be more critical than for your earlier career or careers because you have less time for changing your course than during the first or even succeeding activities.

What is vital is to decide somehow what your skills are, then where you want to use them, and finally how to find a way those skills can be most effectively used.

For now, let's confine ourselves to the question, Change to what? The obvious answer is, Change to one of your favorite skills. But it's not that simple. Do you change to medicine when you're already 60? Do you make buggy whips because that's your favorite skill? Do you enter the ministry despite the fact that the field is already overcrowded?

First, take heart that you have some exciting developments coming up to which you can devote the rest of your working life. The late David Sarnoff, retired chairman of Radio Corporation of America, predicted what he saw would happen by the end of this century:

Food. "The western nations . . . will be able to produce twice as much food as they consume, and if political conditions permit, advanced food production and conservation techniques could be extended to the overpopulated and undernourished areas."

Raw Materials. "Technology will find ways of replenishing or replacing the world's industrial materials. The ocean depths will be mined for nickel, cobalt, copper, manganese and other vital ores. Chemistry will create further substitutes for existing materials, and find hitherto unsuspected uses for the nearly 2000 recognized materials that lie within the earth's surface."

Energy. "The energy at man's disposal is potentially without limit. One pound of fissionable uranium the size of a golf ball has the potential energy for nearly 1500 tons of coal, and the supply of nuclear resources is greater than all the reserves of coal, oil, and gas . . ."

Health. "Science will find increasingly effective ways of deferring death. In this country, technology will advance average life expectancy from the Biblical three score and ten toward the five-score mark, and it will be a healthier, more vigorous, and more useful existence. The electron has become the wonder weapon of the assault on disease and disability. Ultraminiature electronic devices implanted in the body will regulate human organs whose functions have become impaired."

Genetics. "Before the century ends . . . science will unravel the genetic code which determines the characteristics that pass from parent to child. Science will also take an inanimate grouping of simple chemicals and breathe into it the spark of elementary life, growth, and reproduction . . . New and healthier strains of plants and animals will be developed."

Communications. "Through communication satellites, laser beams, and ultraminiaturization, it will be possible by the end of the century to communicate with anyone, anywhere, at any time, by voice, sight, or written message."

Travel. "From techniques developed for lunar travel and other purposes, new forms of terrestrial transport will emerge. Earth vehicles riding on air cushions and powered by nuclear energy or fuel cells will traverse any terrain and skim across water."

Defense. "In tomorrow's national command post, the country's civilian and military leaders will see displayed on a cycloramic color television screen a continuously changing, instantly updated computer synthesis of pertinent events around the world . . . The computer will report, in written form, what and where the problems are. Another section will delineate the alternatives, and suggest appropriate actions, and still another will assess the probable and actual results. But in all cases, final decisions will be matters for human judgment."

Air and space. "Around earth a network of weather satellites will predict with increasing accuracy next season's floods and droughts, extremes of heat and cold. It will note the beginnings of typhoons, tornadoes, and hurricanes in time for the disturbances to be diverted or dissipated before they reach dangerous intensity. Ultimately, the development of worldwide, long-range meteorological theory may lead to the control of weather and climate. Space will become hospitable to sustained human habitation."

Those predictions were published by *Fortune* in May, 1965. They have stood up well for more than two decades, in contrast to some prognostications. The point is that there are good forecasts available on which you can base your planning.

Sarnoff's predictions underline another aspect of planning for your career change. There are so many opportunities that their sheer range could paralyze you into no decision of any kind. To aid you in avoiding that fate, return to Chapter 3 with its suggestions on how to evaluate your strengths and weaknesses. In addition, try three exercises to help you take stock and to gain important knowledge about yourself. If you've followed our prescriptions, you've already done this. Do it again. Still other perceptions about yourself will surface with the repetition.

1) Write at least 10 answers to the question, Who am I? This time, try reading meaning into the answers. If you decide you're more of a dreamer than a doer, should you not consider "creative" pursuits vs. "doing" activities? For example, the dreamer may shine as a writer, but not as a manager; the dreamer as a product designer, but not as an engineer; the dreamer as an architect, but not as a builder.

2) Next, list things you do well—specific tasks that have brought praise or personal satisfaction. This time, decide which are the most important, the least important, and concentrate on the former. When you enumerate things done unsuccessfully and/or with little or no pleasure, file them somewhere but don't forget their location. You may need a smidgen of a distasteful experience to work into a new career. It may not prove so unpleasant the second time around. A financial planner flunked math in high school, but had to master it when undertaking that career years later after she reached a dead end as a librarian.

3) With free choice and none of the usual limiting factors, what would you most like to do? Again, put aside for now the frivolous or unimportant and concentrate on what promises to give you the most pleasure *and* a liveable income.

When the renewed perceptions of yourself become settled and you can look at them objectively, begin to use the insights to make decisions about your future.

If possible, match your skills and interests with those that will be most in demand for the immediate future. However, don't strain for a match-up. Often, a senior will find better success in the less prominent areas of endeavor. For instance, the woman who shifted from selling conventional homes to mobile units deliberately slid down in the social scale of jobs. Yet, she found her new career more emotionally rewarding and, eventually, better paying.

When *Not* To Change Careers

Three circumstances often indicate that the better choice is *not* to change careers:

    1) When a brush-up of present skills is only needed.
    2) When it's possible to pursue two careers simultaneously for many years and opt for one as a senior.
    3) When, upon reexamination, opportunities surface in your present field.

Brush-up. If your perceptions tell you that you want to stay in the same field in which you have devoted most of your adult life, fine, but you may still need refresher education or training. For example, suppose you have been in sales all your life. You may know most of what's known about selling machine tools, but now you want a career that will take less than 40 hours a week and little travel. You pick residential real estate. You must study to pass a real estate exam and to learn how real estate and machine tool sales differ.

Or suppose you were with big advertising agencies for much of your career and now want to become an individual communications consultant. Although the fields are related, they also differ. Courses in community colleges and other institutions teach you how to go into business for yourself as opposed to working for others, how to sell yourself as a relative newcomer as opposed to selling a well-known service, and how to handle the legal and accounting problems of a sole proprietorship as opposed to delegating them to a special staff in a large agency.

Or suppose you want to make an apparently radical career shift—from the clergy to sales, for example. The change may not be as dramatic as it first appears. From the days of the Reverend Mason Locke Weems peddling his biography of George Washington (in print and selling to this day), the clergy has to sell. Your job here is to determine what your old and new careers have in common. You seek education and training in the areas where they differ.

The rapid advance of technology during the last 30 years has brought with it a new concern with the problem of professional obsolescence. More and more professionals are finding it essential—even mandated by law—to continue formal learning throughout their careers. It's becoming increasingly necessary for those whose occupation depends on their command of a certain body of knowledge to update their knowledge and skills through frequent formal learning and continuing education credits.

Seniors can sometimes fit into niches in careers closely allied to their former ones by updating training—in moving from electrical to electronic engineering, in shifting from accounting to financial planning, in changing from journalism to writing novels.

Your previous or new employer may provide the reeducation. The American Society for Training and Development estimates companies are spending $30 billion a year on formal courses and training programs. The institute figures it costs companies an additional $180 billion annually for training, such as supervision and learning on the job. Increasingly, employers have eliminated age qualifications for reeducation.

Besides the conventional sources for education, there today exists another tailored for people 60 and older. Elderhostels began in 1975 on a New Hampshire college campus with 200 participants. In 1984, 90,000 senior students took courses on 760 college campuses in the United States, Canada, Mexico, Europe and Israel. The weeklong sessions at each campus offer a limitless variety of classes taught by college professors and other experts in their fields. For a free catalog, write Elderhostel, 100 Boylston St., Boston MA 02116.

Two careers. We have mentioned Fred Waring and his dual careers in music and invention, but there are many other examples. One of the most incongruous pairings is that of an architect in Pittsburgh who is also a podiatrist.

Although Waring and the architect-podiatrist never really dropped either career, their examples offer a clue to you. Try a second career on the side before you burn any bridges. Sometimes you may be pursuing another one without realizing it. Arthur Murray, the dancing instructor, followed the stock market as an avocation so successfully that he now devotes his energies fully to investment management and leaves to others the running of the dance studios which carry his name. Dwayne actually did this when he primarily managed a foundry, with religion a sideline. He dropped the former for the latter when circumstances dictated the move. With her hypnotism and nursing, Martha combined two careers in a variation on the two-career theme.

Unsuspected opportunities. You may not have exhausted the challenges in your present career. For example, management is management no matter what the field. Military officers have discovered this over the past 20 years. When many of them have reached their late 40s or early 50s, they're lieutenant colonels or lieutenant commanders and have gone as far as they can go. They're out.

Many at first are absolutely sure there is nothing they can do. They are acutely conscious they have been in an insulated, artificial environment. Their first instinct is to go for more education. One who actually signed up for courses in a small college got hired as a business manager for the institution and soon found himself too busy to take more education.

Others have found rewarding work as office managers for law and accounting firms. Still others go with defense contractors and perform liaison functions with the Pentagon for their new employers. Many medical officers find a niche as medical directors for large and middle-sized companies.

Sometimes an unsuspected opportunity lies lurking in the weeds. An architect, retired but not happy about it, decided to move to a condominium with his wife. None they saw pleased them because they didn't offer the open country feel that he and his wife were accustomed to.

He went to one location where a builder planned to erect a colony of more than 200 condominiums on a former public golf course. However, he had construction plans only, none actually yet built. On the spot, the architect made alterations in the basic interior layout on tracing paper that would give him and his wife the open design they preferred. Impressed, the builder offered the architect a job as his on-site specialist in modifications for the prospective buyer.

Eventually, the dreamer must become a doer—write that book, oversee the translation of the design into a new model car, confirm that the architectural drawings are faithfully converted into an actual house. Even Oscar Wilde wryly acknowledges this in yet another aphorism: "(Action) is the last resource of those who know not how to dream."

PART II

The Jobhunt

The next 12 chapters will show you how to hunt for work in ways refocused from those you used when younger. The methods seek to capitalize on the advantages seniors hold over juniors, especially experience, varied abilities, and the freedom to accept more risk. Most advantageous of all, seniors are in a better position than juniors to create their own jobs and to offer solutions to problems troubling potential employers.

8

The Rights and Wrongs
of Jobhunting

Chuck Abbott pounced on a blind help wanted ad for an "experienced claims adjuster" because it sounded just like the work he'd been doing for the past quarter-century. Ever since he had accepted Pyramid Life Insurance's deal for early retirement, he regretted it. He was only 56, for God's sake! Even with the Social Security equivalent Pyramid would pay him until he reached 62, he was not making ends meet with his former employer's pension of a niggardly $1,024 a month. The Social Security equivalent of $584 gave him a monthly income of only $1,608, plus about another $400 from investments.

It wasn't enough, but he had no choice except to take Pyramid's deal because management hinted broadly that there could be no guarantee that he'd have any job with them if he didn't accept the early retirement package. For a while, he drove a school bus, but he couldn't endure the unruly kids. Next, he joined a Dodge automobile agency, but had to sit around 60 hours a week in the showroom to earn a pittance. The blind ad was a godsend.

He heard no response, however, and mentioned the silence one day when he met Ed, a friend who still remained with Pyramid.

"That may be 'cause Pyramid placed the blind ad," said Ed. "I'll bet you applied for your old job."

"The bastards! They led me to think they'd eliminate it."

"No way. They're operating exactly the same way they always have."

Chuck tried to pump Ed for more details. The friend clammed up, however, belatedly realizing that he'd already talked too much.

Abbott used the incident as the basis for an age discrimination suit. His lawyer won an out-of-court settlement, of which the attorney got 30 percent as his fee. The remainder seemed hardly worth the trouble, especially because he didn't win his old job back, lost Ed as a friend, and didn't win a new claims adjusting position with another insurance company. He feared he lost it because the other insurance company discovered he was litigious.

The True Role of Luck

At first, Abbott thought he was lucky to have grounds for a "successful" age discrimination suit against his former employer. It proved to be unlucky because it sent him on a wild goose chase.

Although luck does play a role in jobhunting, it won't play a good one unless you have paved the way with intelligence, creativity and patience. In the sixteenth century, the great French aphorist and essayist Michel de Montaigne wrote, "Experience has taught me this, that we undo ourselves by impatience. Misfortunes have their life and their limits, their sickness and their health."

So, Abbott let apparent good luck rush him into bad luck. He even thought he was playing it safe by suing. He never thought that "the only means of conservation is innovation," in the words of Peter Drucker.

Good luck stems from innovation which springs from creativity. The need for creativity in business increases steadily, Drucker points out. He estimates that demands on the creative abilities of people have doubled in every generation. A major reason for American economic leadership, he believes, is not popularly accepted capital formation—in many European and Japanese industries, it equals or exceeds that in the United States—but the higher use here of creative managers. For every $100 spent for direct labor in 1900, the typical American manufacturer spent $5 to $8 for managerial, technical and professional personnel. Today, more is spent on the latter than the former.

In Chapter 2, we discussed how to enlarge your creativity. Now we will show you how to put it to work.

How's your creativity quotient? Most individuals display one of three self-defeating attitudes toward innovation: (1) they dismiss it as pretentious nonsense; (2) they employ a faddist approach, relying on the superficial use of currently popular programs such as Quality Circles or yoga; (3) they scarcely think about it at all.

The third is the most common and most dangerous attitude. Many seniors don't consider themselves creative. Since they wish they were, they shut the painful subject from their minds. In so doing, however, they may stifle the creativity they do possess.

Even the most prosaic individuals have at least a spark of creativity in their make-up. You have it. You need it to get that better job. You can put your creativity to work by:

1) Orienting the problem.
2) Obtaining the facts.
3) Searching for ideas.
4) Letting the ideas incubate.
5) Evaluating the ideas.

Your problem seems obvious, to find a better job. Yet, probe deeper. Do you want the same kind of job? Slightly different? Radically different?

Next, you need facts that bear upon your problem. Are there plenty of your old kind of jobs around? What about those that are slightly different? How much retraining will you need for radically different work?

In searching for ideas, be on the lookout for idea combinations, refocused ideas, recycled ideas. Quality Circles, for example, were recycled to Japan from brainstorming in America just after World War II, then re-exported back to America.

Incubation involves more than rest. It involves leaving alone, to let the idea gestate. Abbott didn't let his idea of a lawsuit incubate; otherwise, he might have put it aside.

Incubation gives you the perspective to evaluate the idea. When you have taken three basic steps in evaluating ideas—the "loose" ranking, the tighter appraisal, and the consideration of possible improvements—you next analyze on another plane. How much trouble will this job-search idea cause? Will it force a move? Will it upset your family? How quickly can you implement the idea? Sometimes you can enhance the idea with timing or some other characteristic.

When Chuck permitted his creativity the chance to work on his job problem, through problem orientation, fact-gathering, idea-searching, incubation and evaluation, he came up with a new solution, as we shall see later. Along the way, however, he called on other qualities besides creativity.

Managers on average have longer tenures in their jobs (8.8 years) than the norm for all workers, says Challenger, Gray & Christmas Inc., a Chicago executive placement firm. Yet, that span has fallen even more dramatically than for all workers—from 12 years in 1981.

Other Jobhunting Qualities You Need

A Labor Department study shows that 71 million people in the United States labor force hold jobs for an average of 4.2 years compared to 4.6 years only three years earlier. Instead of thinking of a career, people are thinking of serial careers.

So, after creativity, your first jobhunting quality is to accept that you
are one of hundreds of jobhunters of all ages. Your age is irrelevant. Even
unions now try to teach that you're just one of the boys (or girls) if you're
an early retiree. The International Brotherhood of Electrical Workers Local 134 in Chicago holds two evening sessions a month to help older
workers plan for retirement. The three-hour meetings include a talk by
A.S. Hansen Inc., pension fund adviser, and a self-evaluation form to
help workers focus on their fears and needs. Many large corporations
hold such meetings, but few involve hourly workers. The Chicago union
began the seminars a few years ago as a way to sell an early retirement in-
centive program. About a third of the eligible workers retired early, giving way to younger jobless union members.

The second essential quality is the ability to start afresh, ignoring either
that you were fired from your previous job or that you don't like your
present work. Employers who use early retirement like a scythe have
poor personnel practices, but it's pointless to waste time bemoaning that
fact. Likewise, why waste time and energy lamenting your present fate in
an unsatisfactory job? What you really want is a better position. Concentrate on that above everything else in your jobhunting.

Many early retirees do so, sort of. They flock to new ventures, although
some experts discourage it. Hambro International Venture Fund, a New
York venture capital firm, gets two or three applications a week from
former corporate executives. Six months ago, Hambro was getting two or
three a month. Edwin Goodman, Hambro general partner, attributes the
rise to mergers, restructurings and company-induced early retirements.
Challenger, Gray & Christmas says it tries to discourage some executives
if they are over 50 and don't have marketing skills. They're still looking
to the past and the good old days when they had a staff and other support
mechanisms of a big corporation. Another recruiter, Gilbert Tweed Associates, New York, points to the fact that it increasingly gets résumés from
former executives who tried going it alone but want corporate jobs again.
Tweed and other recruiters advise, throw away your tin cup; you can
never beg your way to a better job.

The underemployed find it particularly difficult to begin anew, probably because they don't absolutely have to. Although they won't skid if
they stay in a rut, that rut can become their graves.

The third quality you must have is a hard-headed realism about the
forthcoming search. It's a full-time task in itself to find another job. In
fact, the underemployed senior has a leg up on the underemployed in the
hunt because he or she will have more time to devote to it. Perrin Stryker,
the author and consultant, says, "Whatever their reasons, nearly all anx-

ious to change jobs can expect to find the process a lonely, miserable experience." Indeed, finding a new job is about the most difficult, embarrassing and patience-exhausting venture a senior can undertake.

Why? Because most seniors go at it even more stupidly than juniors do. They have forgotten how, all too frequently, or they never knew how and lucked into a job in the past. Seniors typically send out résumés broadside because they've heard that jobhunting is a numbers game. That's true, but it's largely a waste of time and postge to send mailings out in carload lots. About one job applicant in 250 is invited in for an interview.

Your hard-headedness must give way to intelligence. Use the rifle instead of the blunderbuss to aim your résumés and other approaches at the right people.

Successful jobhunting is successful self-selling. When you fail, either the merchandise is faulty or you don't know how to sell it. In extreme cases, seniors may suffer from a lack of faith in both themselves and their salesmanship. Good job salesmanship starts with good self-knowledge. So, you need to analyze yourself as though you were a Space Shuttle, to sharpen your understanding of yourself.

To summarize, you need some seemingly contradictory characteristics as a senior to land that better job. You should polish your creativity. You require tunnel vision to ignore your age. You must concentrate on what you want in a better job, not what went wrong in the job you had. You must be hard-nosed, but still have the brains to figure out ways to get in to see people you want to see. Finally, you need to learn or relearn how to sell yourself.

You can use parts of the conventional numbers game system to supplement your main program. The greater the number of auxiliary avenues used, the greater the chance of success. The main parts of the game are mailing résumés to carefully selected recipients; using every device you can think of to generate interviews, especially making personal contacts through friends and referrals; reading business news for leads; and keeping your eyes and ears alert for tips.

How To Use Parts of the System To Get Interviews

Here's an appraisal of the reliability, usefulness and effectiveness for seniors of the conventional means of getting contacts for interviews:

Executive search firms. Forget them. They want people already reasonably happy in what they're doing.

Newspaper ads. A study shows these percentages of employers didn't hire *anybody* over a single year through help wanted or situation wanted ads: Pittsburgh (89%), Chicago (87%), San Francisco (85%), Dallas (81%), Houston (79%), Salt Lake City (75%). The percentages don't account for the jobhunter's ages. If there were a percentage of employers who didn't hire any seniors through newspaper ads, it would be nearly 100 in every city in the country. So forget them, too—or almost. If you must answer ads, tailor your résumé to the specifications given in the ad, omit all else, and give no salary range if none is asked for or a broad one if it is.

Your own ads. Almost worthless. Most replies will come from employment agencies and salesmen. If you must do this, concentrate on journals in your field.

Private employment agencies. In contrast to search firms, they'll take you, probably for a fee. The failure rate is 95 percent.

Government agencies. They *have* to take you. The failure rate is 80 percent. They deal, of course, with large volumes, and you become a number.

College placement bureaus. Better for recent graduates than for seniors. Yet, register by all means. They can do no harm and may do some good.

Job vacancy registers. Both government and private registers charge a fee of $75 or more. For most private registers, the employer pays the fee, and so gets the loyalty. Use them, but don't expect miracles.

Book résumés. Even if widely circulated, they have dubious value because they are not tailored closely enough to the potential employer's problems.

Résumés in imaginative packaging. Don't even think of doing it. Hold your creativity for better payoffs.

None of these is likely to help the senior. They're not fatal, but they do waste time. However, there are three conventional bits of advice for job-seekers which, if seniors were to follow them, could prove disastrous.

The first is the counsel that the job-seeker should keep vague about what he or she wants to do so as to be free to take advantage of whatever vacancies may arise. Such advice might well serve jobhunters in their twenties who don't know what they want, but not seniors. On the contrary, the senior must be as specific as possible. This is the principle way people 50 or older get jobs.

The second piece of bad advice is that jobhunters should act very carefully because employers have the upper hand and would resent anyone telling them how to solve a problem or how to do anything. Again, such a recommendation holds value chiefly for youngsters. Yes, some employers do object to anyone telling them how to solve anything, but you want nothing to do with them. You want prospective employers looking for answers to problems and new ways to do things.

Third, employers seek only people who can write well. Professional résumé writers help perpetuate this one; unless the employer is a publisher, writing is not his or her prime concern. This myth persists because it sometimes seems that only the best written résumés net the interview. In Chapter 16, we'll show you how to write like Hemingway, at least as far as correctly addressing your job prospect.

The Assumptions for Success

Once you have identified the dubious routes to job interviews and the three major fallacious recommendations in jobhunting, you can more easily see the correct assumptions for success:

1) You must decide exactly what you want to do. The secret of dealing with the future is to nail down what you have in the present—and to see the different ways in which the basic units of that can be rearranged into different constellations, consistent with the goals and values that direct your inner nature. Unhappily, "skills" has become a scare-word, probably from your early jobhunting days when you found yourself in the Catch-22 situation of not being able to get a job because you lacked the skills which, in turn, you could only get if you found a job. Take heart. You have more skills than you realize. It's unlikely that you will need to retrain. Retraining is "in" today, but too much of it is wasted because it's unfocused or misfocused. If you must retrain, wait until you know what you need to retrain for. Seniors also tend to try to market their lower skills, apparently under the misconception that they're easier to sell. Wrong! They're harder to sell because there's more competition in the lower-skill areas. Cultivate your most esoteric skills because the competition falls away progressively as the degree of difficulty rises. Also, avoid some of the crowded fields. For instance, office work currently provides jobs for nearly half of all American workers and has been the strongest source of job creation in this century. However, office automation is now taking the bloom off that rose, and it's likely that gains in office employment, as a result of automation, will slow over the next few years; it's possible that sometime in the 1990s, the level of office employment will begin

to decline, says a report from Congress' Office of Technology Assessment.

2) Using research from your own survey, you should determine precisely where you want to practice your skills. At first, Chuck Abbott thought he wanted to pursue his profession in the Southwest, but his survey revealed too much competition in Arizona and New Mexico where he thought he wanted to live. He decided upon Vermont, instead. It's worth noting here that unemployment figures are *very* misleading anywhere in the country. They are gross numbers, yet give the impression that you compete against every single one of the jobless. You do not—only against those with the same skills as you possess.

3) You need to study the organizations that interest you and then approach the one individual in the targeted organization with the power to hire you for the job you decide you want. Take heart from the fact that more jobs always exist than is apparent superficially. Musical chairs, expansion, low visibility and the chronic need for good management and professional men and women account for this. Often, such openings are not listed. Indeed, they may never get listed because some employers prefer to fill them privately. However, why limit yourself to a job that already exists? Why not persuade an employer to create a new position just for you? Yet, whatever you do, *contact the personnel department last unless you seek a job there*. In most companies and organizations, the personnel (or human resources) department is at the bottom of the social and executive totem pole. It rarely hears immediately of middle- and high-level vacancies even within its own organization. Even when it does know of vacancies, it seldom has the power to hire, except for its own account. Personnel departments are best at screening *out* applicants. If you receive a letter in response to your résumé that it "has been referred to Personnel," don't hold your breath waiting for a job with that organization.

Those three keys to success for any jobhunter are vital for all career-changers and, consequently, for 80 percent of the seekers over 50. Ignore them at your peril because then you will court failure.

The three keys may sound self-evident (and they are), but they are not easy to accomplish. On average, it will take you three to nine months, full-time, to achieve them successfully. The higher level the job you seek, the longer it will take because decisions normally take longer the higher the job level and salary. If you don't believe this and prefer to find a job fast, it will take you almost as long to land one the chaotic way, and you will probably either end up underemployed or out on the street again within a year. If you are over 50, under 22, a female, in a minority, an ex-mental patient or an ex-felon, you *must* do it according to the three keys.

A Do-It-Yourself Project

For seniors especially, jobhunting is a do-it-yourself project because you know yourself better than anyone else and because you have a loyalty to yourself to a degree that nobody else can match. However, you can buy outside help if:

1) You know exactly what kind of help you need and want.
2) You know precisely what the outsiders can do and not do.
3) You know where to locate them.

Here are typical resources you may need:

1) Help with deciding precisely what you want to do as to vocation, personal growth possibilities, and the degree of responsibility with which you will be comfortable.

2) Help with a personal survey to help you decide where you want to work for the rest of your life.

3) Help to research the hiring organization and to identify the person empowered to hire you.

4) Finally, help with the whole process of the jobhunt, particularly the tactics and strategies of it. This involves questions of timing, emphasis and deletion. Seniors particularly tend to give the prospective employer too much information. An advisor can serve like an editor—cutting, reshaping, and refocusing the presentation.

Where do you get such assistance?

First, from *yourself.* You are far and away the best, provided you can muster the objectivity to act temporarily like an outsider. In effect, if you do the whole jobhunt process yourself, you are learning your new job or career ahead of time. It's ideal education and practice.

Second, you should study *books, pamphlets and other printed materials.* This is the best outside resource, as you already know. Otherwise, why are you reading this book?

Third, *free professional help* can give you valuable insights. When you have friends and fellow alumni, why pay when most people are generous with advice? Appraise it carefully, though!

Fourth, sometimes you can use *professional help for a fee.* Perhaps a vocational aptitude test would be wise. Your own profession or the one you have chosen may have a useful service.

Use your professional help—paid or unpaid—to monitor the state of your hubris. Occasionally, an unemployed or underemployed senior goes unbalanced on the side of conceit. He or she decides idiots abound. The senior grows steadily more rigid, reckless and contemptuous, in dramatic contrast to most jobless seniors. He or she goes off the track psychologically. Dr. William Menninger, the psychiatrist, says, "Six essential qualities are the key to success: Sincerity, personal integrity, humility, courtesy, wisdom, charity." A person suffering from hubris rarely can summon any of these qualities. Tragically, he or she seldom realizes the lack. An outsider does and therefore is your best bet to advise you on how to revive them.

If you go for a paid consultant, he or she may be sincere and skilled, sincere but inept, or an outright charlatan. It's hard to tell at first. The best way to find out is from clients. The consultant's own referral is nearly useless; would he or she recommend a dissatisfied client? Find one on your own, preferably more than one. If you can't locate even one, beware. Also, comparison shop among at least three potential consultants as to fees and what they will and will not do. Remember: Buying a consultant is like buying a friend and just as risky.

A big problem with professional advice is that it's homogenized. Outplacement and similar firms are in the business to make money. For efficiency, they package their counsel. From them, you get just about the same advice as for every other unemployed or underemployed person. That's not enough. You must get help tailored for you and the problem solution you want to provide your prospective employer.

Frankly, it's much safer (and much less expensive) to enlist a family member or a job-seeking peer before you "buy a friend."

Ultimately, only you can decide what you want to do. Every man or woman during the course of the first career should identify posssible succeeding career(s). You didn't? You will have to do the job belatedly— but not hastily. The rest of Part II tells how.

And you must do more than decide *what* you want to do. You also have to find peers you believe you can enjoy working with, including a reasonable number of approximately your own age. This goes far toward making the climate of your next job enjoyable. That, in turn, helps make the job a success.

Chuck Abbott Comes Through

Our friend Abbott went through these exercises. He had no trouble knowing what he wanted to do—insurance claims adjusting. He had difficulty finding people he could enjoy working with, including locating enough people in his own age bracket.

It took him six months to find the solution: Hire two other jobless adjusters and start a service for smaller insurance companies.

The experience taught him the truth of a comment by the seventeenth century Thomas Fuller: "If you are too fortunate, you will not know yourself. If you are too unfortunate, nobody will know you."

9

Hire Yourself

Consider these statistics on self-employment. After the first year of jobhunting, about 17 percent of the frustrated seekers drop out of the market, nearly all to start their own businesses. Unfortunately, the majority of the new ventures fail within another year. So, the evidence is compelling that many seniors go into self-employment without proper preparation and as a way, subliminal or otherwise, to avoid or cut short the difficult experience of jobhunting.

Do It Right

The self-employment phenomenon is so common among unemployed or underemployed seniors that it merits special treatment. Some seniors make a success of going into a small new business—and more power to you. It's fine to do this *provided* you are not doing it just to escape the jobhunt.

That's the first question to ask yourself if self-employment attracts you. Unhappily, the dream seems to appeal mostly to early retirees who have spent the bulk of their business lives with a large public or private business. Some of them, such as Deere & Company, even offer a three-day seminar on starting a new enterprise. So did others among the 59 percent of 512 medium to large companies which had big cutbacks between 1982 and 1985, according to a survey by the Conference Board, New York.

Refugees from such an environment are the least likely to succeed, we regret to report, because they have depended on staff support so long that they have forgotten or never knew how to perform functions outside their expertise—notably in law, finance, and marketing.

The initial shock arrives when you learn you must pay a lawyer to set up your company. The next comes when you discover the capital needed to keep a venture afloat. Still another dawns on you as you gradually discover how hard it is to sell your product or service. Even if you have sold

95

giant widgets for 30 years, you will experience a radically different reception to your midget widgets. Giant Widget Corporation, your former employer, was a long-lived, well-known manufacturer. Your Midget Widget Inc. is unknown. You find you must cut prices to sell anything. That means you make little or no profit in the early going. Your bank is unsympathetic, calls your loan. You scramble for more financing. Your father-in-law provides it, with great reluctance. Soon, both your business and your marriage are bankrupt.

The second question to ask yourself if attracted to self-employment is: Do you have strong opinions and attitudes toward things and do you express them? You are not likely to succeed on your own if you don't. As a sole proprietor, you will need such qualities to offset the nay-sayers that surface at the first sign of trouble.

The third question: Do you prefer to work on your own or do you wish to work with others? Do you need almost constant companionship to be able to function? If you do, self-employment is not for you because the individual proprietor is often lonelier than the Lone Ranger.

The fourth question: Do you need to achieve? We mean here, do you need unmistakable evidence of achievement? In the corporate world, especially, achievements are usually joint efforts. It's often so difficult to assign credit that nobody gets it. If this bothers you, self-employment may be your answer.

The fifth question: Can you talk and write well? You must, to make a success of a small business.

If you can answer yes to at least three of the five foregoing questions, it's probably a good risk for you to go into business for yourself. If you cannot, we advise finding a job with another employer. Look for a smaller one next time. That's the usual pattern for early retirees, frustrated by their former environment of hundreds or thousands of employees. For the first time in several decades, more than half of the country's workers are on the payrolls of businesses with fewer than 100 employees.

Five Case Studies

What follows are five case studies of seniors who wrestled with the question of self-employment vs. working for others. We give you the facts in these instances but not the true names. We let you decide what you would do in each case. At the end of this section, we'll reveal what the individual actually did and how it turned out thus far.

Michael

At 50, this executive vice-president did not become president of a major airline, a post he had been promised. He felt he had no choice but to quit. To this day, he doesn't know why he failed to get the job. The predecessor and the man who did get it aren't talking to him.

After eight years with various transportation companies and 17 years with the airline, he had a solid reputation in the industry. With a B.A. from Yale and an M.B.A. from Harvard, he had impeccable educational qualifications. He had held a high elective post in an industry trade association and served on two boards in addition to that of his former company. Upon his resignation, he resigned the latter post but remained on the other boards. He had no money problems because of the golden parachute he had previously negotiated with the airline.

At first, he didn't even consider going into business for himself, but sought a comparable job with another airline. There's only one executive vice-president or equivalent per airline, however, and he found few openings. A railroad courted him to become its president. He talked at length with a bus company and an aircraft manufacturer.

Out of the blue came a wealthy investor suggesting that he become the top man in a new trucking company he was proposing. Michael would have a free hand in management, provided he put up one-fifth of the capital needed to start. The investor would put up the other four-fifths. Michael could raise his share.

What course did he take, the railroad job or the new trucking company where he would be essentially going into business for himself?

Jean

When the corporate president retired, whose secretary she had been for 35 years, the new president kept his own secretary. Jean didn't hold that against him. At 53, she didn't want to leave the corporation which served as the family she never had. The corporation offered her secretarial jobs with two different vice-presidents. At 60, one would retire before she would and in a few years present her with the same problem she faced now. At 51, the other vice-president didn't pose that difficulty, but she didn't like him very well.

The corporation suggested she join a new venture in the high technology field that it was financing as its head of secretarial services. That tempted her, and also set her thinking along other lines. Why not start an independent secretarial service for the new venture and other enterprises whose secretarial needs were sporadic or not heavy enough to merit full-time secretaries?

What did Jean do, go with the new venture or start one of her own?

Jake

As a machinist and 62 years old, he could retire early. If things got tight financially, he could readily find part-time work in any of a dozen different machine shops in the city. Jake's passion for years had been clocks. He kept as many as 50 in his house at any given time in various stages of repair. In the past, he often sold some for tidy profits. He had long wanted to start a clock business from his home. Did he succeed in doing so?

Elizabeth

A diabetic, she had to take a disability retirement at age 52 because of failing eyesight caused by her illness. She had been the editor of her employer's monthly newspaper and resolved to keep active by becoming an author of articles for her former publication, as well as for other employee journals. She found this increasingly difficult because she couldn't read her source notes. She partly solved this by recording all her interviews, mostly by phone, and grew adept at transcribing like a secretary. Her special large-type computer screen also compensated for her poor vision.

Her progress came to a tragic halt when she suffered a stroke that paralyzed her right arm and leg. What could this woman do to become a self-employed, productive member of society?

Jonathan

He majored in English at the University of Michigan, which fitted him for little except public relations. He worked for a PR firm in Detroit, then switched to its major client, an automotive supplier. He became a speechwriter for the president, and a good one. However, the president lost his job in a power squeeze, and so did Jonathan because he had become too closely identified with the ousted officer. That gentleman soon hooked up with one of the Big Three auto companies, bringing Jonathan along with him. The speechwriter next began writing speeches for the auto company president at a salary double what he had earned formerly. That president eventually was out, along with Jonathan's former boss and the speechwriter himself. History repeats itself.

The auto company president ferreted out a new connection in short order, inviting Jonathan to join him. Did he?

●

Michael did not go into business for himself as president of the new trucking company. He accepted the presidency of the railroad. He recognized that his whole business career had been as a fuctionary in an established organization. His skills lay in administration and risk assessment, not in taking risks whose challenges could not be precisely appraised. Although he had a few regrets in the years that followed, especially because the trucking firm he might have headed became a fierce competitor under the helm of an executive recruited from an established trucker, he knew in his heart that he had made the right choice.

Jean started her secretarial support business, getting as her first client the new venture financed by her former employer. She rented in the same building as that venture a suite of offices that she sublet to manufacturers' representatives, generating income both from the rents and the work she performed for her tenants. In addition, she did overflow work from regular tenants in her buildings. Her income was more erratic than formerly, but her work much more varied and interesting. She never regretted her decision.

Jake failed in his clock business because of management deficiencies, not mechanical shortcomings. He didn't know how to price his services. His accounting "practices" amounted to slips of paper on which he jotted notes, many of which he subsequently lost. He drove customers away because he seldom could keep delivery promises. He had to take full-time work in a machine shop for a while to pay off debts. His interest in clocks had to remain a hobby.

By dint of willpower and endless exercises, *Elizabeth* recovered sufficiently from her stroke to write a best-selling book about her ordeal. She became genuinely self-employed, working at home.

Jonathan had perhaps the most difficult decision of the five. He enjoyed speechwriting and would have earned a handsome salary if he had followed his second boss on his odyssey. Yet, he had been burned twice. He decided to become a freelance speechwriter, working from his home. At first, the assignments came mostly from his two previous bosses. Gradually, his reputation spread and he won jobs from other executives in Detroit. His income never matched what he had once earned, but his inner stability (and his writing) improved.

•

So you still cannot resist the urge to try business for yourself (despite the fact that half go belly-up in a year and two-thirds within five years)? You recognize that self-employment will take at least as much effort as getting a job after 50?

To you dedicated people, we offer the following suggestions.

Where To Start

First, look on the bright side. About 28 established businesses exist for every new one that's started in a year. This keeps the bankruptcy/failure rate lower than you may think. In a good year, of 10,000 businesses, only 62 fail. Even in a bad year, only 186 fail out of the 10,000. So, if you make it during the first tough years of your new venture, you will probably survive, but allow at least five years for a fair test.

Begin at the same place you commence for jobhunting—self-appraisal. What is your expertise? What do you like best to do? Do you possess legal, financial and marketing skills, three areas where small businesses most often founder? If you don't have one or more, do you have ready and inexpensive access to such expertise?

Everything rests on how you start up. Never, never think that self-employment poses fewer risks than jobhunting. It poses more, probably in the order of two or three to one.

Experts say the 10 riskiest small ventures are local laundries and dry cleaners, used car dealerships, gas stations, local trucking firms, restaurants, infant clothing stores, bakeries, machine shops, grocery or meat stores, and car washes.

Consulting offers the best chances for triumph because employers have trimmed their staffs so sharply that they must hire consultants to take on projects and because consulting demands little capital, the lack of which is the major cause of small-business failures. The consulting fields that are flourishing the best include communications, personnel, engineering and marketing because that's where most cutbacks have occurred. Another thriving consulting area is financial planning, especially for corporate refugees from finance, accounting and tax departments, or for retirees from banks, accounting, insurance and law firms.

Between 2% and 3% of the U.S. working population is involved in external consulting, calculates Robert Kelley of Carnegie-Mellon University's business school.

Other promising fields for seniors' ventures:

- Sales representation where the senior knows the territory.

- A service business in appliance repair, plumbing, minor construction, or electrical repair if you can do most of the work yourself. The inability to hire competent help is another common reason for the failure of small businesses.

- A new or specialized product, if you don't need many employees. Examples include making models of classic cars or other classic items, ethnic items, or reproductions of original art such as small sculptures or drawings.

- A specialized retail operation that grows out of a hobby such as collecting antiques, coins or stamps.

Because of the popularity of computers, software tempts some seniors. Experts estimate that it costs at least $100,000 to market a new program, an ominous sum for a single proprietor. Even well-financed firms such as Ansa Corporation have had trouble going against Ashton-Tate Inc. and Lotus Development Corporation, the heavyweights in the hottest markets—spreadsheets, filing, and word processing. Successful firms have found market niches. Springboard Software Inc.'s Newsroom costs only $60 and composes newsletters. Borland International Inc.'s Turbo Lightning offers a computerized thesaurus for $100. Yet, the niches are filling rapidly. One new entrepreneur developed a food industry accounting package, only to discover belatedly that a competitor already offered such programs.

Before you leap, find someone who has already jumped and interview him or her. Mildred, a divorcee, wanted to start a business offering consultation to recent divorcees on how to survive the trauma. She found several public and semi-public agencies who offered this service, but no private consultants. The reason was that few divorcees could afford to pay for help. The few that could didn't need aid. She abandoned the idea and went to work for a semi-public organization funded by a foundation.

Elaine, a 62-year-old lawyer who had spent her entire working life as a member of General Electric's corps of lawyers, retired to public service law, specializing in helping elderly people in New York City and local environs with legal problems primarily involving housing. She spent two years before retiring from GE in setting up a private law firm to do this, first lining up as sponsor an organization in Westchester County that ran nursing homes and medical services, then getting legal support from the local bar association and financial aid from a foundation.

She raised the money, by far the most difficult part of her project, in the same way you would go after a job—through research. She went to the library and consulted such directories as:

● *Annual Register of Grant Support*, published by Marquis Academic Media. It costs $59.50, including mailing and handling if you order it from Marquis, 200 E. Ohio St., Room 5608, Chicago, IL 60611.

● *The Foundation Directory* lists 4,400 U.S. foundations which accounted for 92 percent of all grants made in 1983 and 1984. Its publisher, The Foundation Center, 79 Fifth Avenue, New York, NY 10003, also offers personal assistance in locating grant possibilities at its New York headquarters or in the three other information-gathering centers it operates in Washington, Cleveland and San Francisco. For more on the one nearest you, call 1-800-424-9836.

The directory costs $65, another indication of how valuable is your local business section of the public library.

Elaine also followed the advice of Matthew Lesko in *Getting Yours* in considering public money:

1) If you seek a government grant, look at both federal and local possibilities.

2) Forget logic when looking for government money. For instance, the Department of Labor funds doctoral dissertations; the Department of Agriculture funds many entrepreneurial ventures, and so on.

3) Talk to government people directly responsible for dispersing grant funds, whose names you can get from a public information officer (PIO). Most PIOs will readily give you the contacts, but don't stop with just the PIO. Government grant-hunting is such a labyrinthine process that you need information directly from the person most closely responsible.

4) When you have pinned down the right source, ask to see a copy of a successful application. You have the right to see this under the Freedom of Information Act.

5) If you learn you can get a grant, but only a small one and only for a year, accept it and hope that the government people can learn to love you in that time.

Elaine despaired of ever getting public financial support, but finally secured some from a small foundation in Westchester County. As a female, Elaine also got advice from the American Women's Economic Development Corporation. Counsel over the phone costs $5 for up to 10 minutes. Longer counseling costs $25 up to 90 minutes. The phone number from New York City, Alaska or Hawaii is 212-692-9100. If calling from New

York state, it's 1-800-442-AWED. If phoning from anywhere else, it's 1-800-222-AWED. You can charge the consultation on major credit cards.

Women are going into businesses of their own at a rate six times faster than men. Between 1980 and 1982, more than 2.3 million women started their own ventures, resulting in a total of 3.1 million businesses owned and operated by women, or 22 percent of all sole proprietorships. Computer firms are the most common start-ups by women. Some 45 percent of all women's firms are in the service sector, 30 percent in retail trade. Women face problems in starting their own business, such as these:

- Lack of capital or access to credit.
- Lack of credibility with banks. This goes beyond capital and credit questions and includes difficulty in persuading banks to service their billings and other accounts.
- Not knowing how business operates because of inexperience. The average female entrepreneur has had less than 10 years of experience in the business world.
- Inability to win government contracts, even on the local level. This often is the initial mainstay of a new male-run venture.

No Place Like Home

The majority of new business ventures start at home, or the place closest to it, the fabled garage. For one, it's the least expensive place to begin. For those who still have responsibilities for elderly relatives, it's often the only answer. For years, many fought traffic and waited for trains and buses, and they welcome the new five-second commute.

Nobody knows exactly how many people operate out of their homes. The best guestimate is 11 million. Statistics are hazy for three principal reasons. First, part of the underground economy functions from the home, not reporting all income and not wanting publicity about it. Second, zoning inhibits disclosure; the codes may prohibit businesses in residences, and practitioners want to keep a low profile. Third, 19 states still have laws that prohibit businesses in the home, stemming largely from attempts to stamp out child labor at the turn of the century. If these were all actively enforced, they might seriously stem senior labor today.

Virtually every kind of business imaginable is practiced in the home, but these stand out:

- Writing, painting and other artistic pursuits.
- Manufacturing, such as clothing, craft articles, toys, etc.

- Child care, elderly care and other human services.
- Miscellaneous business services including typing, bookkeeping, accounting, and secretarial.
- Communication services including public relations, advertising, and newsletter preparation.
- Computer-related services such as data processing, market analysis, and demographic studies.
- Professional services such as psychotherapy, executive recruiting, architecture, and interior design.
- Direct sales, such as Amway, Tupperware and the many people who sell on commission.
- Mail order, such as jewelry, shoes, clothes, recipes and so on.

Questions and Answers on the Home Front

So, you're sure you have the entrepreneur's personality. To help answer some questions you may have about a home business, let's have a talk with Regina who is ready to take the plunge. Regina, let's look at your idea of financial planning. What do you really know about it?

"I majored in accounting in college, and I took the six-part, home study course offered by the College for Financial Planning and passed the exams. I'm now a Certified Financial Planner." [Address and phone: 9725 East Hampden Avenue, Denver, CO 80231; 303-755-7101.]

It sounds like you have the education and training for it. How about experience in doing it?

"Well, I've always been interested in stocks, bonds, and other financial matters. Since my daughters left home, I've been working part-time for an accounting service. During the tax season, I prepare tax returns for H & R Block."

Then, you really mean you want to set up as a sole proprietor tax preparer?

"Definitely not. I'll prepare tax returns for clients, but only as part of the whole financial planning service."

Where do you plan to operate this service?

"In my home. Since my husband died, I've had what was our first-floor bedroom remodelled into an office, with an outside door. I use one of the girl's bedrooms for my bedroom now."

Have you gone to your Zoning Board to learn if your property is zoned for business?

"They would take six months to rule and then probably turn me down. There are several home businesses operating in my neighborhood. They all rent postal boxes at the Post Office and give that as their business address, with a second phone number in their homes for the businesses. They've had no trouble, as long as they don't put signs on their houses. Parking is no problem because I have a wide driveway for my two-car garage, and I'd rarely have more than one client at a time since I would see people by appointment only."

Most in-home businesses must attract customers from within a radius of about one mile. Have you checked out what you could draw from that area?

"I disagree about the one mile. People came from further distances than that for the accounting service and for H & R Block. I have six clients lined up already; only two of them live within a mile of me."

Okay, your point is well taken. Do all of them live within five miles of you? That's generally considered the outer limit.

"One lives about ten miles away."

All right, all right. That just shows there are few hard rules that apply to home business. Now, consider what kind of return on investment you can live with. Do you need this business to help you maintain your lifestyle when your husband was alive?

"Yes, but I have a cushion that can keep me going with no more than my six clients for two years. A financial planning practive grows from referrals by satisfied clients and from listings in directories such as those of the International Association of Financial Planning and Institute of Certified Financial Planners. I belong to both. Within two years, I hope to have at least 10 clients. I had none until recently."

Then, you aren't doing this just to keep busy? Remember, if you do not eventually make money, the IRS may disallow any business-related deductions you claim.

"This is no hobby! If I don't make money in three out of the next five years, I'll quit. Even the IRS recognizes a viable business if it's a money-maker in three of five years."

You've thought a lot about this. What's your business plan?

"I just told you mine—ten clients within two years, at a minimum. I've attended small-business seminars and read books on the subject, especially *How To Survive & Succeed in a Small Financial Planning Practice* by Andrew M. Rich."

What about your tax liabilities?

"I'm a tax preparer, remember? I've taken the Business Tax Workshop offered by the IRS and have a copy of IRS Publication 334, the *Tax*

Guide for Small Business. I've also registered my business name with the state. It's a legal requirement, which is a dodge to hit you with a business-privilege tax. I pay it. What else can I do?"

What about other accounting requirements?

"I'm an accountant. If I can't handle that, I don't belong in this business. Also, a nonaccountant should retain one. I do have a problem with one of my clients that I guess you could call accounting. He's a slow payer. I finally went to my bank which agreed to offer third-party credit. It costs me 3 percent of each charge—far cheaper than chasing deadbeats myself. One bank wanted 6 percent. I shopped around."

Do you have liability insurance?

"It's available for financial planners. Thus far, I haven't seen the need for it. If my business grows, I'll consider it more seriously. I've expanded my homeowner's insurance to cover my computer, photocopier and other business equipment."

You seem to have all this pretty well figured out.

"I hope so. I have a good idea that serves a need. I have experience. I've invested thought and a little capital in it. All I need are a few more knocks on my door or rings of my phone."

Why did you choose self-employment rather than working for someone else?

"I did work for someone else and didn't particularly care for it. I like my independence. I like to see measurable results. If I flop, I'll have only myself to blame. I like the excitement of that challenge."

10

Getting Ready To Find That Job

"You got to accentuate the positive and eliminate the negative" go the opening words of a Johnny Mercer song. It's good advice for jobhunters, especially for those seniors who tend to accentuate the negative.

You've decided not to go into business for yourself. You will try to find a job with another employer. The traditional jobhunting "system" is to send out résumés broadside, register with employment agencies and other surrogates, monitor the help wanted ads, and go on any interviews that surface from these activities and others, such as introductions by friends.

This haphazard approach has never worked very well for anyone. It scarcely works at all for seniors because no help wanted ads are addressed to them, agencies and other employment surrogates don't really want seniors, and neither do many personnel departments.

Furthermore, four out of five seniors must change or redirect their careers to find new employment. As a sales manager seeking a new man for the midwest territory, would you even want to interview a 55-year-old whose résumé indicates he has been in engineering most of his working life? If the résumé came to you via an agency or, less likely, an executive recruiter, you'd probably wonder what ailed these people to waste your time with irrelevant applications.

From Irrelevant to Relevant

That's how too many employers consider seniors—irrelevant.

The issue of irrelevancy is the basic reason why jobhunting or career-changing is more difficult for seniors than juniors. People over 50 have to jump a hurdle not facing those under that age.

However, seniors are on the verge of becoming far more relevant in the job picture and must be ready for their coming change in status. By the

107

1990s, there will be acute labor shortages, especially in job categories that seniors can best fill, the low-tech or no-tech areas.

"Older persons are our great unutilized source of labor . . . A growing weakness of American society is that it regards the old as consumers but not producers, as mouths but not hands." So wrote Malcolm Cowley, literary critic and essayist, in *The View from 80*, published in 1980.

Between 1965 and 1984, America's population aged 16 to 65 grew 38 percent, to 178 million people from 129 million. During that period, jobs increased 45 percent, to 103 million from 71 million. By the end of 1984, the number of jobs exceeded 105 million, a rise of nearly 50 percent since 1965. More than half this growth took place since the energy crisis in the fall of 1973—years of "oil shocks," of two recessions and the near-collapse of the smokestack industries. Even the 1981-82 recession, despite its trauma, barely slowed the rapid pace of new-job creation. At its bottom, in the fall of 1982, there still were 15 million more jobs than there had been in 1973, despite record unemployment.

In Japan, jobs in the past decade have grown about 10 percent, half the U.S. rate. Western Europe has had job *shrinkage*, about 3 million fewer than in 1974.

The U.S. economy now has about 10 million more jobs than even optimists predicted a decade-and-a-half ago. The new jobs didn't come from the sectors that for almost 40 years through the 1960s produced virtually all new jobs in the U.S. economy—government and big business. Government has barely maintained its employment levels since the early 1970s, and big business has been losing jobs since then. From early 1979 to early 1984, the Fortune 500—the nation's biggest manufacturers—permanently lost around 3 million jobs.

The significant point is this: Nearly all job creation has been in small- and medium-sized businesses, and almost all of it in entrepreneurial and innovative businesses. The next most important aspect is: As important as high technology is, it's not yet the big job creator, accounting for no more than 10 percent of the jobs created in the past 10 years. Its big job-creation period won't start until after 1990.

New-job creation is largely in low-tech or even no-tech businesses. A survey by Dun & Bradstreet Corporation showed the following percentages of the companies it surveyed in these industries expect to create new jobs in 1987:

Finance, insurance and real estate 34.5%
Services..27.9%
Wholesale and retail..27.8%

Construction	27.6%
Manufacturing	26.0%
Mining	22.7%
Government, all levels	21.5%
Transportation and public utilities	19.2%
Agriculture	8.3%

This American development, suggests Peter Drucker, "is probably a managerial breakthrough: The development since World War II of a body of organized knowledge of entrepreneurship and innovation . . . The American development clearly disproves the most widely held and most serious explanation of the economic crisis of the past 10 years, and the most widely held and most serious prediction for the decades to come: the 'no-growth' theory."

Our economy is growing in ways totally unforeseen by advocates of the "greening of America." Why, then, have we had unemployment rates as high as 7 percent in the mid-1980s at the same time that we have been creating new jobs at a rate unprecedented since the 1870s in this country? Largely because of a phenomenon not foreseen by most economists after World War II and whose significance is still not fully recognized by many of our public opinion leaders. It's the rapid increase in the number of working women. The number of women in the workforce more than doubled between 1950 and 1980, from 5.1 million to 11.7 million.

Most citizens of the Republic have missed—and are still missing—the significance of these facts. Most continue to view issues of retirement and age with a mindset shaped by and inherited from the Depression of the 1930s. So rigid is this mental and emotional attitude that the leaders of American public opinion were—and still mostly are—ignoring the staggering changes that have occurred since the 1940s.

Seniors are the prime victims of this time warp—discriminated against, yet on the threshold of a period when they will be essential to our national well-being. As a senior, you must prepare yourself for the immediate future when you will move with bewildering speed from being the irrelevant to becoming the relevant member of our workforce.

Temporarily Self-Employed

Unfortunately, the future is not yet here, but you need a job now and must still cope with current biases and distortions. The following suggestions can help you today. While you jobhunt, consider yourself as temporarily self-employed because looking for a new position or changing careers is a job in itself. Your objective is to find a job, nothing else. Keep regular hours, and plan at the end of each day what you will do the next. Keep a log of your progress. Delegate some of your activities; for example, your spouse may be able to do some of the library research for you.

Above all, organize your job searching. Schedule all library research for one time period, telephone interviewing for another, direct interviewing for still another.

Consider what you disliked most about your last job. The atmosphere of perpetual crisis? Your organization should minimize the feelings of pressure during your period of self-employment. As to your potential employer's penchant for crisis, concentrate your researches on evaluating it.

The endless meetings? Of course, you will have to attend meetings with potential employers eventually, but we will give you suggestions later on how best to shine under these circumstances.

Did the dictatorial boss get you down? Then, one of your major objectives is to find someone with whom you can be compatible. Concentrate your informational research on the personality of the individual you may work for.

Did you chafe at the company's roller coaster economic fortunes? Focus on a more stable employer next time.

You get the idea. You also must understand by now why jobhunting must be a full-time task.

So, how can a person already employed possibly carry on a job search at the same time? Not easily.

William Gould, managing director of Gould & McCoy Inc., New York, and president of the Association of Executive Search Consultants, says that once an already employed jobhunter starts making enquiries through trusted friends, it will take eight to 12 weeks before word filters back to his or her company. Once you start interviews with prospective new employers, however, "expect word to get back to your company in four to six weeks," Gould says, adding, "Prepare for the possibility of discovery and immediate dismissal."

All told, about 4.5 million people are hunting at this moment for new jobs while still holding their present positions. If we do a straight extrapolation, that means about 1.2 million seniors are doing so. (Approximately 27 percent of the labor force is 50 or older.)

What, then, do employed seniors do about jobhunting? The same thing unemployed seniors do, only at somewhat different hours:

● Put the odd hours to the task—evenings, lunch hours, weekends.

- Use weekends for the tough task of determining what you want to do because you need as much uninterrupted time as possible for this.

- Schedule appointments for just before or after lunch, or late afternoons. If the prospective employer knows you already work, he or she will usually accommodate you. Some will even see you on a Saturday.

- Press into service the holidays that not everyone observes, such as Martin Luther King Day or Presidents' Day.

- Take your whole vacation or vacation days or sick leave days and convert the time into jobhunt days.

- Ask for time off without pay for your search, although do this as a last resort because the employer will naturally want to know why.

Is it unethical to jobhunt while you're still employed? Only if you neglect your present work, and your present employer can always fire you if you aren't measuring up. By the same token, you have the right to prepare for something else ahead of time.

What *Not* To Do

Job-seekers over 50 should avoid the following in their search:

- *Panic*. It broadcasts that you feel irrelevant, magnifying the wrong image. Even if you feel reasonably confident at first that you will quickly get another job, panic may threaten after a month or two of no results. On average, the hunt takes four-and-a-half months, but it may require even more time. Nobody blames you for concern, but stifle even that. Project the image of calm confidence. That probably requires acting ability. Everyone possesses just a little ham within. Draw upon it. Practice before your spouse, even before a mirror if no suitable audience is available but yourself.

- *Overeagerness*. It's panic's first cousin. Even if a miracle happens and you get an offer within a few weeks, don't accept it impulsively. You need more than one offer anyhow, primarily for comparison purposes. Look further. Consider your first offer your confidence-builder. As with panic, practice your thespian abilities to appear calm and pleasantly interested.

- *Overconfidence*. Occasionally, a senior suffers this malady. It's as bad as overeagerness and nearly as harmful as panic because this kind of jobhunter simply doesn't know reality. He or she does little or no self-appraisal, thinks that a new job will turn up almost automatically in the same field and location, and is altogether too casual about the search itself. Even if the new position does surface, it's likely to have the same inherent problems as the last and the same results—severance, but quicker than formerly.

Also, don't jump the gun on salary if you think someone is interested in hiring you. "It's the domain of the potential employer to bring up the issue of compensation," believes Minneapolis consultant Greg Ohman. When the matter does surface, bring up all aspects of it—insurance and medical benefits, pensions, vacations, even the company car if that's appropriate—in addition to salary itself. Benefits may account for 35 percent or more of salary these days. A 1984 U.S. Chamber of Commerce survey revealed that the average benefits among 1,154 companies cost $7,842.

● *Delusion.* Take time—a week or more is not too long—to do a thorough self-appraisal. Analyze what went wrong at the former job, whether you want to switch careers, and where you and your family want to live. While you must analyze what went wrong in the last position, don't overdo it. Over-analysis will do more harm than good.

Also, don't underestimate the stress of leaving your former position, which sometimes hits you weeks after the event and all the more forcefully because of the delay. Peter Drummond-Hay, a consultant with Russell Reynolds Associates, Inc., points out that leaving a longtime employer, particularly when fired or forced out, has "many of the characteristics of a divorce"—and is similarly traumatic.

● *Self-indulgence.* This may take the form of moping. "Get your mourning out of the way and get on with it," advises William Gould.

Or your self-indulgence may take the form of a long vacation. If you feel you must get away for awhile, keep your absence as brief as possible. You need to get working on the job search.

Or your self-indulgence may take the form of laziness and drifting. Develop a plan, target employers, and go after them relentlessly.

● *Self-consciousness.* Too many seniors do not bring the family into the situation, perhaps not even informing them at all for weeks. They fear their relatives will think less of them for being unemployed or underemployed. Put aside such foolishness. The more who know you're jobhunting, the better. One who knows may provide the exact contact you need. That won't happen if only you know you need a new job. Besides, the stigma of joblessness or underemployment is not as severe for seniors as formerly because so many are in the same predicament.

● *Evasiveness*. "Never, never lie—never stretch a point," either on résumés or in interviews, William Gould counsels. Be willing to address failure as well as strengths. Discuss openly and fully what went wrong at the old job, if asked, which you almost certainly will be about why you left your last position. On the other hand, there's no point in volunteering negative information if the subject never comes up. For example, if you are a recovered alcoholic and alcoholism didn't figure in your last severance, say nothing unless asked specifically.

● *Bitterness*. It will slow you down and turn off potential employers. If you do feel bitter, don't show it. Use your dramatic abilities as in the cases of panic and overeagerness.

Improving Your Chances

Besides avoiding the don'ts, you can improve the odds immediately and dramatically of getting a new job if you:

● Give enough time to the search, up to 40 hours a week.
● Take the initiative in the hunt by knowing as much as possible about the prospective employer.
● Concentrate on smaller businesses. Two-thirds of new jobs have been created in that area every year since 1969. In 1985, small business accounted for 1.3 million of the 2 million new jobs and 2 million of the 3 million new positions created in 1986, according to a Dun & Bradstreet survey.
● Identify and prioritize your skills—(1) Supervision; (2) Toolmaking; (3) Inspection, for example.
● Be gently, but not obnoxiously persistent in the time you spend in the search and persistent in returning in a week or two to the places that interest you. You will never know if something has opened in the interim unless you return.
● Take the label off yourself if nothing turns up in your old line. Instead of saying you are a steelworker, say you have great skills

with your hands. Instead of labelling yourself as a locomotive sales-man, call yourself a marketer of high-tech equipment. Give your skills a new name, a new twist.

● Expand your horizons to as many industries as possible. For example, go to aluminum and plastic manufacturers if you find nothing in steel; all three fields have common denominators. Similarly, use as many entrees to potential employers as possible.

● Highlight your qualities that you think make you better than the next job seeker—patience, quality work, persistence in solving problems, or whatever.

● Get friends and relatives to do preliminary research.

● Send short notes of thanks quickly to all involved with every interview—the potential employer, the introducer(s), receptionist, secretary—regardless of the outcome.

● Keep up your personal appearance—clothes, posture, voice, facial expression.

● Keep up your attitudes; make it clear you know that no one owes you a job; you should have the job because of what you can do for the employer.

Times Are Changing

Have you forgotten how much has changed since you won your first job? Nardi Campion, a senior, reminds us, "We were before television. Before penicillin, polio shots, antibiotics and frisbees. Before frozen food, nylon, dacron, Xerox, Kinsey. We were before radar, fluorescent lights, credit cards and ballpoint pens. For us, time-sharing meant to-getherness, not computers; a chip meant a piece of wood; hardware meant hardware, and software wasn't even a word.

"In our time closets were for clothes, not for coming out of, and a book about two young women living together in Europe could be called *Our Hearts Were Young and Gay*. In those days, *Playboy* referred to J.M. Synge's *Hero of the Western World*, bunnies were small rabbits, and rabbits were not Volkswagens. We were before Grandma Moses and Frank Sinatra and cup-sizing for bras. We wore Peter Pan collars and thought a deep cleavage was something butchers did . . .

"We thought fast food was what you ate during Lent."

David Sargent, also a senior, reprinted the foregoing in the March 24, 1986 issue of *United Business Investment Report* (now retitled *United &*

Babson Investment Report), adding, "We were before so much, one wonders what we were after."

At some point in those days, we were after a job. At this point, we're looking again. Times have changed. So have jobhunting techniques, especially for seniors. We have just recounted them, now we'll summarize them.

Eight Roads to Successful Senior Jobhunting

You can best find a new job after 50 when you cultivate within yourself these traits in the search:

1) *Know the real work world*. Many employers don't *dislike* you. Some of their best friends and relatives are over 50. They even may be in that age category themselves. They may secretly or subliminally harbor biases against your age group. They may docilely follow unwritten hiring rules that discriminate against you. They may think they cut costs by letting you go, a misconception generated by skewed accounting practices that seem to make it cheaper to keep juniors. That's the real work world, and you had better understand how it functions. Perhaps you've learned your most forceful lesson when you had no choice but to retire early at 55 or even younger.

2) *Do the jobhunting yourself*. Spend a lot of time at it, as much as 40 hours a week if possible. In the conventional jobhunt, the seeker sits at home most of the time waiting for something to surface as a result of his résumés or his surrogates' efforts. Of course, something might materialize, but odds are heavily against it for seniors. Keep track of your weekly jobhunting hours. If they're under 30, you're not hunting hard enough. If they're over 40, you're putting in too much time and will wear yourself out, a more serious threat to seniors than juniors. Delegate some of the tasks, or apply time management techniques to your efforts, just as you would to a regular job. For example, eliminate unnecessary tasks, such as answering help wanted ads. Studies indicate that a job searcher using conventional approaches spends only about five hours a week in the hunt. If you spend 35, is it not reasonable to believe you will be seven times as successful?

3) *Do self-analysis before you hunt for the job*. We're said it before, we say it now, and we'll say it later: Know precisely what your

best skills are, and know precisely how you want to use them—the type of activity, the type of employer, and where you want it located.

Various surveys show that somewhere between 20 and 60 percent of all working people are underemployed. Whatever the accurate ratio, it's evident that these persons did not perform good advance self-analysis. Otherwise, they would not be in such a fix. A 55-year-old has potentially 10 years or about 20,000 hours of work ahead of him or her. Does it make sense to make a commitment of such duration for your life without investing 40 or more hours in analyzing what you want to do?

Precision must be an integral part of your study. "I want to work with people"—it won't do. "I want to do salary administration"—better, but it could be even more exact. "I want to do salary comparisons within an industry and region as a means of keeping competitive; I want to develop a merit system as a means of getting fair value for the work performed; I want to develop a grid system of job evaluation so that comparable pay is dispensed for comparable but different jobs"—now we're getting somewhere.

4) *Get all information possible about potential employers.* When you know what you're looking for, use as many different roads as possible to find the information. Go to your business library and read news clippings about the employer. Check such directories as *Moody's, Thomas Register* and any others your library provides. Unearth both present and former employees of the organization and interview them as though you were a reporter from *Business Week.* Read the potential employer's annual and quarterly reports for as far back as you can get them. Good business libraries keep them for at least three years.

More than a dozen ways exist for you to find such data. Studies indicate that most job seekers use two or less.

5) *Decide if the potential employer interests you.* This decision can come only after you know a lot about it. We should approach with caution the judgment side of jobhunting. The decision concerning your interest in a particular employer boils down to this:

- An analysis of whether the job fits your talents; you are unlikely to change your talents significantly to fit the job.

- An appraisal of the key facts that interest you.

- A diagnosis of the potential job situation to define basic problems and parameters, to clarify still further your objectives, and to identify a solution.

• An appraisal of the risks, concentrating on taking the right risks rather than on eliminating or minimizing them.

• A hunt for positives. What's good about this potential employer? Rank-order the plusses.

• A search for negatives. What's wrong with it? Rank-order the minuses.

• A comparison of the plusses and minuses.

6) *Determine how to pique the potential employer's interest in you.* In essence, this involves developing a strategy whereby the employer courts you, not vice versa. How can you do that? By providing a solution to a problem that your research shows the potential employer faces.

7) *Focus on the job you want, nothing else.* In the beginning, ignore pay and benefits; concentrate on these only in final negotiations.

8) *Communicate effectively with potential employers.* Coax or hype yourself into your best performance in approaching and interviewing potential employers.

Is all this too much to absorb? Don't worry. We'll go into it in more detail in succeeding chapters. The most important things you ever learn can be absorbed after you're 50.

11

Decide What To Do Next

An artist won first prize for his drawing. In accepting the award, he remarked to the judge, "This isn't my best work."

"Why didn't you submit your best?" asked the judge.

"Because I haven't done it yet," replied the artist.

None of us has done his or her best work—yet. Job-seeking seniors, in particular, have not. When asking themselves what they should do next, most answer: The same thing. That may be a good reply, but more likely it's a poor course of action. If what you did before didn't pan out, why will it next time?

- "Because I'll pick a company next time that doesn't discriminate against seniors."
- "Because I'll find the right boss."
- "Because I'll choose a manufacturer with better products."
- "Because I'll never get mixed up in office politics again."
- "Because I'll never take my job for granted again."
- "Because I'll never work again for an employer that condones nepotism."

Note that none of those replies come close to admitting, "I did a lousy job, but will do better next time." If you can say at least that, you are starting true self-analysis.

Self-Analysis

One dictionary defines self-analysis as "the application of psychoanalytic techniques and theories to an analysis of one's own personality and behavior, especially without the aid of a psychiatrist or other trained person."

In describing the origins of psychoanalysis, Sigmund Freud wrote, "In the years 1880-82 a Viennese physician, Josef Breuer, discovered a new procedure by means of which he relieved a girl, who was suffering from severe hysteria, of various symptoms. The idea occurred to him the symptoms were connected with impressions which she had received during a period of excitement . . . He therefore induced her . . . to search for these connections in her memory . . . He found that when he had done this the symptoms in question disappeared for good."

Thus far, we have advised you not to spend too much time thinking about what went wrong on your last job. Done too soon, the thoughts can disintegrate into stewing on the one hand or pollyannish rationalization on the other. Either will inhibit you and distort your conclusions about what you want to do with the rest of your life.

Now that you've developed some ideas about your future, hopefully undistorted by the trauma of your most recent work, we want you to analyze those latter job experiences. With a more objective analysis of these experiences, you may be able to "exorcise" the evil spirits that tripped you last time. Such exorcisms, together with the ideas you've formulated for the future, should combine to give you a better fix on the work you wish to do henceforth.

Let's see how such procedures will work for Frances, Bert and Max.

Once Upon a Time . . .

Frances had risen to become dining room manager of a private club. She began as a dishwasher at age 18 and rose to become a waitress, a hostess, and finally manager. She retired after 40 years on the job at age 58.

She thought vaguely of "taking it easy." She lived with an older brother and sister, all three unmarried, all three fanatic sports fans. They all retired on the same day and bought season tickets to the Pittsburgh baseball Pirates, football Steelers and hockey Penguins.

The Pirates performed indifferently in the field, and the trio attended less than half of the home games. The Steelers played exciting football, too exciting because the older brother suffered a heart attack in the stands. Paramedics saved his life, but his doctor said no more excitement, forbidding him even to watch athletics on television.

Frances and her sister didn't want to go without him. Soon Frances saw "taking it easy" as a hard life. Finances did not trouble her, but boredom did. Did she want to spend the rest of her life moping around the house?

The Pirates were sold to new owners but remained in precarious financial straits. She volunteered to help sell tickets. She used techniques honed from four decades of dealing with club members. She jollied along the complainers. She sold the right-field seats just as she persuaded diners to take pot roast because the kitchen had run out of steak. She squeezed in the later arrivers and found something for people who forgot to make reservations. So successful was she that the Pirates hired her as one of their salaried ticket representatives.

In thinking things over about her future, she realized she feared boredom most. She wanted some excitement in her life that she no longer could find in the club dining room. She found it in helping to save the Pirates, a job she really fell into. Sometimes that happens when all you really know is the kind of life you want in the future.

Bert got pressured into early retirement at 62. He didn't wear a green eyeshade or garters on his sleeves, but he was not in the forefront of accounting practices either. At first he blamed his severance on age discrimination and even toyed with filing suit. He consulted with four lawyers, but was shocked at the fees they would charge and at the helter-skelter way they seemed to run their businesses. He valued order and calm in anything in which he was involved.

He and his wife lived a quiet life, well-organized and planned for the future. He wanted that for the rest of his days, he realized, after he abandoned the idea of suing his former employer. The law firms he had visited needed better organization, he decided. Bert went back to each of the firms with a scheme for office management, with himself as the manager. The largest hired him.

Max enjoyed selling but disliked travelling to other cities connected with the seven jobs he had held during his 35 years in the "game" as he called it. In his worst moods, he wondered if he was another Willy Loman from *Death of a Salesman*. While still on his present job, he resolved he would never travel out of town for business again.

He did market research on selling positions that didn't entail travel. He ruled out telephone sales because none would pay enough. He needed an income of at least $50,000 a year. He investigated insurance and stock brokerage, but vetoed both because they required extensive training. He considered retail sales of big ticket items such as office equipment, home appliances, and autos, but didn't like the income prospects for any. More systematically than either Frances or Bert, he examined the best roads to a career decision.

Pulling It All Together

To find precise directions to a new career or job, inventory your skills, then match them against your predilections.

As a senior, you've lived long enough to develop many skills, probably more than you realize. In effect, interview yourself, using a memory device, OCCUPATION:

O—Old job: What went wrong with it, and why?

C—Career: Do you want the status quo, redirection, or something completely new?

C—Compensation: Can you afford to take less next time?

U—Unemployed or underemployed: Which are you and why?

P—Part-time or full-time work: What do you want?

A—Age: Does yours worry you, or do you ignore it?

T—Time: Can you afford to take enough to find the next job that's right for you?

I—Industry, business, or not-for-profit: Which would you find most comfortable to work in?

O—Organizational structures: Which would you prefer?

N—Near or far: Would you move if the job were right?

If Frances had taken the OCCUPATION test, she would have answered that her old job was boring; she wanted a new career; she could afford to work for less; she was unemployed by choice; she would prefer part-time or seasonal work; her age worried her because she felt she was growing old without finding anything that demanded her commitment; she had enough time to look; it didn't matter what kind of employer or organizational structure she found herself in; and she couldn't move because of her invalid brother.

If Bert had taken the OCCUPATION test, he would have replied that he was a square peg in the round hole of accounting; he wanted to redirect his career; he would ask for at least as much compensation as before; he was unemployed against his will; he wanted full-time work; age worried him constantly but he would learn to accept the inevitable; he had enough time to look; he preferred a business climate with considerable organizational structure to it; and he preferred not to move because his house was paid for after years of saving.

Max was the only one of the three who did take the test. He found that all his old jobs had a common drawback—too much travelling to other cities. He saw no need to change his basic career of selling or to accept lower compensation in his next job. He decided he was underemployed because he wasted too much time in travelling. He wanted a full-time job. His age didn't bother him particularly, except for the fact that travel troubled him more than when he was younger. He had plenty of time to hunt for something new. He wanted something connected with either industry or business because he had spent his entire working life in for-profit activities. As to organizational structure, he wanted as much freedom as possible because he had it in the past. Somewhat to his surprise, he decided he would not mind moving to another city. He had always liked Pittsburgh, one of his stops for years, and found a real estate connection there.

The Search for Skills

As already stated, seniors may overlook their most salable skills, their higher levels, under the illusion that their lower ones would find more takers. Not true. Competition escalates the lower you go.

The Bible of career counseling is the *Dictionary of Occupational Titles* (U.S. Government Printing Office, Washington, D.C., 1977.) It breaks down skills into Data (information), People and Things. The lower the skill, the more prescribed it is and the more closely the boss defines the job and supervises you. The higher the skill, the more discretionary it is, the more freedom you have to define the job yourself, and the less direct supervision you experience.

For example, under Data, the highest skill is synthesizing it, followed in descending order of difficulty by coordinating it, analyzing it, compiling/computing it, copying it, and comparing it.

For People, the highest skill is mentoring (guiding/teaching) others, followed by negotiating with them, supervising them, persuading them, speaking with them, and helping them.

In the Things category, the highest level of skill is setting up the task, followed by precision work, operating/doing the work, manipulating it, tending it, and handling it.

Each higher skill level embodies all those below it. For example, in the Data category, a person synthesizing data also coordinates/creates it, analyzes it, compiles it, copies it and compares it. At the next lower level of coordination, there is no synthesis, but all following functions are included.

In the People category, a mentor deals with others as a guide and teacher, and so on down the list. In the Things group, a set-up person on a machine or task can do all the rest, but his or her skills are so valuable that they are reserved usually for just this function, even if the individual can do everything else.

From the foregoing, we can draw these conclusions:

First, the lower the skill levels you think you can claim, the more you will have to fit in.

Second, the higher the skill levels you can honestly claim, the better you can make the job fit you. Also, the higher the skill levels, the less likely it will be advertised and the more ingenious you will have to become in unearthing ways to find it.

Third, the bright side of the foregoing is, you'll encounter less competition for the position once you discover it because far fewer people know about it than about an advertised one.

To have skills is not enough. What have you done with them? Here lies the major advantage you have over juniors. You can draw upon your long experience to cite chapter and verse. An employer doesn't care particularly that you know labor relations, can supervise a factory shift, operate a word processor, run a club's dining room, do accounting or sell mattresses. The employer wants to know how you can solve his or her particular problem, and every employer—whether in industry, business, or nonprofit activities—has a problem, usually more than one.

As a starter, think of all the problems you've solved over the years. In narrative form, describe the problem and how you tackled it. Give the particulars of your solution and the benefits that resulted.

Max went through this exercise, describing his experiences in the mattress trade. Here are three of his case histories.

"A major home furnishing chain with six stores in Buffalo, Erie and local environs began to delay its payments. My early inquiries brought the expected explanations—customers are paying slowly because of the recession, business is off until spring, competition is hurting us.

"I knew the first and third reasons were valid. I persuaded my employer to join with the chain in a co-op ad campaign that offered longer credit and special prices. The competition was hitting one of its six stores in North Tonawanda where Bethlehem Steel was curtailing its steel operation. I prevailed on the chain's management to close it because it had long been a marginal store. I suggested it donate the facility to Goodwill Industries for one of its second-hand outlets and take a tax credit. Goodwill was already a major factor in the second-hand home furnishing market and would give the nearby store selling new merchandise (including *my* competitor's springs and mattresses) a hard run for their money.

"My suggested strategy worked well. The ad campaign spurred business. The closing of the money-losing North Tonawanda store improved cash flow, and the chain began paying us on time again. (Also, the competitor there closed within six months.)"

•

"For years, I had no luck selling to a two-store outlet operated by a husband and wife in the Corning, N.Y. area. The same competitor who caused me trouble in North Tonawanda had monopolized their business for more than 20 years.

"In all the cities I visit, my practice is to cultivate the executive director of the local chamber of commerce because he or she is a great source for the area's business news. It happens that in Corning, Corning Glass Works is the chamber's Big Daddy. Corning Class owns a good deal of the town's business district.

"At lunch one day, the director told me that the company would soon be seeking a new tenant for one of the buildings it owned on Dennison Street. This time, it wanted something other than an arts and crafts store because the town had too many already. The place would be vacant because one was going out of business.

"That afternoon, I changed plans and called on the husband-wife team. Before they could politely turn me down for the umpteenth time, I mentioned my surprise that they had no outlet on Dennison. They had long wanted one, they told me, but rents were out of sight. Furthermore, nothing was available. I said something might soon be. I hinted my company might even help with the lease's costs for the first year, provided of course that they bought our products.

"It took nearly six months to work out the details, but they opened a new store on Dennison and bought our line for all three of their units. What's more, the chamber director buys my lunch every other time now."

•

"My Elmira account had a fire in its place, one of the major hazards in this kind of retailing. I heard about it on my car radio while heading for Syracuse. I immediately turned back to Elmira; I had been there just two days earlier.

"The fire was bad—no hope for a fast clean-up, which we had been able to help accomplish in past disasters. The management was fighting with its insurers and trying to decide what was salvageable. Their state of shock had not yet allowed them to look seriously for new or temporary quarters. They were relieved and surprised when I volunteered to search.

"With the help of realtors, I found two possibilities within 24 hours. Upon my advice for its irony and promotional possibilities, they chose an old firehouse that the city had for sale. We provided a rush shipment of our products and gave counsel on how the management could get fast delivery from other suppliers. Within ten days, the store was back in business in the firehouse."

•

When Max reread his narratives, he was struck for the first time that the common denominator of real estate ran through all of them. That fact helped convince him that he should and could shift to that field in redirecting his career.

Making the Decision

Max made the decision about what he should do with relative ease. You may experience trouble with it. Here's advice on how to go about the survey:

1) Look at your present career first. Even if you have already written this off, check again. You may have overlooked a niche. Business communicators can move from employee publications to public relations to advertising because they use the same basic skills in all. A toolmaker can make dies, operate the machines that need them, function as an inspector or set-up expert, or perhaps serve as a foreman.

2) If a toolmaker becomes a foreman, he or she has redirected a career. That's a common route for seniors. Find the corollaries for your career. A good manager can manage almost anything. Someone good with his or her hands can move to many related fields. A good salesperson can sell almost anything. Construction activities make logical adjuncts for architects. Lawyers can move readily from private practice to legal departments of corporate or government employers. A truck driver can operate lift trucks or construction equipment. Use your creativity in your redirection.

3) Find a completely new career. Fields which had the greatest demand in 1987 included computer-related (especially software design and robotics), engineering (particularly genetic, electrical, mechanical, manufacturing, and plastics), languages (notably Arabic, Russian, Japanese, and Chinese), retail banking, market research, statistics, business teaching at the undergraduate and graduate university levels, skilled machine work (both on machine tools and in tool-and-die), and secretaries (in some areas of the country). Check demand preferences periodically because they change as often as fashions in clothes. The Sunbelt is the fastest-growing section, although the decline in oil has cooled the Southwest considerably. If a career in any of these fields or areas doesn't appeal to you, don't

worry. Glamour careers draw heated competition; why subject yourself to it? We will always need good repair people, good professionals, and good practitioners of every skill.

4) Determine if what you want to do has any demand. If you make the best buggy whips in the world and have identified a viable market, go into this field. However, it's common sense for most of us to choose something less specialized. Labor Department statistics show that since 1983 more than three-fourths of new jobs were in these three major, higher-paying occupational categories—managerial and professional; technical, sales, and administrative support; and precision production, craft and repair. On the other hand, only one-tenth of jobs created over this span were low-end, minimum-wage jobs. The job growth rate for the three highest paying occupational categories has been 50% faster than the rate for all job categories. At the same time, the high-end jobs' share of all jobs has increased, while the share of the low-end jobs has decreased. Somehow, the service sector has become unjustly associated with low wages, perhaps because we see so many fast-food outlets advertising for workers. Actually, the most lucrative jobs to be had these days are in the service sector. It also accounts for most job growth, in a diversity ranging from consulting on human resources to operating computers to providing financial services.

The Question of Retraining

Career counselors love to advise retraining, more education, a brush-up at least. Sometimes it's good advice; more often it's not. The reason is that the retraining is premature, taken long before you know what you should retrain for. If you take accounting courses, you discover belatedly that what you really need are courses in financial planning. If you take secretarial retraining, you find too late that the demand for secretaries in your area is low. If you brush-up on your public speaking ability, not a single potential employer seems interested. The best bet is to wait until you know the gaps in your store of knowledge for a new or redirected career.

Of course, all bets are off if you wish to switch to a profession that requires extensive education. Law and medicine come first to mind, but others do, too—financial planning, the arts, religion.

Unnecessary retraining can cause more serious losses than time and money. It can do irreparable damage to your psyche when you learn it's useless. In these days when standard universities, community colleges and technical schools all beat the bushes for students, beware of their hard sells for "adult education."

The Route of Volunteerism

There's still another way to learn what to do with your future, especially for executives who had to retire—volunteer your expertise. The opportunities for meaningful volunteer activity are widespread. You decide what you want to do and where you want to do it in the same manner you look for a new paying opportunity—by research. A good place to begin your studies is with The National Council on the Aging, 600 Maryland Ave., SW., West Wing 100, Washington, D.C. 20024. It boasts one of the largest libraries in the country on senior-related volunteer activities.

If that's not convenient, you can offer your skills and experience for the benefit of your community through executive service corps (ESCs). One of the oldest, the Chicago ESC, is considered a model for other city service corps and, with support from a Mott Foundation grant, is conducting training programs for those interested in establishing similar programs.

In Chicago, more than 450 retired educators, doctors, builders and other professionals have volunteered their managerial and business skills to not-for-profit organizations and public agencies according to Pamela Smith, the Chicago ESC's communications manager.

"ESC is a unique arrangement where everybody wins," she explains. The volunteers may uncover talents they had half-forgotten they possessed. Users of the expertise get consulting help they otherwise could not afford. Corporate supporters find their charitable dollar is greatly enhanced.

One of about 20 similar organizations around the country, Chicago's ESC receives financial support from more than 100 corporations and foundations, but is largely run by volunteers.

In 1985, Chicago ESC consultants contributed more than 25,000 hours to nearly 200 organizations in the Chicago area, including educational institutions, arts and recreation groups, and health care agencies. According to ESC members, the consultants benefitted as much from the experience as did the agencies they worked with. For example, Louis E. Lynch, formerly a vice-president with Kraft Foods, says, "ESC activities [can help you] recover some of the mental and physical stimulation enjoyed in the days before retirement."

Founded in 1978, ESC was modeled on the International Executive Service Corps, which sends retired executives overseas to advise corporations and governments in developing countries, and the National Executive Service Corps, which provides volunteer consultants to national charitable organizations.

For more information on present local ESCs or starting a new one in your area, contact NESC, 622 Third Avenue, New York, NY 10017 or call (212) 867-5010.

Whether you decide to labor for pay or for free, do it with all your heart and skill to make sure that your next work is your best yet.

12

Learn How To Start Jobhunting

Come all you rounders that want to hear
The story of a brave engineer.
Casey Jones was the rounder's name.
On a big eight wheeler, boys, he won his fame.

The caller called Casey at half-past four.
He kissed his wife at the station door.
He mounted to the cabin with the orders in his hand,
And he took his farewell trip to that promised land.

So go the first eight lines by T. Lawrence Seibert of the most famous of all railroad songs. At the time of the tragedy, according to one legend, Casey, throttle-puller of the Illinois Central's crack "Cannonball," was driving No. 382, making a run for a sick friend. The train was wrecked at Vaughan, Mississippi, and Casey died at the throttle.

Alas, American railroad companies are all in danger of becoming legends now with curtailed trackage, reduced passenger traffic, and freight being taken from them by trucks, waterways and airlines. Builders of equipment and supplies for these companies have also suffered a parallel slump.

Hal, a 57-year-old salesman of locomotives, had to take early retirement because the market for his product was only 20 percent of what it had been 35 years before when he graduated from Penn State.

His research told him that he should deal with something related to capital goods that also possessed an element of high technology. Furthermore, he wanted to work only part-time in the future. Why did Hal want high-tech capital goods? Did he need more education and training? Did his desire to labor only part-time affect his decisions? We will answer

131

those and other questions and point out analogies for seniors in different circumstances—for those who want full-time jobs, who require work with a low-technology content, or who seek employment in disciplines other than sales.

Aren't You Glad You've Already Started?

If you have followed the precepts detailed thus far, you've already started the process of finding another job by first deciding what you want to do. Now, we deal with the second step—positioning yourself to start jobhunting. Do you simply begin mailing résumés, telephoning likely prospects and knocking on doors? Not unless you are willing to accept the most likely result, a disheartening flurry of rebuffs.

Some of the positioning goes on already for you because of demographic changes progressing like a tidal wave. In the future, jobs for seniors will be easier to find, but not yet.

Because of the 20-year decline in the birth rate that started in 1957, today's labor force is increasing more slowly than earlier. The Bureau of Labor Statistics estimates that workforce growth is currently averaging 1.3 percent a year, about half the annual growth rate in the 1970s when the economy absorbed the post-war "baby boom" and an increase in women workers.

Fast food restaurants and other businesses that depend on young workers are already finding it difficult to fill jobs. "Today's shortage of teenage workers will spread to other age groups," according to an analysis by Morgan Guaranty Trust Company. "In the next five years—and into the 1990s—employers will find themselves in the unaccustomed position of scrambling for workers."

Over the long term, personnel policies will be a greater factor in success or failure than in the past. "Companies that invest heavily in training . . . may well find that the payoff is unusually high," Morgan Guaranty notes.

Peter Morrison, a demographer at the Rand Corporation in Santa Monica, CA, says that "an inevitable consequence of the baby bust is a shortage of entrance-level workers." Higher immigration may solve part of the problem, but he points out that "the best people are going to be very much in demand, both men and women." Women will make up 46 percent of the workforce in 1995, up from 40 percent in 1975, and "jobs by men and women will be very much alike" with shrinking pay differentials. In the face of short supplies of skilled workers, many women may find it easier to win such company benefits as flexible work hours.

Managing and maintaining a skilled workforce in the future will require "imaginative" personnel policies, Mr. Morrison advises.

"There is going to come a time when quality younger employees are going to be scarce," says David Gamse, director of the American Association of Retired Persons' Worker Equity department. "Older workers are going to be an important factor in the work force."

To help older persons achieve their growing workplace ambitions, AARP in 1985 formed the Worker Equity department. Using a mix of techniques, including business partnerships, worker education programs, and litigation, the worker-equity staff is addressing key community and constituent groups.

One target audience consists of those midlife employees and preretirees who either hope to keep on working or, after retiring, to reenter the job market. To help such individuals, the department has established a network of volunteers to educate employees and companies about preretirement planning and work options.

In addition, the department offers a variety of preretirement and life-planning guidebooks and programs that can be used either individually or in group sessions sponsored by business or community organizations. The materials, says Denise Loftus who oversees the department's preretirement efforts, cover all aspects of retirement planning.

"The program, at heart, is motivational. The real issue is getting people to look ahead," says Bill Lerch of Atlantic Electric, a southern New Jersey utility that first began using AARP preretirement materials in 1985. "Everyone talks about financial and legal matters and Social Security, but I think the real issues . . . are usefulness and 'what does my life mean now?'"

The department is also establishing support for older workers within the business community. It is, says Gamse, a crucial connection. "We can talk and talk about how wonderful older workers are but if a company is convinced older workers cost more money, they are not going to hire them."

To correct corporate misperceptions and to better understand the problems of business, during 1985 the department sponsored two weekend conferences attended by executives from leading U.S. firms, labor leaders and government policymakers. "The meetings," says Anita Stowell who runs the department's business partnership section, "are designed to look at those factors that create disincentives to the hiring and retaining of older people." So far, the AARP-sponsored sessions have focused on two issues affecting the employability of seniors: pensions and health benefits.

Although initially cautious, the business community has increasingly warmed to department efforts to openly discuss its concerns about older workers. One early outgrowth of the sessions is the formation of a research agenda by AARP to develop statistics and other data related to the value and contributions of older employees.

In addition to such bridge-building programs, AARP is also monitoring the activities of those employers who may be ignoring the provisions of the Age Discrimination in Employment Act (ADEA). It has filed numerous friend-of-the-court briefs in cases that allegedly involve age discrimination. Such a brief is a means by which interested parties other than the litigants can present arguments in a lawsuit. In two cases—involving discriminatory retirement practices against fire fighters and airline personnel—the Supreme Court handed down decisions along lines recommended by AARP.

To receive preretirement planning or Worker Equity publications, write to the AARP Worker Equity Department, 1909 K Street NW, Washington, DC 20049.

Researching Your Ideal Job

The climate-building efforts of AARP and other organizations to win more senior jobs are welcome, but the responsibility for locating new work still rests largely with you. Once you have generally decided what you want to do, you still must specifically pinpoint with whom you wish to do it.

A factor in this decision must be time. How long can you afford to hunt? Today, the average for all persons, regardless of age, is 18.4 weeks, or about four-and-a-half months. For seniors it's longer, both because of biases against the 50-plus group and because you want to make this your last and best job search.

Allow about one month of jobhunting time for every $10,000 in annual salary you seek. If you want $40,000 a year, at least a four-month search for you as a senior is not out of line. Younger jobhunters can reasonably expect to find something sooner. So, under the one-month-per-$10,000 formula, you would need 8 months to locate a position paying $80,000 a year, and that would probably be the minimum.

Regrettably, the downside on the salary scale rarely means less time will be needed by people 50 and older to find a job. If you wish a $20,000-per-year job, it will still take you as a senior *at least* two months to find it under the formula. The reason: The lower the job scale, the tougher the competition.

Many outplacement specialists don't like the idea of any formula. "What it really gets down to is how hard are you going to work at finding another job," says Donald Sweet of Costello, Erdlen & Co., Boston.

The Story of Hal

Hal, the former salesman of locomotives, decided he needed to earn $40,000 a year but didn't want to work more than 1,000 hours annually, or about 20 hours a week during a 50-week work year. That's $40 per hour, below what many self-employed consultants charge, but he was willing to trade a guaranteed income against the uncertainty of commission sales as a manufacturers' representative or the roller coaster earnings of a consultant.

How did he arrive at the $40,000 figure? By matching his budgeted living expenses (plus 15 percent, the standard fudge) and desired savings for eventual full retirement against his income from his early-retirement pension and investments. Without any added income, he discovered he was $40,000 a year short if he kept his former lifestyle of a golf club membership, a Chris-Craft on Lake Erie, maintenance of a paid-for home, and a posh vacation annually.

Doubling the formula in the preceding section, he calculated that he needed to support himself and his wife for eight months while looking. For that period, he required a cushion of $26,666 (two-thirds of $40,000). Near the end of his financial calculations, he cashed in some of his investments and set aside the $26,666 in a money market fund for living costs. Although he lost some investment income by doing this, it was not as much as he at first feared because he would still earn about 6 percent from the fund.

He did not include jobhunting expenses because he couldn't estimate accurately what they would be. Furthermore, he resolved to do all the jobhunting research himself, so that would cost him little except for photocopying, postage, shoe leather and gasoline.

When You're Still Employed

Perhaps one-third of all jobhunters do it while still employed. The ratio is lower for seniors, an estimated one-fourth. The employed senior has one major advantage over the unemployed—he or she has an earned income, at least until the present employer learns what's going on. However, severance may well come before new work is found. So, go through the same exercise as Hal did, but you can deduct the income months needed according to how long you think you can get away with staying on the old payroll.

Some seniors are more comfortable informing the boss at once and negotiating several months of pay as a severance settlement. Use the same formula as a basis for your negotiations.

Unfortunately, Hal did not. He suffered from the it-can't-happen-to-me syndrome, so his severance came like a car wreck on the thruway. It was over before he knew what happened, and he got only his early-retirement pension.

He resolved never to be taken by surprise again in the job market and systematically began to research for his next job, which he promised himself would be ideal. He considered self-employment until his wife, Sheila, discovered most of the self-employed worked even longer hours than Hal's 10 to 12 a day as a locomotive salesman. She put her foot down, the first among several factors that made him reject sales consulting and representing work. Knowing him as well as she did, Sheila also persuaded him that he had operated too long under a corporate umbrella ever to be comfortable working completely on his own.

After discussions, they decided that the new employer must meet these criteria: have a product on the leading edge of environmental and technological development (unlike the locomotive), be an employee-oriented organization (more so than his former company), be relatively small and flexible (his former firm was one of the 10 largest in the nation), and permit him to continue earning his living in the pleasant city on the shores of Lake Erie (where they had lived all their lives, but he had always been too busy for them to indulge fully in their passion for boating).

Six Questions To Ask Yourself

After agreeing on these basics, Hal found it easier to answer six questions that every senior seeking new employment should ask about researching for the ideal job:

1) What skills do I have that I can demonstrate I possess?

Selling technologically complex products was Hal's prime skill. As an electrical engineer out of Penn State, he had both the education and experience to be either a salesman or an engineer. The optimum use for such skills would be as a sales engineer for a product that requires electrical or electronic engineering. A decade ago and also three years earlier, his employer had sent him back to Penn State for brief refresher courses.

What refresher education have you had? Can any of your skills be combined? For example, as a former member of a corporate legal staff, can you combine your legal and business expertise to join a venture-capital organization? How can you demonstrate your skills?

2) Where and how do I want to use these skills?

First, Hal wanted a job in his hometown. He wished to sell a technically advanced product that would require his engineering training. Next, he sought part-time work from his home. Hal and Sheila decided on the office-at-home requirement to minimize travel. Finally, he wanted substantial freedom to handle the job on his own, but with the employer's support when needed. That was the way he had operated selling locomotives.

The desire for part-time work is no longer the drawback it once was. Today, employers are more flexible about working schedules and places. At least an estimated 11 million people operate from their homes.

3) What employee-oriented, relatively small organization wishes me to sell (make, promote, repair, serve) a product or service in a place that I like?

In the beginning, Hal rejected this question's wording as both too broad and restrictive. It was too broad, he argued, in that he knew he wanted sales, engineering, or a combination of the two. Why even introduce the possibility of manufacturing, advertising or servicing? And why suggest that he might deal with a service rather than a product? Sheila rebutted him by pointing out that this was the *research* phase. Why not at least investigate other avenues which he could abandon if the detours looked unpromising? On the restrictive side, he thought the requirements of employee orientation and size might limit the number of possible organizations that would turn up. Again, Sheila countered him by pointing out that he wouldn't know until he studied the situation. If the wording did, indeed, prove too restrictive, he could broaden it later.

In rewording this question to fit your own circumstances, start with the ideal. Dream a little at this point. If the dream turns into a nightmare, alter the language as your research dictates.

4) What are the names of organizations that meet my criteria?

Hal soon discovered he had to get more specific in answering the third question before he could tackle the fourth. He needed to decide first on whether he wanted to deal with a product or service. He picked the product category. What product? He considered machine tools, construction equipment and materials handling machinery, but none of them excited him. In his researches, he visited the Materials Handling Institute. There he encountered MHI's affiliate, AIM, Inc. (Automatic Identification Manufacturers) who produce bar scanning systems that automatically identify products. (Many also keep track of sales and inventories.) That excited Hal from the standpoints of both technology and the environment. The industry scarcely existed as a recognized entity before two decades ago. In that short time, bar-code equipment sales have soared to nearly $1 billion annually.

He next had to choose what he wanted to do with the product. Research reaffirmed that he wanted to combine sales with engineering. Then he found the beginning of the answer to the fourth question—from AIM's membership roster. It was only the beginning, because he next had to investigate how each member measured against his other criteria of size and employee orientation.

5) What are the organization's problems where I might be working?

Hal got in touch with everyone he could think of who might know anything about any of the companies on his list. He found these common denominator challenges within the fledgling industry: difficulty in persuading potential customers that automatic identification would pay off for them; the public's hazy understanding of what automatic identification is; spotty sales coverage, often by manufacturers' representatives; conflicting and emerging technologies.

Hal saw marketing as the thread going through all the problems. The more he learned about this industry, the more enthusiastic he grew about it.

6) Who can hire me?

Hal found himself interested in an industry mostly populated by small companies. Furthermore, he encountered a complication—several different methods of selling—that could influence who might hire him. He could work directly for a manufacturer of automatic identification systems; he could set himself up as a representative of several manufacturers; or he could go into business on his own as a systems analyst for automatic identification and sell his service to potential users to help them decide what they need. In the first instance, he discovered the manufacturer would teach him the technology. If he became a manufacturers' representative, the companies he would represent could teach him, hopefully. If he took the third route, he found he must first know about computers and scanning technology. The "how" emerged in Hal's case as the first route. Therefore, he determined to go to the company president in every possible case.

Enter Emily and Ted

Hal is a self-assured salesman, accustomed to large dealings through years of contacts with top executives. How would people lower in the ranks answer the foregoing six questions? Let's try them on Emily, a 55-year-old just let go as the editor of an employee newspaper, and Ted, an unemployed tool-and-diemaker whose employer of 40 years sold out to a conglomerate which will henceforth do its tool-and-die work on the West Coast.

To demonstrate her skills, Emily showed the publications she had edited or helped to produce. Likewise, Ted showed exhibits of the smaller tools and dies he had made.

Neither had problems with the second question, either. Emily owned her own personal computer and wanted to do some of her writing and editing at home, but she also would work in an office. Ted recognized he would have to labor on his new employer's premises, and did not want to move to another city.

For the third question, Emily dreamed more than a little. She reworded the question to, "What organization, such as a publisher, could use my expertise and experience in business writing?" However, her research revealed that it's difficult to come up with a fresh business subject and even harder to find a publisher. She abandoned the idea of a book and rephrased the question, "How and where can I sell my expertise in business writing to an employer?" Her research revealed the possibility of operating from her home as a consultant to employers on how to improve their employer publications. Ted found himself restricted either to small tool-and-die shops or such departments in larger companies.

Neither Emily nor Ted had trouble with the fourth question, the names of employment prospects. They both well knew the potential employers in the cities where they lived.

For the fifth question, the ex-editor knew from experience what the problems were for the employee publications: inadequate budgets, inexperienced staffs, lukewarm support from the top. She started off by listing those organizations where the problems were the most severe. Ted focused on companies experiencing quality problems, reasoning that faulty tools and dies often contribute to such difficulties.

Problems also arise because of one or more employees. This situation is hard to pinpoint and verify, subject as it is to malicious gossip and exaggeration. Nevertheless, it may be the key to the problem. Check it out as best you can. If you are a manager, such a situation could develop into your next job.

Hal, Emily and Ted soon learned the value of being as specific as possible in answering this and all other questions. Details give added meaning to answers.

As to the person with the authority to hire, the sixth question, Emily focused on the vice-presidents in charge of the publications. Ted unearthed names of vice-presidents of manufacturing or engineering.

Note that the two, like Hal, went as high as possible in the relevant organizational hierarchy. Hal did not go to vice-presidents of sales. Emily avoided intermediate figures between publication editors and vice-presidents. Ted ignored foremen. All three chose the people who, experience told them, had the hiring power. Lower-level figures usually have a say in the hiring decision, but rarely the final voice. Is there the danger here in alienating the lower-level people who might veto you out of spite? It's possible but not probable because they feel the weight of the problem just as much as the person who has the power to hire you. If you can solve a difficulty, neither spite or any other irrelevancy should deflect you from the job.

Note also that none went to personnel departments. Unless you want a position within that department, you usually waste your time there. Will an ignored personnal department block you out of spite? Possible but highly improbable, and for the same reason that bypassed lower-level figures in the area where you eventually want to work won't block you. The key lies in your research that uncovers real problems and that suggests solid solutions to them.

How To Do Your Research

Do it yourself. Do not pay or otherwise inveigle someone to do it for you.

First, only you know what clues and subtleties to look for. Also, you alone know what to avoid.

Second, your research aids in bolstering self-confidence as your job future unfolds. Research can help ignite you *before* your first job interview.

Third, you are learning skills in doing the research yourself. Every worthwhile job has some element of search about it. The tool-and-die-maker must seek the best way—perhaps completely new—to form the tool or die. An editor must do the research, or know that a reporter has done it, for every article in the publication. Hal visited a library and talked to friends for two months before he happened upon automatic identification systems. He only dimly knew it existed before finding the Material Handling Institute. Even then, he devoted another two months to learning about the industry and the manufacturers in it before he felt himself ready to make his first approach to a person with the power to hire him.

How did he accomplish the research? By reading, primarily in the library. He wrote AIM's 54 members, plus several others he uncovered from his studies, asking for their annual reports, technical literature and anything else in writing they could send him. Fifty-one companies responded with mailed materials. Although the volume of it almost overwhelmed him, it also cheered him because the response signified an alert, energetic industry. When he ran into questions that no reading could answer, he went to see people, many of whose names surfaced from his reading. They were usually executives from companies in northern Ohio, western Pennsylvania, and New York.

Do such informational interviewing with caution and skill. The interviewee can easily mistake your search for information as a cover for a job interview and resent the apparent subterfuge.

Hal had no problems. He frankly told each person he saw that he had retired early and wanted to get into a new business. He wished to learn if bar scanning was as interesting as his reading had led him to believe. Most of his contacts showed the zeal of missionaries about their industry. Two said to come back to see them when he had made up his mind. Another offered him a sales job on the spot. He pleasantly put them all on hold.

Emily, the editor, faced different research problems. She knew her business as well as *The Associated Press Stylebook and Libel Manual*. Yet, she didn't know precisely which organizations were experiencing trouble with their employee publications. Even business libraries don't receive many that she could examine for telltale signs of trouble (less frequency in publication, rapid turnover of editors, declining size, deteriorating quality of paper, poor writing). Yet, she belonged to two associations of in-house editors and/or communication managers—the Council of Communication Management and the International Association of Business Communicators. Using her membership rosters, she requested copies of publications from organizations in her areas of interest. She soon amassed a private library to study.

Because she had many friends in communication, she invited a few to lunch and discreetly pumped them about what they knew concerning problems in their fraternity. It was fun.

As a tool-and-diemaker, Ted had to solve still other research challenges. He had to unearth companies in his area suffering quality problems. This is occasionally reported in business journals, seldom in local newspapers, and almost never in company publications. He skimmed the business magazines, found nothing, so forgot the libraries. He needed to talk to people. His brother-in-law is in the purchasing department of a large local manufacturer. He heard rumors. Ted followed through and learned of three possibilities in other companies. He knew a foreman in one and skilled people in the other two. The foreman pooh-poohed the rumors, but in such a way that indicated he was lying. The friend in another had heard nothing, but checked and confirmed the rumor. The rumor seemed to be true in the third, also. Lo and behold! Ted had three possibilities.

It's worth noting that Mrs. Casey Jones had done a bit of research herself, as the last lines of the ballad tell us:

Mrs. Jones sat at her bed a-sighing
Just to hear the news that her Casey was dying.
"Hush up, children, and quit your crying,
For you've got another poppa on the Salt Lake Line."

13

Determine Where You Want To Work

"If you don't know where you are going, you will probably end up someplace else," says Laurence J. Peter.

When you limit your searches to the want ads, to the tips of friends, and to the employer-driven vagaries of employment agencies, you don't really know where you're going. You're a misguided missile destined for a random target at best, or a disaster at worst. If you happen to hit a bull's-eye, it's luck. Odds are enormous that you will misfire and damage mostly yourself. You wouldn't be the first to reply to a blind ad by your present or former employer.

Solving the Equation

When Hal, the locomotive salesman, was laid off (for that's what it was despite his early-retirement pension), he and Sheila, his wife, went through the exercises of deciding what to do next and how to start jobhunting. They decided the "where" of the equation presented these unknowns:

1) The where as to the organization
2) The where as to the person who can hire
3) The where as to the problem
4) The where as to the place

The Organization

Most seniors start jobhunting believing there aren't many jobs waiting out there. The truth is, there are too many. Whether you realize it or not, the range is overwhelming. The numbers distract, tricking you into using buckshot instead of a few rifle shots. You bring down nothing with the scattered fire and blame the failure on too few targets.

You read in the paper about a candy company opening a new plant in an industrial park and mail your job application, getting it back eventually marked "address unknown." A major company in your city advertises for an expediter. Before replying, you check it out with a friend in the organization who says he would recommend the job "only to my worst enemy." You don't answer the ad, but "the worst enemy," whom both you and your friend know, gets it and thrives. Another friend alerts you to an opening in his employer's purchasing department. You call for an appointment, to learn that the job is already filled. An employment agency sends you 40 miles to a neighboring town to interview for a job as an "inspector in analysis." The company actually wants someone to do vector analysis. You don't even know what vector analysis is.

The National Alliance of Business, a group dedicated to finding jobs for the disadvantaged, estimates that America will gain 16 million new jobs over the next five years. While the majority of these will be entry-level positions, not all will be. Somebody will have to train and supervise the new people. Somebody else will have to manage the trainers and supervisors.

And that's only the beginning. The workforce in the United States is highly mobile; from 300,000 to 800,000 members, depending on the state of the economy, make a change *every month*. That's 300,000 to 800,000 openings per month. In addition, include the new jobs created. Even if NAB is wildly optimistic, our labor force has been adding a *net* of 200,000 new jobs per month, on average, for some years. We're the envy of the western world in this regard. So, even in the worst of times, 500,000 new job openings turn up every month in the U.S., and 1 million in the best times. (That's 300,000 openings from restlessness in bad times plus 200,000 from innovation, or 800,000 from restlessness in good times plus 200,000 from innovation.)

What's more, many job openings exist that few know about. Business and industry, for instance, usually want relative privacy in seeking new top managers, especially if they are looking outside the company. They do it as quietly as possible to minimize upset within the ranks, to avoid a flood of irrelevant candidates, and to forestall possible bad publicity outside. During a normal year, some 750,000 management vacancies turn up, only one-third of which are filled within 12 months. Jobs may remain open for a long time with little or no fanfare because not enough people are around who have the required skills or mix of abilities. If you repair pipe organs, for example, you might find more work than you could handle in any major city in the United States.

Wait a minute! you shout. What about the 8 million unemployed (or whatever the current unemployment figure is)? They exist, no doubt about it, but you don't compete with every one. In fact, if you have many skills or if they are of an unusual nature, then you compete with very few people. Furthermore, the unemployment numbers the government issues monthly are filled with anomalies. They include many people not really looking for work—students, people who have given up hunting, sharpies who make a career of collecting unemployment compensation. Of course, competition does exist. We merely say that it's not as severe as the ball-park figures suggest.

Actually, there's no such thing as a "job market" in this or any western country. The situation frustrates you *and* employers. The typical hirer would be delighted to call a job broker and order three qualified applicants as simply as a stockbroker can suggest three stocks that meet your qualifications. Today, that happens only at the lowest job levels.

There are tens of thousands of organizations that hire people, no single one doing it precisely like another. Your task is, first, to identify the organization that interests you; next, to discover how it hires new employees. An added complication lies in the fact that many hire in several different ways and don't follow the same practices twice in a row. They may use executive recruiters for high-level positions, the old-boy network for middle-range people, and help wanted ads and employment agencies for entry levels. The rare drop-in may get a job at any level, and that's where you could fit in—if you're lucky.

However, why depend on luck? You can spot potentials who may hire when you have completed the research described in the last chapter. Your research will also reveal that the Fortune 500 and other large companies are scarcely recruiting at all, except for highly specialized jobs. They are mostly paring down their employment rolls. So, concentrate on middle-sized to smaller companies for the best results.

For example, an optoelectronics operation in San Jose, California, attracted Hal the most among all the companies active in bar-code technology. Its reputation as an employee-oriented firm, with a stated policy of no or limited layoffs, reassured him. Its size—nearly 1,000 employees—alone disturbed him. Its decentralized organizational style, however, could offset size, he reasoned.

As back-up possibilities, he chose Pannier Corporation and Allen-Bradley's Sensing Products Business Unit. A doubt nagged him concerning Allen-Bradley because he found that Rockwell International had recently acquired it. Although the press releases concerning the transaction claimed Allen-Bradley would remain autonomous, he knew such promises are honored more in the breach than the observance. He decided to concentrate on the San Jose prospect first and Pannier second. As far as he could determine, both used the mixed bag of hiring practices common to American industry.

As a business communication specialist, Emily pinpointed six companies in her area which had, or seemed to have, problems with their publications. In consulting, she knew she would need more than one client, so she planned to go after them all. To get her foot in the door, she counted on the increasing trend in industry to take on free-lancers.

Free-lancing is especially noticeable at companies with no-layoff policies, says Jerome M. Rosow, president of Work in America Institute, a research center in Scarsdale, N.Y. "In more sophisticated companies you see tighter staffing margins that are below 100 percent to avoid layoffs, so they use temporary workers for unexpected peak loads," he says. Nor are the temporaries confined to clerical help. They run the gamut of professional positions from author (as a speechwriter, for example) to zymologist (a fermentation specialist, for instance). Nor are the jobs routine, because management tends to try out free-lancers first on new and chancy work. And the pay is good—sometimes 50 to 100 percent more than total compensation for regular employees.

You will soon discover drawbacks to consulting, however—notably, the usual short assignments that force you to spend a quarter or more of your time selling your services and the antagonism of regular employees who resent your pay and consider you an interloper.

As a tool-and-die maker, Ted spotted three manufacturers with quality problems and decided to go after them. His first choice resulted chiefly because of geography—it was closest to his home. Although he knew this could prove to be a poor reason for his choice, he made it in the absence of any stronger criterion.

If you're a highly skilled blue-collared senior, you enjoy great advantages over juniors. Younger people tend to have lower manual skills than their elders, largely because such abilities can take years to hone and because many juniors suffer from indifferent education in mathematics, mechanical drawing and other basics of much blue-collar work.

The Person Who Can Hire

Once you have picked the organization(s) you want to work for, you must next identify the person(s) with the authority to hire you. Ask friends and other contacts who might know. Double-check their information against what you have learned from the annual reports and other brochures you collect from the organizations.

With exceptionally good fortune, you may need to search no further than annual reports and brochures for names of individuals. Yet, the odds are high that you require more sources. Go next to your business library where your librarian can help you with many directories. Among them are:

- *American Men and Women of Science*
- *American Society of Training and Development Directory*
- *Consulting and Consulting Organizations Directory*
- *Directory of Corporate Affiliations*
- *Dun & Bradstreet's Million Dollar Directory*
- *Dun & Bradstreet's Middle Market Directory*
- *Dun & Bradstreet's Reference Book of Corporate Managements*
- *Encyclopedia of Business Information Sources*
- *F & S Index of Corporations and Industries* (current articles from newspapers and magazines about employers)
- *Moody's Industrial Manual* (and other Moody manuals)
- *Standard and Poor's Register of Corporations, Directors and Executives* (and other S & P reference volumes)
- *Thomas' Register of American Manufacturers*
- *Who's Who in Finance and Industry* (use to learn more about an individual once you have identified him or her as a person with the power to hire)

Many good libraries keep their own files of news clippings and other information about organizations in your area. Use your relatives and friends to help gather this information. You can't hear or read everything, but a good contact network can at least expand your reach.

If you still get nothing from such sources, try informational interviewing, the major purpose of which is to find names, indirectly if you can. It's a last resort; skip it if possible. Many managers will be suspicious about your disclaimers concerning informational interviewing. If you bluntly ask who has the authority to hire, you blow your cover completely. Instead, inquire who, if anyone, in the organization recruits at colleges and universities, how most in the workforce are hired, and who, if anyone, runs training. Answers to questions such as these should give you a clue.

Hal didn't know a soul with the San Jose firm, not having called on the organization in his field trips. He learned that the nearest sales office to Erie was in Dayton, Ohio. Upon telephoning, he reached a helpful salesman who gave him the names of the three top people in the company. Sometimes it's as simple as that.

As a fledgling communications consultant, Emily did not find it so easy. Communicators don't take to consultants well, and the very mention of the word may freeze them. After one such experience, Emily got smart and never used the word again, and just asked for the top person's name to send him (or her) her newly-prepared brochure. She got the names in five of six cases, but remained in the dark as to hiring practices because none yet made extensive use of free-lancers. She discovered she first had to educate potential clients on the advantages of her service, especially lower long-term costs and higher professionalism.

As a tool-and-diemaker, Ted's buddies in his union gave him all the names he needed. However, he decided they were virtually useless because the companies hired through their own employment offices or agencies. He wanted to avoid both. He wrote to their vice-presidents of manufacturing or engineering, banking on the novelty of the approach at this level to win an appointment.

The Problem

Before you dredge up individual problems, do an overall survey of the organization. For example:

- What's its staff turnover?
- Does it help pay for employees' education?
- Does it have a formal training program, in addition?
- How does communication flow in the organization—strictly downward, usually upward, both ways?
- Is there a "smoking gun" in the background—obsolete products, high costs, nepotism?
- Has the organization expanded, contracted or stayed at about the same size over the past five years? Why? How?
- Any merger or takeover in the offing?
- If it has publicly owned stock, how is it doing?
- What's its image in its community? In its industry?
- Does it have a centralized or bottom-up organizational structure?

Again, interview directly for your answers as a last resort. You will be pleasantly surprised at how readily you can find such information in the library or from friends.

With a broad profile compiled from replies to these questions, you're prepared to put the problems of the potential hirer in better perspective. Even so, how do you pinpoint specific problems? Here are suggestions.

First, choose problems you can manage. This seems obvious, but unfortunately big projects seem to mesmerize even seniors. It's unlikely that you will impress IBM if you claim you can solve their corporate-wide marketing problems. If you approach that giant with a suggestion of how to better market its lap-top personal computers, you may get a better reception.

Often, the problem is simpler than that—the person holding the job you seek can't perform; the section has trouble with customer complaints because it misses delivery dates.

Second, address the hirer's problem, not yours. Try to read his or her mind. You may uncover a problem which stands out to you, but not to the person who could hire you. This is not the time to risk educating the hirer. Rather, learn through your contacts what motivated earlier hires. A desire for a subordinate who will keep the organization out of trouble? Someone who can calm complaining customers? An expediter who gets things done? Whatever your research indicates is the problem in the hirer's mind becomes the problem you must address.

You can read minds through educated guesses about the organization, by talking to competitors or associates, and by "accidental" meetings with the individual in settings outside work. This last could be during association meetings, at church or synagogue, or even on the street.

Third, talk the hirer's language. Some people hate to hear of problems. Speak instead of concerns, challenges, and issues. Some have little or no sense of humor, or the opposite. Stay serious or tell a (clean) joke, as appropriate. Some hate details; others thrive on them. Again, speak as your intuition dictates.

On another level, you must define your expertise in language with which the hirer has empathy. If the organization is expanding, it probably must do a lot of training. Mention your experience and skill as a trainer when you can legitimately do so. If the organization faces stiff competition, cite what you did to counter competition in previous jobs. If cost-cutting is the issue, give examples of how you've done this in the past.

Hal shrewdly guestimated the San Jose firm's problems—lack of full geographic market coverage for its bar-code technology. It sold its bar-code readers in northern Ohio, Pennsylvania and New York out of

Dayton, Ohio. Living in Erie, Pennsylvania, he resolved to use this gap in his approach to the top people in San Jose.

As the communications consultant, Emily used her brochure as an entree and gained a meeting with five of the six prospects. In two of the five cases, she discussed how production costs can be reduced while still keeping up quality. In a third case, she learned the communications manager sought a new editor. She offered to help recruit one. In the fourth and fifth cases, writing skills were below par, and she proposed seminars to improve them.

With only one did she encounter trouble seeing the manager with the authority to hire. There, the company had just discontinued its publications and didn't yet want to be reminded of its possible mistake. She put that one in her file to check again in a year. Four welcomed her with a cordiality that surprised her until she discovered they all feared, rightly or wrongly, that their top managements doubted the need for their continued existence. They badly needed reassurance and ammunition to fight the real or imagined battles.

Tool-and-diemaker Ted saw the vice-president of production at the company nearest him after a series of rescheduled meetings (a bad sign, usually). The session was short and not sweet. Although Ted identified the person who could hire him, he misfired on the problem. It had nothing to do with poor tools and dies; it involved poor employee attitudes, the official contended. "There's no need for a new tool-and-diemaker. Thank you very much." It didn't seem to work with the second or third either, until the third vice-president phoned him back and said, "I've been thinking your proposition over. You may have something. Come in. We'll give you a try."

The Place

The fourth "where" in determining your working future is the place. If you want the place to remain your hometown, skip this section. If you've had enough of rust, snow or tornadoes and yearn for warmer or otherwise welcoming climes, read on.

First, try to answer from home as many questions as possible about the distant organization, hiring person, and his or her problems. You can do this by consulting the directories we listed earlier; subscribing to the newspapers there; contacting the local chamber of commerce or equivalent for any available information; checking with the appropriate state, county and local government agencies; and uncovering personal contacts from the desired area. You may find these last if you look hard enough—friends of relatives or friends, old school or military service buddies, chance people you have met during the course of you career.

Second, go to the desired place to check its ambience, preferably before you make a single contact with a potential employer. If it hits you as Fort Pitbottom, why waste any more time on it? Often, you already know the place from previous visits before you had any idea of ever working there, liked it, and choose it now because of the favorable impression. Even so, return to confirm your earlier perceptions. Although you don't want to pitch directly for any jobs now, make the visit serve the double duty of field trips to the organizations that interest you.

Hal faced a special challenge. The optoelectronics firm's headquarters of San Jose boasted a better climate—both economic and weatherwise— than Erie, but he liked Erie. He was born there, lived there all his life, and knew it was neither Dreary Erie or the Mistake on the Lake. Therefore, he faced a problem because he wanted to stay in his home city, but the optoelectronics company had no sales office there.

Research often uncovers dilemmas such as Hal's. He solved it by taking his wife on a vacation to San Francisco. During its course, they visited nearby San Jose where Hal had wrangled an appointment with the company's top man. At first the official was cool about hiring someone with no experience in identification technology and who also wanted to operate out of his home. Then, Hal played his trump. His former employer would seriously consider switching to the company's bar scanning system if he became its sales representative.

As a communications consultant, Emily faced no problems of geography at the moment. Yet, she began to see that she might eventually have to broaden her horizons as she ran through the locally viable clients. For that reason, she pursued a possible assignment with a Lutheran college 60 miles away that needed help preparing a brochure to recruit new students.

As a tool-and-diemaker, Ted didn't think the place would become an issue until he struck out on his first contact. Yet, he knew he couldn't win them all. He eventually won with his third choice.

Where Do Pensions Fit?

A fifth consideration sometimes surfaces in determining where to work. Your present pension should not figure in how you look at the organization, the hiring person, his or her problems or even the place where you want to spend the rest of your working life.

If you think too much about your pension during your searches, you may be tempted to give inadequate attention to your research on the other four "wheres." Some organizations and their hiring representatives may try to take advantage in compensation of the fact they know you have a pension (more on this later). You want nothing to do with them. If they think they must be that penny-pinching, let them keep that problem without bothering you with it.

Your pension may even distort your decision about the place to work. If your pension enables you to afford to live in a retirement community such as Sun City, you're not likely to find work there that will truly satisfy you.

Still another reason for ignoring your pension now is that you may lose it, in spite of the government's Pension Benefit Guaranty Corporation. Although a reduced payment is more likely now, even that is questionable, all the more reason to treat your pension as a reserve cushion. Before one of his battles, Napoleon figured he had 16 regiments. "Sire, you have 20," corrected one of his generals. Napoleon turned upon him in a rage. "I know that, but I want to conjure up the extra four if I need them."

So, try to keep your pension completely out of the equation at this stage.

The Balancing Act

Balancing the where with the how and what is a juggling act. At one point, Hal feared every tenpin he had in the air would come crashing down, all because of a slight mistiming. The optoelectronics company man said they had plans for stronger sales representation out of Erie or Buffalo. Hal at first thought the plan was already well along. Not so; it was in the formative stage, and Hal's timing turned out to be perfect.

Early in his search, tool-and-diemaker Ted thought he had lost the show by guessing wrong on the problem. He recovered from his miscalculation by doing it right on the third round.

If you don't recover in time, you'll knock yourself out with a tenpin. Instead of that, you want to end up in an office and an interview with an interested potential employer.

Now, at last, you are ready to acquire the best job of your life.

14

How To Get the Interview

Some claim that the best writers get the best jobs because they write the best letters and résumés to secure interviews.

Nonsense. No letter or résumé, by itself, ever won the job. Interviews, however, *do* win jobs. A letter or résumé is one way to get an interview, but not necessarily the best method. For a senior job seeker, the most effective approaches to gain an interview are (by rank order):

1) *Through a contact.* Seniors have a marked advantage here over juniors because they have been around longer to develop the contacts. If you know the person yourself, so much the better. In the more likely case that you don't, find a conduit to him or her. It's astonishing how often you can dig up some mutual friend or acquaintance. Be as certain as possible that the contact will be an effective advocate for you. You can usually determine this after one arrangement for a meeting. If you sense anything amiss, don't use that person again.

2) *Through a direct phone call* if you simply cannot find that mutual friend or acquaintance. In this and the previous approach, you must be prepared with a quick pitch that will catch the listener's interest. This should be a brief reference to the potential employer's problem you have already identified and the solution you propose for it. Problem identification is crucial to successful jobhunting, especially for seniors. There's nothing mysterious about it. In effect, you do the same thing that a good salesman does—offer a product or service that will benefit the customer. James H. Rand, one of the founders of a component of what is now Unisys Corporation, started as a salesman of office equipment. He visited Frank A. Munsey, the eccentric publisher and financier who was opening banks in Baltimore and Washington. He persuaded Munsey to give him a letter of introduction to his Washington manager. Rand then rushed to the manager and succeeded in selling him $25,000 worth of equip-

ment. Only after the interview did he discover he had forgotten in his zeal to show the manager the letter. It read, "Learn all you can from this man, but don't buy anything from him if you can help it."

3) *Through another person with the organization* if the first two methods fail. When you can't easily reach the person involved with the problem, perhaps he or she is part of the difficulty. The author had trouble seeing the vice-president of human resources at a bank. He was acquainted with a loan officer (who will see anybody), visited him, and eventually was passed along to the relevant individual.

4) *Through an outplacement firm or other paid intermediary.* While not an ideal method, more and more discharged managers use it because the former employer pays for it. Think twice about using it if you have to pay for it; you can probably do just as well or better yourself. Outplacement firms may exaggerate their effectiveness, or traumatized managers may select one for the wrong reasons, chiefly related to desperation or even panic. The $150 million-a-year outplacement business involved more than 130 firms in 1986, up from 43 in 1980, according to James Kennedy, a directory publisher.

5) *Through a résumé or qualification letter* if you can't get the interview by the first three methods. A qualification letter is merely a résumé in letter form. Outplacement firms routinely require résumés, which they will usually write. Don't let your representative, if any, do so for reasons we go into next.

The Importance of the Résumé

Although the résumé or qualification letter is the course of last resort in gaining an interview, it's nevertheless important because:

- It's a calling card.
- It serves as an agenda for the interviewer.
- It jogs the interviewer's memory after you've gone.
- It goes where you can't, such as a distant city.
- It's your self-inventory on paper.

You don't write your résumé, you *rewrite* it, refocusing it for every interview by restating the problem that you judge the interviewer faces. Make it your work, not the outplacement firm's or anyone else's. If somebody else writes it, it cannot help but sound more like the other author than you. This must be one of the most personal documents you ever pen. There is no sense in adhering rigidly to some format dictated in a book, by an outplacement firm, or by your brother-in-law whose résumé won him an interview. This document aims at selling *you*. Emphasize the biographical facts that will best sell you. If you seek a sales job where appearance is important, include a picture of yourself in the résumé. If you want a research position, highlight your education after your accomplishments instead of at the end as is customery. If your experience is broad and you think it will help sell you to an employer, let your résumé run to two pages if that's what it takes. The widespread dictum that a résumé should be confined to one page makes no sense if your accomplishments run to two pages.

Yet, you may not even show the document to the person who has the power to hire you. Many such people never ask for it, although you should always have it ready if called for. Consider it like a drama script that an actor memorizes. The audience may never read the script, but they'll hear its words and see the actor interpret its meaning. You are both the author and actor.

It's unnecessary and irrelevant to put it in some eccentric format, such as a simulated telegram, in doggerel verse, or in purple ink on pink paper. Type it using a black ribbon on good quality white paper of at least 20-pound weight. Don't print it because you will change it often. If you can operate a word processor, or can persuade someone else to use the computer for you, that's ideal because of the frequent changes.

Here's fundamental advice about a résumé:

- State your objective as specifically as possible. Some specialists give the opposite counsel, but we disagree as it relates to seniors with their special challenges. This is the portion you most likely will change to fit the circumstances. Vaguely stated objectives are most likely to get vague responses—"We'll keep this on file for when something comes up that fits your goals," or, "We have nothing open right now that would call for your undoubted abilities." As a senior, you seek a niche; you'll never find it if you don't define it.

- Emphasize your achievements rather than your duties. Employers want to know how you performed, not just what you were supposed to do.

- Buttress your points with data. If you headed a department, state *accurately* how many people you supervised. An employer can easily check numbers.

● Avoid trivia, such as details of your daily routine or the titles, publications and dates of all the articles you ever wrote (unless, of course, you apply for a writing job). You can normally cover the writing question with a sentence such as, "Tearsheets of 43 articles I have written are available upon request."

● Try teasers if possible. As in romance, a little mystery can make you more interesting. If you have done something unusual but not relevant for the particular job, you can use a throwaway line, such as, "Climbed Mt. Everest, 1966." The analogy with romance is not far-fetched. Look upon your résumé as a special kind of letter to woo the person with the power to hire you. Unless you're self-employed, a job is a marriage between you and the employer. If you wish to be self-employed, it's a marriage between you and your clients which requires still another kind of wooing document.

The Résumé as a Calling Card

A jobhunter saw the secretary take his résumé into the office of the boss. Through the partially open door, the applicant spied him tearing it up and throwing it in the wastebasket.

When she returned to report that he couldn't see him, the senior asked, "May I have the résumé back, please?"

The secretary retired in confusion to the inner sanctum. She returned to say, "I'm sorry, it was accidentally destroyed." She handed him a quarter.

He took the quarter, reached into his briefcase and extracted another copy of the resume. "Tell him I give two copies for a quarter."

He got the interview, but did he get the job? It would make a good story to say he did, but he didn't. He won the interview for the wrong reasons, a lot of embarrassment, and a little remorse.

A résumé serves as an extended calling card. Consider your timing in handing out your conventional calling cards (if any)—usually during or just after a meeting with someone you don't know or don't know well. If you surrender it before the meeting, you do so with some reluctance and because the secretary or the person with the power to hire you asks for it.

Follow the same practice with the résumé. Try to make your presentation orally and in person before you surrender the document. Above all, resist the request to mail it when you telephone for an appointment. Excuse yourself by saying, "I'm revising it, but it will be ready at the time of the interview."

That most likely will be a true statement because you should revise it for nearly every interview. Sometimes, you will be forced to give it before you want to. So be it, but write off your prospect to nearly zero and go to the next one on your list. The reason: A drama is almost always more effective when performed than when read.

The Résumé as an Agenda

There is one circumstance when you can safely give your résumé early in your meeting: When the interviewer is inexperienced and doesn't know how to run the session. Then, the résumé helps him like a prompter in the wings of a theater. The key here lies in the speed and accuracy of your appraisal of the interviewer's competence. Signs of incompetence include much hemming and hawing, repetition, obvious nervousness, off-the-wall questions. Then, you do the interviewer a favor by the early surrender of your life story.

However, do you want to work with, for, or near such an individual? Peter Drucker said, "So much of what we call management consists in making it difficult for people to work." We amend that to ". . . difficult for people to find work."

The Résumé as a Reminder

When you face lots of competition for a position, your résumé can serve the invaluable role of making you stand out from the others. Again, you wish it to shine like a beacon through its quality, not its eccentricity.

Have several copies handy if the interviewer asks for them because he or she may want to send them to others who have a voice in the hiring decision. This is a form of reminder. If the interviewer doesn't ask for copies but also says he or she will seek the views of others, offer them anyhow.

Obviously, you should present clear fresh copies. Or is it obvious that you should do so? Not from samples the author has seen—faded photocopies or so dogeared that a dozen interviewers must have handled them already. That's a reminder you don't want to reinforce—the lack of jobhunting success thus far.

The Résumé Goes Where You Can't

One job offer gets made every 1,470 résumés that the average company receives. So, why bother sending any at all? As we explain, you may never do so. Yet, sometimes you have no choice because your prospect is in a distant city.

Hal, the ex-locomotive salesman, lived 2,000 miles from the headquarters of his prospect, a company making automatic identification systems. He mailed his résumé. It won him the interview because he focused on a problem—marketing penetration—that he could help solve.

The Résumé as a Self-Inventory

This is the most important purpose of the résumé, still vital even if you never show it to a person with the power to hire you. A good résumé forces healthy introspection, a quality not always present in job seekers, especially in seniors who may not have had to think about themselves for decades in terms of career goals. The résumé distills the self-analysis we've been urging upon you. It converts your conclusions to print.

It does even more. It focuses your thoughts, bringing to the surface ideas and notions that may never get into the résumé but which reenter your mind for use if needed. Ernest Hemingway said, "I always try to write on the principle of the iceberg. There is seven-eighths of it underwater for every part that shows." The seven-eighths that doesn't show strengthens the part that does.

In categorizing your life, which is what you do in a good résumé, you should try for more than a list of dates and accomplishments. You should also think deeply about their significance.

Hal, the former locomotive salesman, listed his major sales in the first version of his résumé. Then, he thought again. As he didn't intend to remain in the field and so wouldn't be talking to people who knew that market, his numbers wouldn't mean much. So, instead of writing that he sold 12 units to Canadian Pacific Railroad, he said, "The twelve units represented the largest single sale by any U.S. locomotive manufacturer outside our country since World War II."

A communication manager's instinct was not to mention in a résumé his former alcoholism. On second thought, he added this: "As a reformed alcoholic and member of Alcoholics Anonymous, I have special insight into the addictive or potentially addictive employees and am prepared to develop oral and/or written communication programs directed to them."

Cleverness is the most widespread of writing commodities. It can be brushed over empty or shoddy events in your career like varnish, and sometimes it conceals holes. You fill the empty or shoddy holes with good wood as a result of your statement, and that's important in itself. Full honesty underlies all successful job searches.

As a tool-and-diemaker, Ted needed physical stamina as well as dexterity to perform good work. Did it make sense to mention his diabetes? Upon reflection, he decided that it did for reasons that ran deeper than a dislike of evasion with a potential employer. He turned it into a positive with this statement on his résumé: "In the 40 years that I have been successfully coping with diabetes, I have developed a self-discipline which has served me well in learning, practicing and improving my skill to produce tools and dies of the highest quality."

Rewriting the Résumé

Here's the mediocre résumé statement, unfortunately typical of many: "I carried out an active nationwide technical recruitment program, involving employment agency contacts, college interviewing and considerable advertising. The program made possible extensive organizational growth."

Here's a better version: "I recruited technical personnel. I sparked lab expansion from 90 to 500 people. I developed new supply sources for technical manpower by interviewing in 50 colleges and universities. At conventions and colleges, I scoured the country looking for suitable employees. I increased inquiries from 50 to 75 a week by means of advertising."

Never exaggerate your accomplishments; the overstatements can come back to haunt you. Some outplacement firms and professional résumé writer's push the jobhunter into exaggerations. The jobhunter says, "I was on the team that developed the new product." It comes out of the professional résumé writer's typewriter or word processor as, "My team developed the new product," unmistakably implying that you led the team even though that was not true. You may tell the professional, "Sales for the widget doubled in the five years I was a member of the marketing force." It comes out, "I doubled sales of the widget in five years." Not true, because the sales force of which you were only one of 40 members doubled sales in five years.

If you think your contribution to some activity can't be measured in specifics, think again. Here's a typical vague résumé statement: "I was responsible for overall planning and execution of public relations programs. I disseminated information and promotions. I was the liaison for mass media and other agencies having similarly oriented programs in world affairs, particularly the United Nations. I conceived and executed long-range programs. I served as a catalyst for world affairs and peace projects. I prepared releases, brochures and news bulletins."

Here's the rewrite: "Directed an anniversary program called 'Perspective of Peace.' I was responsible for placing 2,000 publicity items in newspapers, eight articles in national magazines, broadcasts on 21 domestic radio stations and four television stations, and 20 news stories on a worldwide basis through the U.S. Information Agency. I secured the participation of 600 colleges in World Affairs programs. I persuaded 125 national organizations to stimulate peace programs, including the YMCA, the League of Women Voters, and the U.S. Chamber of Commerce."

No one can or should write a résumé exactly like another, so avoid the potted variety.

In writing your résumé, besides keeping to specifics:

1) Use simple, hard, picture-creating words. Avoid passive verbs, abstractions, polysyllables (except for effect).

2) Write short sentences with active verbs. Use "I." This is no place for false modesty.

3) Keep your paragraphs to three or four lines. Single-space within the paragraph, and double-space between them. Although you want brevity, avoid telegraphic wording.

4) Highlight only one of your skills, that which appears most relevant for the potential employer. Hold in reserve others to bring up in the interview. You blur the focus with more than one. People who read résumés have tunnel vision and are easily distracted. If they seek an engineer, and you also talk about your sales experience, your résumé may go into the slush pile. You seek only an interview with the résumé, not the job. In rare instances, a résumé may win the job, but don't hold your breath.

5) Keep your cover letter brief and don't highlight your résumé. It's supposed to be a highlight in itself.

The Ideal Résumé

Sorry, there's isn't any. Tailor your own, and be comfortable in the knowledge that it may never be shown, even to the person who eventually hires you. However, it remains the basis for your search. To prove this point, bear with John Morgan in a case history of his own résumé. He prepared a conventional one, listing his job objective, work experience, career-related experience, education, and personal data, in that order.

It was a good résumé. An outplacement firm reluctantly said so, and every interviewer praised it. Yet, it didn't lead to a single job offer.

Discouraged, Morgan decided to go into a business he called Advocacy Communications. To sell his services, he prepared a brochure that read, in part:

Advocacy, *n.* active support

Communications, *n.* the act of imparting thoughts, opinions or information by speech, writing or signs

Advocacy Communications, *n.* 1. active transmission of your message.

"Eschew obfuscation" goes a jocular sign you can buy in a variety store. Although such words are in the dictionary, Advocacy Communications uses others to get across more directly. That's because the man behind the firm has been making his living as an advocating communicator for 33 years . . .

Advocacy Communications, *n.* 2. compound support, verbally and graphically, for the client.

"Me Tarzan, you Jane," the memorable line from an early Tarzan movie, is immortal because it combines brevity, simplicity and force. So does Advocacy Communications help you to speak, write or show your message as quickly, understandably and forcefully as possible . . .

The brochure was based on Morgan's résumé. It won him some consulting business. More importantly, it got him an interview which led to a full-time job.

Jobhunting is a numbers game. The more interviews, the better the chance to connect.

When All Else Fails . . .

Sometimes a prospective employer gets as frustrated as the potential employee in failing to win an interview. General Electric tried to hire Charles P. Steinmetz, the electrical genius, from Osterheide and Eickemeyer, a small electrical firm in Yonkers, N.Y. Steinmetz went beyond refusing GE's job offers. He wouldn't even accept interviews out of a feeling of loyalty to his present employer. GE solved the problem by buying the company.

This could even happen to you, although perhaps not so dramatically, if you are so good at your work that employers seek you, not vice versa.

15

If You Don't Interview Well

You'd better learn to do it better. A good interview with the potential employer is the key to winning the job.

Fortunately, you can learn to do it better because it's a learnable skill. Practice helps. Even those going-nowhere sessions arranged by well-meaning friends can serve as exercises.

The Typical Interview

It starts with innocuous conversation about the weather, sports or a current event. It then grows more focused with questions about you and your background. Answer briefly because the crux is yet to come. It's the description of the job to be filled. That's your cue to ask pointed questions about it, particularly probes to determine if you have the correct fix on the major problem.

The customary interview then takes one of two courses. You are routed to other managers in the organization (that's good), or you're told your application will be considered. Thank you for coming (that's bad).

To forestall the second course, we have several suggestions.

How To Interview Better

Think back on the occasions in your life when you had to make a presentation, whether to your boss, your spouse, or your friends. Did you undertake it "cold"? How did it turn out? Not well, probably. A job interview is a presentation, and you'd better prepare for it.

1) Know the job problem facing the person with the power to hire. Have at least one other potential problem in reserve to discuss, and have tentative solutions in which you figure. Put this on paper; at the least, jot down notes.

163

2) Rehearse what you want to say and how you want to say it. Ask your spouse or friend to play the role of the interviewer. If that doesn't work well, try for an audience that offers constructive criticism—but try out you must. Look upon the exercise as the New Haven run to iron out the kinks before Broadway. You court disaster without this step.

3) Eat and drink normally as you would on a regular day. However, if the appointment is at 2 p.m. and if you often have a drink with lunch, skip it this time. You don't want to smell like a distillery. More importantly, you want to be up naturally, not alcoholically.

4) Dress well for your performance. The conservative style is best if you don't know whether the interviewer favors blue jeans or blue suits. If you do know the interviewer and have seen him or her always dressed casually, scale down your sartorial conservatism, but not much. He or she may suffer a "dress for success" attack when seeing you. The interviewer is probably just as uneasy as you.

5) Stand straight and tall. Observe normal social protocols about shaking hands if the interviewer extends his or hers, sitting when invited to do so, and drinking coffee or tea if offered. Even if you don't particularly like coffee or tea, take it this time. The idea now is to fit in.

6) Keep the interview on track, tactfully. The interviewer, not you, is the likely wanderer. Unlike you, he or she probably has no script, nor even, sometimes, a clear idea of what skills are needed for the job. If pressed, the interviewer will probably specify the same abilities as had the previous jobholder. Yet *why*, if that person is leaving? Even if the individual's departure is amicable, must you as the successor handle the position exactly as your predecessor did? You need answers on such issues, which is part of your "track-keeping" chore.

7) Keep "on track" yourself. You can easily get bogged down in the details of your autobiography, for instance, if you tend to babble when nervous or if the interviewer wittingly or unwittingly leads you on. Watch yourself.

8) Never argue or interrupt. This would seem obvious, but seniors, particularly, tend to do it when tense.

9) Correct the interviewer's misconceptions about you, but not about the problem as you see it. You may have it wrong at this stage. The interviewer is closer to it than you. At this point, reject the argument that the hirer can't see his problem because it's just a tree in the forest.

10) *Listen*. So important is this that we devote the next section to it.

Is Anybody Listening?

Many factors contribute to difficulties in listening, but these stand out:

● *Inadequate background information*. We hate to admit we lack information, so ignorance and pride combine to produce a listening failure. Mixed in with this is the common psychological fear by the listener of admitting he or she doesn't get the point, and therefore doesn't measure up to the speaker's expectations.

● *Selective inattention*. We hear what we want to hear. A common one in job interviews concerns salary. When the interviewer says they "give merit increases," we may hear it as "automatic boosts."

● *Selective memory*, a corollary of selective inattention. An example is the applicant who never had a failure in his or her career. Why search for a job now? Needs a change.

● *Selective expectation*. The senior, particularly, may over-anticipate a reference to age and so leaps in at the most oblique mention of the subject. Relax. Wait until, or if, the interviewer gets to the matter. Even so, the employer will have to exercise caution in this area because it's illegal to bring it up unless it's a factor in some activity, such as professional sports.

● *Fear of being influenced*. If the interviewer let's fall some opinion about politics or economics with which you disagree, don't turn off, even though that's precisely what often happens.

● *Bias*. If we take a dislike to the interviewer, it will be hard to hear what the individual says.

● *Boredom*. It can happen, even in a job interview, particularly if the person goes on and on about his or her career. We turn off, to return to find that the conversation has taken an unexpected turn, the beginning of which we have lost.

● *Mental listening only*. We hear the literal words without the connotation of body movements, facial expressions and vocal tones.

What can we do to improve our listening during a job interview? One improvement is up to the potential employer—the listening environment. If the individual permits telephone and other interruptions, you must concentrate harder and also wonder whether you want to work for such a person. Also, unobtrusively reposition your chair if you need a better view of the speaker. Listening involves seeing as well as hearing the speaker.

An improved emotional attitude toward listening will go far toward overcoming many barriers to listening—selective inattention, selective memory, selective expectation, fear of being influenced, bias and boredom.

Boredom may be as much your fault as the speaker's. You have failed to listen creatively. You have probably showed your boredom and dampened the other's enthusiasm so that he or she isn't thinking and verbalizing well. Conceal your boredom. *Act* enthusiastic and you'll *be* enthusiastic. Act bored and you'll be bored. Ask leading questions that may stem the flow of reminiscence or diatribe. Try to smile when you're bored. Nod your head at appropriate moments. Force yourself to be attentive. An amazing thing may happen when you work this way at listening. Soon, you grow genuinely interested. Your alert listening has acted as a catalyst on the speaker whose ideas sharpen and whose choice of words takes on a new aptness.

If you are biased and fear being influenced, you may subconsciously take refuge in ostentatious boredom. However, a whole new world may be yours if you allow yourself to be influenced just once and drop your cherished biases.

Empathy enhances listening. Webster defines it as "the capacity for participating in another's feelings or ideas." With this trait, you can look into the other's mind and hear far more than just the words. No one knows exactly how empathy occurs, but it begins with an interest in the other individual, followed by sympathy and understanding. It is the best catalyst in the world for breaking down all the barriers to good listening. To some extent, you can foster it by forcing interest, enthusiasm and sympathy for the other. This becomes easier with practice.

Put yourself in the other's shoes, understanding his or her emotions, suppressing your own emotions and ego in the effort to understand that of the other. Empathy is the best antidote, too, for selective inattention, selective memory and selective expectation. If you're in tune with the speaker, you will more naturally hear everything.

Try as we might, however, we don't always achieve the ideal relationship with the person who has the power to hire us. What then?

First, we should accept the reality that all of us tend to be selective in what we retain among all the words we hear daily. Our goal is to broaden our selection.

Ask questions if you don't understand. Almost always, the other will be flattered, not contemptuous. If you do drift, curb your errant thoughts and get back to the sound track. If you have lost the thread hopelessly, apologize and ask for a repetition.

Be physically alert when you listen. Don't slouch when you stand or slump when you sit. Look directly at the speaker. Psychological studies indicate that most of us are more alert mentally when we stand or sit erectly and look at the speaker.

In the first job interview, we should spend about 80 percent of the time listening. If you sense the ratio is radically different than this, that you are speaking much more than 20 percent of the time, then ask a probing question or two about the organization's problem(s). The interviewer will be only too glad to expound on the subject. It probably has dominated his or her workaday thoughts for weeks.

In successive interviews, the listening ratio for you can decline, perhaps to as low as 20 percent as the other wants to hear more about how you propose to solve his or her problems.

Finally, speak up, slow down, and—listen.

Take Charge

Take charge during your first interview, despite your listening for about 80 percent of the time. Get the interviewer to talk about the job, the organization, its culture. Avoid the subject of compensation at first; that comes later. In the most successful interview, it comes naturally from the interviewer when he or she tries to sell you on the job.

Taking charge includes an understanding that you are as uneasy as the potential employer. He or she has or should have five basic questions in mind:

1) *What attracted you to us?* This goes beyond the reputation as an employer; it involves concerns about your motives.

2) *How can you help us?* Can you perform the tasks we need to do, help meet our challenges, help solve our problems?

3) *Will you harm us?* Will you make us regret we ever heard of you?

4) *Who are you?* Will you get along with the rest of the people on the staff? Can *we* get along?

5) *What do you want for compensation?* What's the least we can get away with? How high are we prepared to go?

Don't be surprised if the interviewer never gets to some, or even any, of these questions. Many employers have less experience than you in interviewing. If the questions don't surface soon, bring up numbers 1, 2 and 4 yourself. Answer number 3 through indirection by dwelling longest on number 2. If your interview nears an inconclusive close, you can get some sort of reaction from the employer by stating what you want in pay and benefits. If the response is a decided "no," you still have gained something. You can write this one off and not waste more time on the prospect. If the reply is a guarded "that might be possible" or something similar, you have a live one. If the potential employer says, "I'll have to take that up with my associates," or, "We weren't planning to go that high," you have trouble. Either the interviewer doesn't want to pay as much as you ask, or he or she hasn't made a firm decision about you.

Assume it's the latter, which it usually is. Some people aren't indecisive; they just don't wish to decide quickly. Once they do make up their minds, they act as forcefully as you could possibly wish. For the moment, assume that's the kind of person you face. Don't press for a resolution now. Offer to answer any further questions. Express your interest in the job and availability in person or on the phone in the immediate future. If you can legitimately do so, state that another organization is interested in you.

Here are typical questions that relate to the foregoing five fundamental concerns that every employer has:

"What are you interested in doing?" This is a tell-me-about-yourself question that generally covers the first four basic anxieties. To allay that fear, you want to show you will be a good employee. Briefly, give your history, your hobbies, your interests, your family background. Sprinkle your history with phrases such as "came early, left late" or "liked that job" or "won the top employee award that year."

"What work do you want to do next?" The employer is really asking if you will fit into the open job. Your answer lies in your experience. You have developed many skills which you can transfer into many fields. Name your skills. If you apply for a known vacancy, first say, "I'll be glad to answer that, but first I think it's important for you to tell me what skills are needed for your open job." When the employer tells you, then answer the original question. Don't forget to do so!

"Have you ever done this sort of work before?" The employer fears you can't do the job and lack the necessary experience or "smarts" to learn to do it quickly. Again, you assuage such concerns by repeating that you have transferrable skills. Use responses such as, "I pick up things fast," or, "I can make myself at home very quickly." A variant on this theme is, "Do you think you can handle this job?" Your reply to this should take into account the likelihood that your interviewer feels pressure to fill the job quickly. Answer yes. Don't elaborate at this point because too much justification could perhaps signal the opposite.

"Why did you leave your last job?" or "Why are you considering leaving it?" The employer fears there's something wrong with you, either in expertise or interpersonal skills.

To answer this one, cite your technical accomplishments and the fact that you have held other jobs for considerable periods. If you were fired, say, "My job was terminated." If not, say, "My boss and I agreed . . ." Say as many positive things as honestly possible about your former boss and coworkers. Occasionally, the interviewer may challenge your stated reason for leaving your last job. Although you want his or her favorable impression, you also need not tolerate an insult. You can reply, "Call my former boss if you doubt my word."

"How much were you absent on your last job?" Obviously, the employer is concerned about absenteeism. If you were seldom or never absent, then you have the perfect response. If you were off a lot, tell why and say you have resolved the difficulty (and you better had).

"How's your health?" Naturally, the interviewer wants assurances here. Give them if you possibly can. If, for example, you had a heart attack, stress your subsequent recovery.

"Why are these gaps in your work record?" The potential boss wants reassurances here, too. Again, explain how the heart attack forced your absence from the workforce, or whatever.

"Isn't this job below your capabilities?" This is a favorite, especially when the interviewer is on the verge of turning you down. Employers also like to say, "I think you'd be underemployed here." One good answer is, "Better to be underemployed than unemployed." Every employer fears the applicant will leave as soon as something better turns up. Rebut this one directly, because when the interview reaches this stage you have little to lose. A good response is, "We have mutual fears. You fear I'll leave soon. I fear you'll let me go. I'll do a fine job here and will stay as long as we both agree I should stay."

"What's your greatest weakness?" The employer fears some flaw will surface in expertise or character. Respond by citing some weakness that has a positive side to it. "I don't take well to close supervision. I like to anticipate problems before they arise." Otherwise, say, "I can communicate better." Everyone can communicate better. This is not a damaging admission.

Because of current laws, employers are prohibited from asking:

- Are you heterosexual or otherwise?
- Are you married, single, divorced, engaged, or living with someone? Do you see your ex-spouse?
- Do you have children at home? Who cares for them?

- How tall are you? What do you weigh? Do you have any physical or mental handicaps?
- Have you ever been arrested, convicted or spent time in jail?
- What type of military discharge do you have? What branch did you serve in?
- How old are you?
- Do you own your own home or do you rent?
- What's your religious background?

What do you do if an employer asks one of the above? You can:

  1) Answer it and ignore the fact that it's illegal.
  2) Answer it, but with the preliminary, "I don't think the question is relevant to the requirements of the job."
  3) Go to the nearest Equal Employment Opportunity Commission office.

Response number 2 is probably the best to give in most circumstances. Yet, do you want to work for someone with such an interest in your personal life?

Often, a job interview runs into dead spots. The interviewer momentarily can think of nothing to say or ask. Be prepared with priming questions: How did your company manage to boost sales last year when everyone else was flat? How's your new product doing? I like your new ad campaign; what's your agency? You pick up the background for such questions, of course, by reading recent news items about the organization.

The Employer Looks at the Job Interview

Have you ever wondered how the employer sees the employment session? Here's what General Foods Corporation advises its applicant-interviewing supervisors:

  1) Don't worry about nervousness—many interviewers are nervous, and almost all applicants are. Relax.
  2) Remember, informality helps an interview. Sit on the same side of the desk with the applicant, or sit facing the applicant away from the desk entirely.
  3) Carry the ball because few applicants have had much experience being interviewed. (Not true for you, is it?)

4) Ask questions, lots of them.

5) Avoid inquiries about race, religion and citizenship.

6) Don't take "secret" notes during the interview.

7) Speak frankly if a rejection is based on technical qualifications. Be less candid if the decision is based on personality, appearance or similar aspects.

8) Don't oversell the job to the applicant; paint the picture realistically. Make no promises you may be unable to keep.

9) Don't select someone far above the level of the job in ability.

10) Be thorough, friendly and sincere. And be yourself. You represent the company to every outsider you meet.

Testy Issues

You won't have trouble with *those* General Foods recipes, but others may appear that will be difficult to "digest." One is the question of age.

The skilled interviewer will never ask it directly, but it slides in with references to the average age of the workforce, the mention of the interviewer's age, or allusions to the need for physical and mental stamina on the job. When you hear this more than once, you should deal with it forthrightly.

For a starter, say you believe age is irrelevant for the job under discussion. However, experience *is* relevant, and you have it. List it. If you are in your fifties, point out that you intend this job to be the climax of your career and to last until you are 65 or 70. When you are in your sixties, assure the other of your intention to work until 70 (if true) and to cap off your career with new accomplishments. Cite your goals.

Sometimes the employer presents another digestive challenge, the psychological test. You have little choice but to accept it. Remember this:

● The test usually reflects more on the tester than the testee.

● Anyone with a knowledge of such tests can influence the results substantially.

● Uncertain hirers rely on them, not people who know whom they want.

Fortunately, psychological tests are less common than in the past.

Unfortunately, much more common today is the urine test for drugs. Take it.

When you go for an interview, you'll often be asked to fill out the job application form before you face your interviewer, if you haven't filled it

out already. Try to avoid doing so because application forms and psychological tests screen more applicants out than in. Here are strategies that
will forestall the application form:

- Tell the receptionist you don't have time now and will fill it
out after the interview if it goes well.
- Tell the personnel representative the same if he or she gives
you the form.
- Tell the hirer you have a few questions first before dealing
with the form.
- Tell whoever asks for it that your résumé (if submitted already) answers the questions or will when you surrender it following the interview.

If none of these works, fill the thing out as gracefully as possible.

Every potential employer wants references. Three should suffice; five
should be the maximum. Here are criteria to consider in choosing them:

1) Is the person well-known in your field? Help from such a
person can be invaluable.

2) It helps only if the reference is enthusiastic. A reference that
is noncommittal or offers faint praise does more harm than good.

3) Is the person well-known in your community? Okay, but this
is less helpful than a person familiar in your field. Don't overweigh
your reference list with this type.

4) Is the reference persuasive and convincing? An enthusiastic
nonentity is better than a well-known person in your field who offers only faint praise.

5) Will the reference speak well of you as an individual and
professional, but mention some other shortcoming, perhaps divorce
or former alcoholism? You can offset this if you are candid during
the interview, although you must fit your strategy to the circumstances.

If you're seriously concerned about what someone might say of you,
don't use that person as a reference. If you believe you must, test what the
reference says by having him or her mail the comments to a friend at
some place where you don't intend to apply.

You have special problems when you parted with your last employer
on bad or even indifferent terms. Count your blessings if that employer
doesn't give references of any sort (increasingly common today), but will
only confirm employment dates. Even in this case, however, prepare the

potential employer for a possible poor review because the two may be, or have, mutual friends or acquaintances and your ex-employer's opinions about you could get out despite company policy to the contrary. Frankly state why and how you left your last job, putting it as positively and honestly as possible, of course. You can even bring up age as a cause of your last departure, if it was and if you judge it won't be an issue this time. "I was 18 years older than my boss," you might explain to the potential employer who is more nearly your contemporary. "I thought him a brash kid, and I'm afraid it showed," or, "The company was on a youth kick. When it offered an early-retirement package, I decided I could afford to move on."

The Wrap-Up

Sometimes, you'll get a job offer on the spot. Your instinct is to accept on the spot. Resist your natural impulse. You want at least two offers for comparison purposes. Put the employer off with, "Let's both think this over and get back together soon."

At the opposite extreme, you'll get rejected on the spot. Aside from damage to your ego, there's no harm done, possibly even a benefit. You now know what doesn't work with a potential employer. In your post-mortem, decide what went wrong, but don't grow obsessive about it. If you don't know (which may be the case), ascribe it to a chemical failure where you and the employer didn't react well together.

The most common outcome of the first job interview is equivocal. The employer has not made up his mind, and probably you haven't either. If neither of you has mentioned compensation up to now, bring it up yourself, even though it's more properly the interviewer's subject. Money usually serves to focus matters.

Assure the interviewer of your interest in the job if you honestly can. If you aren't sure, say you need time to think it over. The employer probably does, too.

Immediately after the interview, write a thank-you letter to everyone you met at the session, including the secretary and employees who "dropped in" to meet you. Some employers use the drop-in technique to give an associate a chance to look at you.

When the potential hirer doesn't set a return date, call within a week to set one if you want it.

When you do get it, great! In your next interview or interviews, you'll *really* be able to sell yourself as to the kind of job you wish to build for yourself and the way you want to solve problems.

16

Create Your Own Job

To create your own job is the best way for a senior to "find" one. At the least, this takes time and true patience. At the worst, this would seem impossible except when you start your own business.

Yet, it's very possible.

The Unborn Job

Consider the problem of the president of a West Coast company that makes and markets bar-scanning devices to identify and keep track of products on the factory floor, in warehouses, on supermarket shelves and at checkout counters. He must cope with technical, production, budgeting, personnel and marketing challenges in a rapidly growing business. He hasn't gotten around to solving them all and knows it.

One day, his secretary puts a letter in his in-basket she would normally route to Personnel—a job application with a difference. It deals first with the company's market coverage in the Northeast, a subject which has drawn discussion in several of his recent meetings. It next proposes a solution to a gap in the coverage by hiring the applicant as a sales representative operating out of Erie, Pennsylvania.

The writer knows so much about the company and its marketing arrangements that the manager wonders if he's a former employee. No, reports his secretary after a check with Personnel. The manager ponders the possibility of a breech in security. Has the subject been discussed internally? Not likely, his sales head reassures him, only four of them ever talked about it in any depth, and their meetings were confidential. Personally, he wouldn't mention it even to his own wife.

Intrigued, if not slightly alarmed, the president asks his secretary to try the phone number listed on the letterhead. He reaches Hal, the former locomotive salesman, who assures him his conclusions come solely from reading and other research, and not from a breech in security. Greatly relieved and growing excited, he invites Hal to come to San Jose. Hal and his wife already plan to do so. He offers to pay Hal's air fare and other expenses for two days.

Recounted like this, it sounds simple. Yet, it wasn't at either end. The president and his associates agonized for weeks over the marketing problem. Due to distractions, disagreements on the best course of action and budgetary considerations, they had reached no conclusion. Now, this fellow turns up. Hang the budget. Forget the disagreements, if this Hal turns out to be the answer. (Of course, we know Hal had not found his way easily to the California company, either.)

Will an Employer Create a Job Just for You?

The answer is a resounding *yes* if you offer convincing proof that you can solve the employer's problem(s).

Most jobhunters believe the best—even the only—way to find a new position is to somehow ferret out one that's vacant and apply for it. That may work sometimes for younger seekers, but less often for seniors because of reasons already discussed.

Organizations exist to make a product, to market an item, or to provide a service. If they have trouble performing their function, they may cease to exist. Even if the difficulty is relatively minor, it may threaten their effective performance. They want to solve it. That's where you come in. You don't flat-footedly call it a "problem" or "difficulty," you dub it a "challenge." In your hunt, you look for trouble and develop solutions.

Of course, employers know the troubles exist, but they haven't solved them, perhaps for reasons that delayed the resolution in San Jose. Hal arrived and sold the optoelectronics company's president on selling its bar-scanning system from Erie. He concentrated first on the city's geographical advantages in the Northeast with the greatest density of population and manufacturing in the United States, and good access to the area by road, air and rail.

Next, he detailed his marketing experience—35 years selling expensive, technically complex equipment, primarily in the Northeast. He emphasized the technical expertise he provided to sell locomotives because he shrewdly and correctly guessed that the company had to offer the same to market its optoelectronics. He pointed out that he could exercise patience in selling because it always took months to sell a locomotive, sometimes more than a year. Again, the company had never sold a bar-scanning system overnight. Finally, Hal told of his interest in continuing education, touching on his success in keeping up with the technological evolution of the diesel-electric locomotive. He brought this up because he said he wanted the company to teach him or tell him how he could learn about optoelectronics. He candidly admitted he knew only the superficial rudiments of bar-scanning technology.

After a day of talks, the discussion concentrated on how the company could teach him that technology. The president had tacitly accepted Hal's credentials as a good salesman and his arguments for Erie as a good base from which to tap the Northeast market. The president would create a job for Hal. Furthermore, the company would teach him the technology. Such a course promised to be easier and more cost-effective than moving an already knowledgeable salesman into Erie or another appropriate city in the region.

Naturally, the decision didn't become final in even two days. The president had to check Hal's references and resolve misgivings about the request to work only 20 hours a week. Compensation proved a stumbling block for both sides because the pay-and-benefits offer was based on a full-time job. Each party agreed to think things over for one week. Hal knew he took a risk in asking for a part-time job. While industry is more hospitable to new time arrangements for work, the hospitality does not extend to management positions which Hal's would be. There, hours are longer and vacations shorter.

The author encountered somewhat similar circumstances when he spotted deficiencies in a bank's employee communication program. After wrangling a circuitous introduction to the vice-president of employee relations, he gave him chapter and verse about them, together with solutions. Following three weeks of meetings with key people in the personnel department, refinements of his solutions and negotiations about compensation, he was hired as director of employee communications, a job that had not previously existed.

He, too, intended to work for the bank part-time. He ended up putting in more hours a week than he ever had before in his life. Fortunately, he negotiated his pay on an hourly basis, with no benefits except for a two-week annual vacation, plus the conventional holidays. Hal did the same on benefits. For pay, the parties agreed to a small weekly draw against commissions, with no upward or lower limit on hours worked. After a month's indoctrination into technology to which Hal willingly devoted more than 200 hours, he began work out of Erie. He expected to put in heavy hours for the first six months. Yet, after only a year he could cut back to under 40 hours. Although he never averaged as few as 20 per week, he enjoyed the work so much that he didn't mind. His wife did, but she wisely kept quiet in light of Hal's pleasure in his new career.

Finding That Niche Anywhere

Are you limited to creating your own job with medium to large companies because they have the resources to take a chance? No. The factor that influences the employer to create a job for you is the severity of the problem, not the extent of resources. If a problem threatens the life of an organization, it *will find* the resources to hire you if you can convince it that you will solve the difficulty.

If the problem is less than life-threatening, it may still dig deep to marshall resources to take you on because every organization must eventually solve most problems to flourish, whether the difficulties are major or middling.

An analogy exists in the way companies hire subcontractors to solve their problems. Here are examples:

- When Polaroid Corporation introduced its SX-70 instant cameras a decade or so ago (when Polaroid was smaller than today), some of them spat out pictures before they were developed. The problem threatened Polaroid's survival. Tiny International Components Corporation, a maker of special-purpose motors, solved the trouble by tracing it to a signal created when the print-delivery motor ran. It developed a motor with a different metal alloy so the signal it produced didn't disrupt the camera's electronic circuitry. The subcontractor sold Polaroid $10 million worth of the motors in the next six years.

- Chicago Metallic Products Inc., a baking-pan manufacturer, designed a pan with bumps in it to enable giant Pizza Hut to make uniform deep-dish pizzas in continuous-belt ovens.

- Canterra Engineering Ltd., finds a profitable niche developing specialty products for customers of every size, mostly in oil exploration. One is a portable earth-boring rig which crews can hand-carry to remote locations where vehicles can't go.

Like International Components, Chicago Metallic, or Canterra, you will be taken on by an employer—whatever its size—if you can solve its problem.

Finding the Problem

Identifying the difficulty is usually as challenging as solving it. Charles F. Kettering, the legendary problem-solving vice-president of General

Motors, said, "A problem well stated is a problem half solved." G.K. Chesterton added, "It isn't that they can't see the solution, it is that they can't see the problem."

Before you approach a possible employer with the idea of persuading him to create a job for you, first make sure it's the kind of organization you want to work for, in a satisfactory geographic area, with a congenial group of associates to work with. How do you learn this? By research. A vital result of such study in most cases is the discovery of a problem.

A good problem statement should include what is known, what is unknown, and what is sought.

Under what is known, consider where and when the problem is occurring, its magnitude, and why it must be solved.

Under what is unknown, list what you don't know about the problem. Ask yourself why it is occurring now and under the present conditions instead of at another time and under different conditions.

Under what is sought, go beyond "a solution." What kind of solution do you need? Will the solution create new problems? How can the original problem be kept from recurring? Do you need an answer now, or can it wait? If so, how long? Does your solution include you? If not, look further.

Where are you most likely to unearth problems that will pay off well for you? Korn/Ferry International, a search firm, says that in the first quarter of 1986, new positions paying $100,000 or more opened up most frequently in financial services (which accounted for 20 percent of the total), health/pharmaceutical (16 percent), public sector (12 percent), electronics (11 percent), real estate/construction (10 percent), leisure (9 percent), merchandising (8 percent), consumer products (7 percent), manufacturing (6 percent), and energy/chemical (1 percent).

Formerly, a senior seeking a new position to be created for him or her at any level would almost automatically look first at high-technology firms. No longer. Fast growth there cannot be guaranteed today. High-tech recruiting slowed during the summer of 1986 from the previous year, reported Deutsch, Shea & Evans, based on a count of help wanted ads. It blames "the continued poor performance of many major computer and electronics operations" and the rash of mergers.

The Bureau of Labor Statistics projects that the following occupations will have the fastest rate of growth in the next decade: Paralegal personnel (98 percent), computer programmers (72 percent), computer systems analysts (69 percent), medical assistants (62 percent), and data-processing equipment repairers (56 percent).

Don't all but paralegal and medical assistance types relate to high-tech? Not necessarily. A paralegal may find work in high-tech, but a computer systems analyst may be in a supermarket chain. Tomorrow's jobs will most likely be in business services. As already noted, the service sector will account for most new jobs through the mid-1990s, and the business service industry—such as data processing and temporary help agencies—should provide more new jobs than any other industry in the economy, says the BLS's Occupational Outlook Handbook. Five of the 10 projected fastest-growing jobs are computer-related. Employment in slumping industries like agriculture and mining will continue to drop, while construction should rebound due to the strong demand for housing. Manufacturing will rise slightly.

So, gauge your search accordingly.

An Alternate Way To Create a Job

There's still another way to persuade an employer to create a job for you—buy him or her out. Many seniors from large corporations are doing this. They are putting their management skills to work in reviving smaller companies in aging industries.

"That's the new American dream, to buy something in the Rust Belt and turn it around," says Robert S. Ehrlich of R.S. Ehrlich & Company, a New York investment-banking firm that caters to small- and medium-sized businesses.

"I see a lot of it," says Timothy R. Sweeney, a Cleveland attorney who represents both buyers and sellers of Rust Belt businesses. "I have a call a week from somebody saying, 'If there are any good businesses for sale out there, let me know.'" In fact, Mr. Sweeney says, "There are a lot more buyers than sellers."

In 1984, Michael J. Fallaw quit as vice-president of sales and marketing at Southwest Forest Industries Inc. of Phoenix, Arizona, and bought ailing Chicago Molded Plastic Corporation. It's no longer ailing and he enjoys his senior years running the business.

In 1983, John W. Moffat left LTV Corporation's Jones & Laughlin Steel Corporation division where he had been assistant superintendent in the basic oxygen furnace department. He was tired of his long association with a declining industry, and so led an investor group that bought money-losing Northern Malleable Iron Company in St. Paul, Minnesota, from Atlantic Richfield Company. It made money during its first month of independence.

Going into a highly leveraged acquisition, though, entails big risks. When Thomas A. Lisle, a former Eaton Corporation vice-president, teamed up with a partner to buy a Wisconsin boat-building company in

1982, he had to sell his two homes in Michigan and move into a modest house in Wisconsin. He's now chairman of Cruisers Inc. in Oconto, Wisconsin, where he can also indulge himself more fully in his major hobby, boating.

Seniors also buy service operations. In one recent month, a refugee from a major Pittsburgh corporation where he had been a financial vice-president bought a firm servicing doctors' patient accounts, an executive with a trucking company bought a nursing home, and a woman divorced after 30 years of marriage acquired an operation supplying nursing services to house-bound patients. Note that they all went into health-related activities, one of the fastest growing businesses in America.

In Pursuit of Leisure

The leisure industry is another boomer that may serve you well in your senior years. For example, travel spending in the U.S. has soared from $93.8 billion in 1975 to $259.4 billion in 1985, according to the U.S. Travel Data Center. Spending for leisure products alone—from skateboards to video cassette recorders—more than doubled in the past decade to $181.1 billion. Electronics Industries Association reports audio and video sales totaled $18.6 billion in 1986 vs. $13.7 billion in 1983. The Department of Commerce reported sporting goods shipments totalling $1.5 billion in 1986 vs. less than $1 billion in 1982. The Book Industry Study Group forecasts book sales of $10.7 billion by 1989, compared to less than $5 billion in 1981. Is something there for you?

Be forewarned, though—you will have to work for the leisure dollar. The 40-hour work week, protected by federal law for nearly half a century, is fiction for many wage earners. Professionals and managers worked an average of 45 hours a week in 1985, while manufacturing employees put in an average of 43 hours. Professionals and managers have less vacation time—an average of two weeks a year—than do their counterparts in every industrial country except Japan. So, you'll have to come up with leisure concepts or products that take less time—for example, the promotion of quick trips to the Poconos instead of around the world, or the manufacture of racketball apparatus instead of golfing equipment.

The Kinds of Problems

Thus far, we have concentrated on where to look for likely employers who will create a job for you. Now we turn to the kinds of problems that most commonly plague employers. They more often involve an employee than a situation, so expertise in personnel management is a priority. Develop solutions to absenteeism, poor motivation, priority-setting, and you can often create a job for yourself.

Another kind of problem is a company or one of its operations in unspecified trouble. Nobody can say its product needs redesigning or its marketing requires an overhaul. Often, this trouble develops from poor leadership, nothing more specific. Are you a person with proven leadership capabilities? Then look for problems in this area.

Sometimes the employer knows he or she must solve a specific problem—inventory control, computer systems analysis, marketing—but cannot find the right person to deal with it. As Hal succeeded in doing, ferret out those specific challenges and offer yourself as the solution.

Ever so tactfully, ask someone within a company or organization that attracts you: What's the biggest challenge you face? It may be common to the whole industry and too big for one person. Even so, try to develop a solution for a small segment of it. The solution to the problem may seem obvious and even trivial to you, but may not be to the employer suffering from it. A chemist with a major tire company discovered that a manufacturer of plastic and rubber kitchen products couldn't keep its items stable in moist heat. The tire company had solved that problem long ago for its tires. The chemist worked in his garage for only three days to adapt the tire company's processes to kitchen products. He took it to the maker of kitchen items and won a new job. The organization didn't solve the technical problem on its own because it never before had a chief chemical engineer.

Even when you run into a stone wall in trying to unearth a problem in an organization which interests you, that tells you something—it hires unduly rigid people, or too many of its employees don't know how to communicate, or it has no structured way of dealing with the public. Your solution: Form a public relations department consisting of you at the start, perhaps more people later; show how the lack of such a unit has hurt the organization in the past by giving it a poor image with the public; develop examples of the benefits of public relations in other companies, particularly of competitors.

As you research the organizations that interest you, two things usually happen. First, your list of such organizations shortens as you can't find problems germane to your concerns. Second, you learn a great deal about those organizations remaining on your list, particularly their problems, their methods of approaching them, and their typical solutions to problems in the past.

No matter what your interests are, here are the kinds of questions concerning a potential employer to find answers for:

● How does this organization rank within its field or industry?

● Is the organization family-owned? If so, what effect has the ownership had on promotions?

● Where are its various facilities?

● What does the organization do?

● How has it grown recently?

● How severe are its internal politics? (Politics exist everywhere; every organization has them, despite denials.)

● What's its public image?

● How has its stock (if publicly traded) performed recently?

● What's its staff turnover?

● How are employee attitudes? (Observe for yourself, if possible. If not, ask.)

● How are promotions handled—generally from within or from outside?

● How long has the CEO been on the job? How long has he or she been with the organization?

● What kind of training does the organization provide?

● How do communications work within the organization? How widely within the organization is information disseminated?

● Does a time bomb threaten the organization, such as a possible takeover, product liability suit, or technological development?

Solving Problems

When you are jobhunting, you feel the pressure. So, you may tend to fret and stew over solving problems. Dr. Jerome Bonner of Harvard University describes four traits that may result from too much pressure:

1) A tendency to narrow the field of observation. If you are afflicted with this trait, you tend to look for and recognize only those clues that seem immediately relevant to the specific problem, passing up less obvious ideas that might lead to a more novel and creative solution.

2) A tendency to abandon trial-and-error methods. Those who fail to consider a number of possible alternatives get stuck on the first plausible one encountered.

3) A failure to be generic in observations. Good problem-solvers are able to see and list the basic attributes of the problem on which they are working.

4) A failure to see possible applications of information that aren't directly related. Good problem-solvers can apply to the problem information that is not directly related to it. They don't become too literal.

When you suffer from fuss-and-fret blocks (and you probably do in the jobhunting pressure cooker), you can overcome them in ways such as these:

- Counteract the symptoms of the barrier. Be conscious of your own reactions to what seems to be a familiar problem, and be aware of the ways in which such a reaction manifests itself. The chemist did this when tackling the troubles plaguing the maker of kitchen items and came up with a genuine solution for it that went beyond the formula for tires.
- Take your time in reaching conclusions. Hal took his time in his search and landed a job more compatible with his expertise and temperament than even locomotive-selling had been.
- Watch out for the routine. This does not mean entirely avoiding routine solutions. Consider them, but look further. In tackling the bank's employee communication problems, the author went beyond the conventional employee magazine and newspaper. He also promoted a cafeteria-style benefit plan more suited to the institution's predominantly female workforce.
- Relax, above all. You won't solve every problem you encounter. When you don't, go on to the next challenge.

Choosing courses of action that provide maximum benefit within acceptable limits of risk is the essence of successful problem-solving. In summary, to solve problems:

1) *Establish objectives.* "Solve the problem" is too general a goal. What *is* the problem? What causes it? Why and how did the problem arise? How can I solve it? How can I involve myself in the solution? Answers to those questions will enable you to give meaning to objectives.

2) *Generate the alternatives.* Don't settle for the first solution that occurs to you. You may end up using it, but think of others before deciding. You may be able to meld the best features of two or three and find a better course of action.

3) *Examine possible adverse consequences.* Avoid creating new problems with solutions to old ones. A textile firm hired a

behavioral scientist to help motivate employees to achieve higher productivity. Lower productivity resulted because employees resented a stranger telling them how to do their work. An ex-foreman recalled from retirement achieved what the scientist could not.

Demonstrating Your Problem-Solving Skills

Identifying a problem and coming up with the solution to it are just two legs on the stool. You need the third—demonstrating your skills. Fortunately, this is the easiest leg to fashion. Here's why.

As a jobhunter, you have a problem, especially severe because you are past 50 years of age. By the professional way you show the potential employer how you propose to solve that problem, you are demonstrating your problem-solving skills. You will especially impress him or her if you show how and why it would be in the employer's (enlightened) self-interest to create a job just for you.

A sloppy jobhunt, a half-hearted manner and a misreading of the potential employer's challenge will prove fatal to your demonstration. Again, a successful jobhunt demands patience and work, an enthusiastic manner and painstaking research. That will demonstrate your problem-solving skills more than anything else. Hal won his new job by demonstrating intimate knowledge of the president's problems, by showing why a sales office in Erie made sense, and by proving his years of success in selling.

Yet, he had to do more than demonstrate by example, the first principle of persuasion. He called upon the nine other principles of persuasion, too.

The second is that he stated his conclusions, making crystal-clear where he stood and why he took that position. He did not let the facts alone speak for themselves. He well knew that the president might not draw the same conclusions he did from the facts. He knew that his conclusions must have logic and must respond to a need—in this case, the need to expand market coverage.

The third principle of persuasion stems from the second. Emotions persuade more effectively than facts, particularly in the short run. In this, Hal carefully orchestrated his use of superlative (and emotional) words. He said his research convinced him that the company possessed the *most complete* line and the *best* products in optoelectronics. He said he wanted to work for the company because it enjoyed the *finest* reputation in its industry. He commented that his study further showed that the company had *one of the most enlightened* personnel policies in America, notably in its policy of no layoffs.

The next principle involves repetition and anticipation. Hal gave his message bit by bit, summarizing what he had already said as he proceeded to the next portion of his message. He was careful to avoid boredom by phrasing the parts he had already covered in new language and new anecdotes and examples from his own experience. He tried to express rebuttals to objections before they came up. For example, he said he wanted to work out of his home, at least in the beginning, thus countering before it arose the negative of the expense of setting up a new office.

Expect resistance, the fifth principle. If you believe your pitch encounters no resistance, think again. The listener may be too polite—or worse, too bored—to express it. Hal kept alert for resistance. When none came after nearly an hour of talk, he said, "Tell me frankly. Am I off-base in any way thus far?"

That drew the first objection, which Hal rebutted with the sixth principle, candor. The president objected to his lack of deep knowledge about bar-scanning technology. Hal admitted it, countering with his eagerness to learn it. He hoped the official would help him.

Hal invoked the seventh principle, personal involvement, by offering to commit a minimum of a year of his time to give his proposal a try. If he sold little, the company was not out a great deal financially, except his small monthly draw.

When the president objected that he would have lost a year, despite Hal's commitment, if the experiment failed, Hal brought to bear the eighth principle, that the desired action was possible. He mentioned again his past successes as a salesman.

Hal stated his motives frankly, the ninth principle. Why not? It was obvious that he wanted to work for that operation. Everyone has self-interest. Use it, because everyone understands it.

Hal guarded his credibility with care, the tenth principle. He gave accurate figures concerning his marketing history. He told his earnings annually for the past three years. He mentioned other companies in bar-scanning which he had studied.

Finally, Hal exercised patience, which could be the eleventh principle of persuasion. Even intelligent people have trouble with new ideas. If you expect to get new or somewhat complicated concepts across quickly, you're doomed to disappointment. As Solomon says in Proverbs, "Through patience a ruler can be persuaded, and a gentle tongue can break a bone."

17

Make Another's Job Your Own

"In two words: im possible." —Samuel Goldwyn

Try as you will, what if you can't tailor-make a job for yourself? Not everyone can, of course, despite the advantages of doing so.

Then, you hunt more conventionally. To unearth leads, you use your network of friends and acquaintances, read the business news to discover expansions, mergers and promotions, read the obituaries and even the help wanted ads.

To get an interview with a promising prospect, try first to arrange an interview through a friend or acquaintance. If you have no success there, telephone for an appointment. If that doesn't work, write a brief letter that highlights your accomplishments, and ask for an appointment. Here's a famous opener: "I have been in Sing Sing Prison 20 years—auditing the books." The author then explained he was an outside auditor.

Common examples of accomplishment openings: "As assistant marketing manager for a leading consumer product, I helped increase sales 12 percent through a new marketing policy." "I recently brought a $25 million contract under financial control within two months, at a substantial increase in net profit."

Next, list a few of your other accomplishments, briefly naming each in separate paragraphs.

Repeat your request for a time and place for the interview concerning the open position. Address the letter to the highest executive you can find in the directories, preferably the CEO, unless your contact(s) suggests otherwise. Do not send your résumé with the letter.

How To Approach the Potential Employer

Once you get an appointment, the following six tips will maximize your chances of making a connection:

1) Know your needs. Be aware of what you want, and don't reshape your desires to the employer's words and other signals.

2) Decide in advance on the size of the organization you wish to join and its location. However, size and location alone don't make for the ideal company. Hewlett-Packard is large but widely acknowledged to be a top-flight employer. Some small organizations are dogs as employers. Usually, though, medium and small companies in medium and small cities and towns are normally more hospitable to seniors than others.

3) Know the compensation you want and stick within a narrow range. Manufacturers sell their products at set prices, sometimes negotiated lower, but only after specific considerations. Why should you do otherwise in pricing your services?

4) Research the organization you are interviewing in advance (as we have advised repeatedly thus far).

5) Research the performance of your predecessor.

6) Know the worms in the apple—in other words, know any negatives about the employer.

How *Not* To Approach a Potential Employer

If you don't have the talents to fit the job, you won't win it. You can also fail to get it if you make stupid mistakes in approaching the potential employer. Here are prime don'ts:

1) *Don't* start a query letter with "Dear Sir/Madam" or "To Whom It May Concern," or send it with typographical errors.

2) *Don't* handwrite anything except your signature to your query and/or "broadcast" letter (in lieu of a full résumé).

3) *Don't* offer a laundry list of the jobs you can fill, instead of just pitching for the one open.

4) *Don't* appear on the employer's doorstep without an appointment.

5) *Don't* call the employer after normal business hours or at his home.

6) *Don't* forget to include your address and phone number.

7) *Don't* call within 72 hours to determine if the organization received your letter and will grant an appointment. The vagaries of the U.S. Postal Service and interoffice mail mean you should allow a slush period of at least three days.

8) *Don't* be dishonest about your talents or yourself or appear for an appointment under the influence of alcohol or drugs.

A Silver Lining for an Existing Job

Although you are going after an existing position, take reassurance from the fact that once you perform any job successfully, it becomes your tailor-made position. *No one*—none of your colleagues, predecessors or successors—can discharge its functions precisely as you do. You are unique. Therein lies your clue: Even if you can't tailor-make the job before you get it, proceed 'on the assumption that you will do so after you land it.

You probably should not tell your potential employer this at the outset, although any wise employer knows the superior employee gradually molds the job to fit his or her way of doing things. So, even when you apply for an existing job, think of how you would reshape it to fit your own talents. Your thinking in this way sends a desirable subliminal signal to the employer, although not yet expressed in words—that you are already thinking of yourself in this position.

Do you believe this approach presumptuous? Most seniors need to show more effrontery on the job front because too many of us are too quiet. We live in the job world tentatively, as if it is not ours. It *is* ours as much as that of any other age group.

Thus, the key to winning an existing job lies in considering it the same as landing a job that never before existed: Unearth a problem, develop a solution or solutions for it, and persuade the potential employer that you are part of the solution.

Yet, filling an existing position poses pitfalls you don't face when creating a new one. Following are four of them.

A. Why Did Your Predecessor Leave?

When a position is unfilled, that's obviously one of the employer's problems, but dig deeper. If the previous holder was fired, find out why. Often, the interviewer won't tell you directly out of some misplaced sense of fairness. Fairness to the predecessor? That person has gone. Fairness to you? Definitely not. Fairness to the employer? Rephrase that—saving the employer's ego?—and you come closer to the truth. The employer may have erred in hiring the predecessor and doesn't want to be reminded of it.

You must then probe, probably with other employees or with outsiders knowledgeable about the inside of the organization. The more dramatic the predecessor's shortcomings, the easier it will be for you to learn the truth and to offer assurances that you don't suffer from similar faults.

Firings often result from personality clashes. That may mean you wouldn't get along either with such a boss. Weigh that possibility with care. Remember these words of Mark Twain: "I don't like to commit myself about heaven and hell—you see, I have friends in both places." In short, did the person who was fired bear most of the blame?

In many cases, the job is open because the previous holder moved to a better position, retired, or died. Then, you often must cope with the Prince of Wales syndrone—"Sal (or Sally) would have accomplished even more wondrous deeds if only he hadn't left (or retired or died)." Your only response can be agreement. (It would help to learn what problem your predecessor was working on at the time of departure and to suggest ways to complete the solution.)

In other instances, there's no clear explanation for the departure, although the predecessor seemed to handle the job to the employer's at-least-moderate satisfaction. Here lies the greatest challenge.

Proceed with caution because you need to know more. Probe as you would with a firing. If the reasons for the departure remain mysterious, put a question mark against this job possibility. The reason may be something personal for the predecessor, but it could also be a personality clash or some other explanation that bodes ill for your future success in this particular position. Why chance it? If you've researched well, this won't be the lone opportunity you've found.

B. Is This Job a Phantom?

At other times, the job that you believe exists or should exist is not as clear-cut as you thought. Here are examples:

● From friends, you learn that a local bank is having problems with high turnover, absenteeism and other personnel difficulties. You're an experienced and unemployed manager of employee communication. You tell the bank that it needs better internal communications through its employee publications. You argue that part of the problem arises because the public relations department under the supervision of its manager issues a company magazine and newspaper with blurred focuses of both internal and external orientations.

You further argue that the proper internal focus will come only when employee publications are moved organizationally to employee relations. Fortunately, the vice-president of employee relations agrees with you. Unfortunately, you find yourself enlisted as an uneasy ally to help win the battle of office politics. Although the vice-president emerges victorious and you are named director of employee communications, the public relations manager is already your enemy and the job is a hybrid—half created and half an existing position that some people don't think you have the right to fill. You start with two strikes against you. You probably should not have started here at all.

• As a manufacturing engineer let go by a large company, you read in the obituaries (a prime research source) that a manufacturing manager died on the job with a medium company in a small town near your city. Using as an entrée a friend of the company's vice-president, you gain an interview with the firm's executive vice-president to whom the deceased had reported. You win a new job within three weeks of losing your former one. Before you expound about how it's easier for seniors to find positions with smaller companies in less populated areas (which is usually true), you discover strange things about the job. The plant superintendent discharges most of the responsibilities you thought you would fill and has no intention of turning them over to you. The former manufacturing manager handled purchasing (in which you have limited experience) and did customer trouble-shooting (which you wish to perform as infrequently as possible). Both you and the executive vice-president acted hastily. You don't belong in this job because it's not what you thought it was.

• You learn from contacts in the industry that a conglomerate has purchased a small machine-tool builder in your city. The machine shop where you labored 40 years, the last 10 as a shift foreman, has declared bankruptcy. Sensing the managerial upset that occurs during many company acquisitions, you contact the new owners of the machine-tool firm, forearmed with the knowledge that this company heretofore never used a second-shift foreman. You learn the name of the new manager, get an interview and sell him on the need for a foreman of the second shift. While this seems like the creation of a new job, it's more closely the filling of a job that should have been created long ago. Alas, however, the conglomerate sells the company within a year and the new owner cuts back to the bone, including your new job. You should have at least factored in that possibility when you researched the position.

● When your boss of 35 years retires, you find yourself in the limbo of executive secretaries who have nowhere to go within the same organization except down. You choose to go out, and take early retirement even though you're only 55. You are correct in assessing the market for executive secretaries in your area and have a choice of two positions with corporate vice-presidents. You choose the younger, 49, because you don't want a rerun of your former experience. Dame Fortune toys with you, however, because your new boss dies of a massive coronary before you have worked for him six months.

In the first two instances, you probably should have foreseen the phantom qualities of the new job. In the second two, you suffered from the luck of the draw. Haven't we said you should minimize the role of luck in your search? Yes, but you can't eliminate it altogether. Luck still enters into jobhunting even when you research conscientiously, focus your search wisely and interview well. Still, the odds are higher then that you will make your own good fortune.

Look around you and you will see that:

1) Luck smiles on people who work hard in hunting for a job.

2) Luck likes the prepared person. People who do the homework on themselves and identify their skills grow more alert to the good chances that come along.

3) Luck falls upon the individual who has told the most people what he or she seeks. In effect, that person recruits helpers in the jobhunt.

4) Luck favors those who want passionately to find a new job. The half-hearted jobhunter is more likely to be unlucky.

5) Luck loves the people who go after a range of jobs, using a variety of approaches to find the right position.

C. Can I Remain My Own Person?

Thus, you must ferret out employer problems whether you wish to create your own job or fill one that already exists. However, in trying to replace someone, you must take care to remain your own person, not a clone of your predecessor. Consciously or unconsciously, many employers want you to conform to the ways of someone you're not. Even if the previous holder of a position was only moderately successful, most employers suffer a mindset. Employer Ed or Edna wants someone just like the departed Sal or Sally. You must purge from the employer's mind a problem he or she may be unaware of.

How? In Chapter 16, we named the principles of persuasion. Now, here's an actual act of persuading—in this case, convincing a potential employer why he or she should consider you as your own person, not merely someone replacing the estimable Sal or Sally. Research your predecessor's performance as carefully as you do the job itself. Hopefully, you will never have to cast any doubts on that performance, but if Ed or Edna mentions Sal or Sally frequently in laudatory terms, you should consider taking these steps:

1) *Lead the listener gently to your point.* Most interviewers would deny, even indignantly, that they have a prototype in mind with whom you must conform to win the position. Don't accuse the other of such a prejudice directly. Rather, approach the likelihood obliquely. For example:

"I admired the way Sal (or Sally) handled Acme's complaint on the late delivery."

"How did you know about that?"

"They told me about it. They liked his clearing it up, with apologies, but when it happened the second time they were really upset. Yet, Sal seemed to have calmed them down."

"The second time? I knew nothing about that."

"Sal handled it so fast you probably didn't have a chance to learn of it."

2) *Don't make the issue any bigger than it really is.* For instance, the employer might respond with this:

"I don't care for that—Sal's covering up the second late delivery."

"He didn't cover it up. He handled it so well Acme forgave him, and no late shipments have happened since."

3) *Tell the whole story.* Relate the full circumstances under which you learned about the late deliveries.

4) *Accent the·positive.* Report that Acme was sorry to discover Sal had quit, but not surprised he won a better job. Tell how you interviewed a few of the company's customers, asking how it could do a better job. (Acme reported the incident of the late delivery.)

5) *Don't exaggerate.* Stretched truth can snap back and hit you. When you are found out (as inevitably you will be if you do this frequently), your credibility is gone. So is the job prospect.

6) *Give the listener his or her say*. When you bring up a negative about a supposed paragon, you live dangerously because the troubled employer might say something like this:

"I must say, I doubt your word."

"I understand. Why don't you check it with Jim Ames at Acme? He told me. I can wait outside or come back another time when you have verified the incident."

In two of three cases, the employer won't check it, or at least not immediately. In the third instance, he will call Jim Ames. You'd better be right!

7) *Itemize the message*. Now's the time to forget Sal and sell yourself. List what you can do for the employer.

8) *Backtrack when necessary*. If you aren't getting across, repeat your points, but in different words if possible. Moderate repetition aids the memory of your listener, but don't overdo it.

9) *Use feedback*. In this instance, it's whether you are invited for another interview.

10) *Keep calm*. Never show exasperation when you fail to persuade. Never accuse or threaten. When you do fail, ask yourself what you did wrong. Perhaps you should never have mentioned the case of the late deliveries.

The author worried about criticizing a predecessor's handling of the bank's magazine and newspaper. The interviewer didn't at first invite him back. Two days later he called him to return and confessed, "I was not competent to judge your critique of the publications. I went to a friend who is, and he supported you on almost every issue. Let's get on with this job discussion."

The key to effective persuasion is your reasonable position, unaffected by side issues and irrelevancies. The episode of the late deliveries wasn't irrelevant because it bore directly on two factors that could determine if you win the job—the quality of Sal's performance about which you believed the boss held an inflated opinion and thus a false standard, and the inference that you let the boss draw about your own competence.

D. Should I Search While Holding Another Job?

Your major problem here in seeking a new job arises if Sal (or Sally) also jobhunted on the sly. Ed (or Edna) won't feel kindly toward you if you do, too.

In your research, find out if Sal revealed his intentions to Ed before he began his search. If he did and if you think you want this job and stand a good chance of winning it, bare your soul to your present employer. He will find out eventually anyhow. You probably have little to lose. Then, immediately inform Ed that your employer knows what you're doing and will give you a good reference (make sure of this in advance). This counts as a strong point in selling yourself.

If Sal did his search sub rosa, Ed probably no longer thinks highly of him, so you don't face the paragon problem. However, you still face the question of informing your present boss about your actions. Our advice: Tell him. Odds are that he'll improve your current deal to keep you. Then, you face a new dilemma: Accept it or continue hunting. We advise that you keep on looking, except in the unlikely event that the only thing you dislike about the present job is the compensation. If you do accept the present employer's better pay, ethics dictate that you stop jobhunting immediately.

A possible outcome of telling your boss you're jobhunting is to be discharged on the spot. At the least, such an action confirms your feelings of dissatisfaction with your old situation. However, you can't use him as a reference. Explain why to the new prospective employer.

A Footnote on ADEA

You may be able to sue your former boss, though, under provisions of the Age Discrimination in Employment Act. For reasons already explained, we recommend other courses than lawsuits or the threat of them to win redress. However, situations do arise when you have no choice but the courts.

The most common situations that force legal action include demotion or lack of promotion based on age and mandatory retirement before age 70. This last one arises because of ADEA's fuzzy definitions of an "executive officer" and "major policymaker." He or she doesn't come under the age-70 rule. Cases have turned up in the courts where vice-presidents and other high officers, who were mandatorily retired before 70, have argued that they weren't executive officials or major policymakers in their organizations.

It is against federal law to discriminate against workers 40 through 70 on the basis of age. In 1967, Congress passed the ADEA which covers most employers except small businesses with fewer than 20 employees.

If you believe you have been discriminated against, you have rights and recourses through the Equal Employment Opportunity Commission (EEOC), state agencies and the courts. A good defense against age discrimination is an understanding of the law.

Under the ADEA it is illegal for an employer to:

- Specifically exclude older workers when recruiting employees. For instance, an employer may not place a classified ad stating "teenagers preferred" or "recent college graduate," nor may an employer recruit exclusively from local high schools.

- Pay workers (or refuse to hire them) solely on the basis of age. An employer may not use the excuse that an older worker will "retire in a few years."

- Pay workers differently on the basis of age. This practice doesn't always take the form of a difference in salary. Other forms may also be illegal—for example, less sick leave or severance pay or "stretched out" pay increases.

- Refuse to train seniors based on age. An employer can't use the rationale that younger workers will "be with the organization longer" and so are more worthy of training.

- Deny a promotion because of age. Seniority sometimes doesn't work for seniors. They get unfairly labeled as "unpromotable" because "they've been on the job too long to do anything else."

- Discharge workers on the basis of age. If a company encounters hard times, it cannot discharge employees with the most seniority (and highest salaries)—who tend to be older employees—to save money.

- Mandatorily retire almost all workers before age 70. As noted, certain executives and high policy-making employees may be exempt from this law, but generally ADEA prohibits forced retirement. For example, police officers cannot be made to retire at age 55.

- Demote older workers based on age. Some employers' common tactics to force a worker to retire include giving seniors smaller accounts, restricting their sales territories, or "laterally transferring" them in actions that amount to demotions.

- Transfer (or refuse to transfer) seniors based on age. A union hiring hall can't give referral preference to "a journeyman under

55"; an employment agency can't try to fill a request for "a receptionist under 40."

● Retaliate against workers who complain about age discrimination. It's also illegal to fire a supervisor who refuses to demote a
senior.

Certain situations are exempt from the ADEA. In some instances, age
can be a legitimate qualification for employment. For example:

● If age is a reasonable qualification necessary to the operation of the business, it is legal. Obviously, it would make no sense
to hire a senior male for a television commercial to model young
boys' clothing.

● Providing a differential level for a bona fide employee
benefit can be legal. Normally, life insurance premiums increase
with age, and a senior may get less coverage than a younger worker
for the same premium.

● Giving a benefit on the basis of seniority can be legal. A
40-year-old employee with 10 years' experience may get two weeks
vacation while a 50-year-old with five years' seniority may get one
week.

● Mandatory retirement at 65 of executive or high policy-
employees is legal. That person must qualify for an employer-paid
pension of at least $44,000 per year.

● Hiring on the basis of ability, regardless of age, is legal.
For example, a 25-year-old engineer may have special skills needed
by an employer, rather than the general experience offered by a senior engineer. Employers rely heavily on this exemption to get off
the legal hook, often successfully.

● Firing or demoting for just cause is legal. If a senior performs poorly, he or she may be fired or demoted.

● Job elimination is legal. The ADEA says nothing substantive about this, so employers usually go this route in laying off and
discharging seniors.

What To Do About Age Discrimination

If you believe you are a victim of age discrimination, you can pursue
your rights under the ADEA. You should:

- Get as many relevant facts as possible in writing. Keep a diary, take notes, make copies of all correspondence relating to the requirements of your job, your qualifications and your performance.

- Discuss the situation with your employer. Talk it over, but don't make accusations. Keep a copy of all your performance evaluations, responding quickly in writing to all inaccurate evaluations or memoranda concerning your performance.

- Try to resolve the matter informally. Aim to do this in early discussions with your employer without bringing in a lawyer.

If this fails:

- File a charge with the EEOC within 180 days of the alleged discriminatory incident (300 days in states that have age discrimination laws).

- Go through your agency's normal equal opportunity process if you're a federal employee, or notify the EEOC of your intent to file a lawsuit. Thirty days after notifying EEOC, you can file suit against the federal agency. The upper age limit of 70 does not apply to federal workers; every federal worker over 40 is protected.

- File your own lawsuit if the EEOC does not pursue the charges in court or if 60 days have passed since you filed the charge.

- File as soon as possible. You can only get back pay for two years before the suit is filed (or three years if the employer's violation is wilful).

- Don't hire an attorney in an age discrimination case until you have decided to file a lawsuit.

- Pick an attorney through legal aid groups or from law firms that specialize in employment discrimination cases. Local bar associations may also have referral services for attorneys skilled in the ADEA. Also, look up recent age discrimination cases in a local law library to get the name of an experienced ADEA attorney in your region.

- Deal with the court's ruling realistically. If you win a lawsuit, the court usually awards back pay and attorney fees. The court may also order that you get your old job back or be paid until you find a comparable position. You can ask for liquidated damages (up to twice the amount of back pay) if you can prove that your employer wilfully violated the ADEA. If you lose (and more recent cases were decided in the employer's favor than the employee's), accept the decision and go on with your life. The saddest career for a senior is perpetual litigation.

You can get information about ADEA enforcement through the local EEOC office listed in the United States Government section of the phone book or by writing to the EEOC at 2401 E Street NW, Washington, D.C. 20507.

The Role of AARP

The American Association of Retired Persons is the most active group lobbying and acting to educate employers and the general public about older workers and age discrimination. Its Worker Equity Initiative is working to change attitudes, policies and practices that result in the unequal treatment of seniors. The major changes AARP is working for on behalf of seniors are:

- Increased employment in both the public and private sectors.
- Equal access to promotion and training opportunities.
- Increased knowledge for seniors about employment protection and retirement options.
- Increased services for older workers in transition, such as those entering the job market for the first time, those interested in second careers, and those who find themselves unemployed late in their careers.
- Elimination of mandatory retirement based on age.

If you insist on taking the legal route in gaining redress in an age discrimination situation, remember the words of Samuel Goldwyn, "A verbal agreement ain't worth the paper it's printed on."

18

When the Promising Interview Fades

"Ethics stays in the preface of the average business science book," says Peter Drucker.

This chapter contains much on this subject because apparent or real evidence of dishonesty or flexible ethics is often the reason the promising interview leads nowhere.

The Career-Counseling Boom

Desperate jobhunters see too much evidence around them of weak ethics among some executive search agencies and career-counseling agencies. The large number of professionals, the majority seniors, laid off in a recession and even in prosperous years fueled the career-counseling industry's rapid growth—and has prompted many complaints about fraudulent services. The complaints spurred many state attorneys general, as well as the Federal Trade Commission, to examine this industry.

Today, 17 states require career counselors to be licensed. Many universities and other institutions offer training in career guidance as part of a degree in education or counseling, and the National Association for Career Development, a trade group, now certifies counselors. "While these changes have helped reduce the number of complaints about the industry, abuses still occur," accused the *Wall Street Journal* on May 22, 1986.

Glowing promises are a bad sign. Indeed, in addition to providing encouragement and coaching, says Nella G. Barkley, president of Crystal-Barkley, a New York service, a counselor should "help (clients) avoid that grass-is-greener syndrome." Generally, counselors offer two services: assessment and lessons in jobhunting skills. A counselor first tries to help a client discover why, say, he or she has become bored with that accounting job, or whether a salesperson who moved up to management would be happier back knocking on doors. Then, counselors teach clients how to market themselves, focusing on making contacts, researching job markets, writing résumés and polishing interviewing skills.

Counseling packages at LifeWork Associates, New York, can run as high as $1,500, but the company will custom design programs with an average price of about $750, payable in installments. International Career Counseling, Waltham, Massachusetts, requires payment up front and charges between $1,850 and $5,000 for a five-year contract, including follow-up services to clients in new jobs.

The Signs of a Promising Interview

The first indication of a good session with a potential employer is when you know you've not misstepped in ethics or anywhere else. This goes beyond intuition. You know you've not exaggerated your accomplishments, "edited" your failures into successes, or committed any sins of omission. And you have said no half-truths because you know they are really lies.

Other signs:

● The prospective boss introduces you to people who would be your colleagues if you're hired.

● The prime interview lasts at least 30 minutes (preferably longer).

● The interviewer takes notes on your problem-solving suggestions.

● He or she concentrates more on your ideas than on yourself, urging you to elaborate on your suggestions.

● He or she asks many "what if" questions. What would you do if the circumstances were this or that? How would you handle this kind of problem?

● He or she does not return material you have submitted, but promises to do so "next time."

● You win an invitation to return.

The best sign arises if the interviewer's syntax shifts during the course of the session from "the holder of this job would have responsibility for . . ." to "you would be responsible for . . ."

If you don't experience all or some of these indications of interest, your interview was not promising.

Sometimes, the job signs can be misleading. The author's wife hired a cleaning woman to come one day a week. She saw the author often staring vacantly at his desk and went to the wife and said, "Mrs. Morgan, you're paying me $30 a day."

"I know, but I can't afford more."

"It's not that. It's just that I'd be willing to take $25 until Mr. Morgan gets a job."

A common misleading sign in a job interview is great cordiality. Hearty joviality is more likely a bad indication. The interviewer doesn't want to be rude and turn you out quickly, so can think of little else to do with you except make affable chitchat.

Your intuition, honed by your experience, also tells you how well you put yourself across. Use some of the tests an actor employs. If the audience is restless, inattentive or shows displeasure, you face trouble. If the interviewer is barely polite during the problem-solving part of your pitch, you need help. The best kind is self-help. Ask if you're on the right track. If you learn you are not, ask how to right yourself.

Through no fault of your own, the interview may start to turn sour if the employer is poorly prepared. He or she may have no job description or one that's grossly inadequate, or there's no clear explanation of the problem. That's *your* opportunity to turn the session around by probing more directly than you would normally about the nature of the "challenges."

When the interviewer's questions show he hasn't read your broadcast and/or query letter or he allows frequent interruptions and other distractions, you can still salvage the session. You can take charge more forcefully.

An applicant's request that the interviewer take no more phone calls until they are finished brought profuse apologies from him. He hadn't realized how upsetting they were. The candidate took the sting out of his implied criticism by admitting that he too suffered from that managerial malady, telephonitis.

Make allowances for the fact that the employer is under considerable pressure—to solve a problem, to fill a job, even to make a good impression on you. Most employers have less experience than you with job interviews and uneasily sense that they show it.

Early Warnings of Trouble

The first ominous evidence of a fade of what seemed a promising interview is when the interviewer's secretary cancels or postpones your follow-up session with no explanation or a vague one; or you have the interview, but with someone lower in the pyramid; or you see the principal who this time is cool and distant and equivocates about your chances and offers no third interview.

Sometimes, the second interview goes reasonably well, but not as well as the first. You may learn then that the employer is also considering another candidate, although you're still in the running. Your best course is to ask if you can answer any further questions or supply additional material. When you are genuinely interested in the job, restate your wish to get it. If the interviewer declines your offer and seems unimpressed about your hope for the position, take that as a bad sign. If you can ethically do so, say you too are pursuing other opportunities.

When or if a third interview continues the downward spiral, you can almost forget this job. Now, you might as well ask the interviewer where and how things went wrong. He or she most likely will reply with something such as:

"Nothing went wrong, per se. You were a viable candidate whom we probably would have hired if _____ hadn't come along."

"What did _____ have that I didn't?" More than ego prompts this query. You need to know how to forestall the problem next time.

If you get dodging answers such as, "The other candidate seems like he'll fit better into our operation," or, "He had a bit more experience than you," press deeper. If nothing substantive develops, drop the issue, wish the employer good luck, and move along.

If the interviewer answers honestly and fully, count your blessings and don't make the same error again. For example, if the interviewer says, "I hired someone with experience in inventory control. Although your ideas appear promising, you haven't tried them in a real-life situation. We can't afford to be a guinea pig because we're so small." Now you know better than to come on next time so quickly and strongly about your statistical inventory control ideas. At the next opportunity, lead the interviewer more slowly and gently to your ideas.

The Causes of Trouble

When your seemingly promising interview proves to be less than that, always try to persuade the interviewer to tell you why. Even when he can't or won't do so candidly, you can guess that PART caused the turnabout—

*P*ay discussion that's unsatisfactory
*A*nswers to questions that go awry
*R*eferences that turn sour, and/or
*T*rouble on the empathic level.

Often, when you run into trouble over salary, your research told you what competitive places pay for similar jobs. If you discover this figure is far above what the employer intends to pay, stop immediately. To go further is a waste of time. However, your research may tell you the range the employer would consider. Of course, you want the high end of the scale. When the employer offers the low end, try for a compromise. If that draws a response that's less than favorable, consider withdrawing.

Until the employer says he or she wants you and you have decided to return the favor, salary discussion tends to be premature. When it's premature, the figure will normally be the lowest the employer has in mind. The first interview usually is too soon for salary negotiations because you almost never can get to know each other well so quickly. Therefore, if you have an invitation to return, don't be concerned at no salary offer. It may be a bad sign if the employer brings the subject up in the first interview.

Salary may still prove to be the stumbling block at the second or third interview. Then, prematurity is less likely the problem. In the next chapter, we will probe those other difficulties, but we leave the matter temporarily with the reminder that compensation includes benefits which can amount to *thirty percent* or more of the total package.

The promising session may also fade when the employer or you give bad answers to good questions, or vice versa. For instance:

"What type of job are you seeking?" an interviewer asks typically.

"I'm pretty open, anything in accounting." Here's a poor reply because the employer isn't looking for anything in accounting. He wants better control of his inventory costs.

"Why are you interested in a little outfit like us?" This is a bad but common question because it implies the applicant has not researched and doesn't know the employer is small.

Yet, you make do and explain you want to work for a small company after unfortunate experiences with a large one. The answer is little better than the question. A better response: "I want a broader range of activities and responsibilities than I could get with a large firm. I'm particularly interested in your problems with inventory control and believe my experience can help you lower your carrying costs."

"What are your career plans?" The question is a little vague, but moderately good.

"Inventory matters interest me." This reply is still vaguer. What do you specifically want to do concerning inventory? Better: "I want to apply statistical controls to inventory management. I have some ideas that I believe would cut costs by 15 percent a month. In my former job, I was confined to payroll accounting. The purchasing and inventory people wouldn't listen to me because I wasn't from their department. Hence, my frustration."

"What other companies have you already interviewed or do you plan to interview?"

"I hope I don't have to interview another one when I get a job here." The question deserves that mildly flip reply. Do not get specific with this answer unless you already have an offer from someone else and want to use it as a lever.

"What do you think of your present (or former) employer?"

"A good outfit, despite the problems I mentioned. I'm leaving [or have left] because I went as far as I could go there [or whatever]." The question is off base, so you should respond generally.

"What salary were you making there, and what do you expect here?"

"I don't think my former salary is relevant here. I've been impressed during this interview with your fairness and would prefer that you name a figure." This is a good answer to the first mention of salary. If the employer names a figure below what you were making, you can reveal what you earned formerly.

"Why do you want to leave your present job?" or "Why did you leave?" are inevitable and legitimate questions and may come even if you have already answered them, at least indirectly. Be patient and courteous. Reply again, in different words. Your show of exasperation here could prove fatal.

Here are sample answers: "They offered early retirement, and I took it because, as I said, I've long wanted to change my career focus and saw your firm's situation as an opportuunity to do so, especially because I'm now only 55 [or whatever] years old and intend to work until I'm 70." Fairly good, and the little dig about repeating your reply probably won't hurt. Yet, the response could leave the potential employer with the impression that you want to use him as a guinea pig on which to make your career-changing experiments. After you comment about your early retirement, a better explanation would be: "I learned of your firm's problem with inventory control. My long experience in financial analysis convinces me that I could apply my knowledge to your situation, with profit to us both."

"Did your old employer offer any alternative to early retirement?" This is also fair, but it poses a possible trap. If your reply is negative, you leave the impression that your former boss didn't want you for anything, possibly because you had made yourself obnoxious over the inventory matter. If you can ethically and honestly do so, say, "He offered a couple of things that didn't attract me because they had nothing to do with inventory control [or whatever]." If he gives you no alternative, say something like this: "When things reach the stage of an offer to retire early, there's no future with such an employer. I was glad to leave to pursue my ideas on inventory control [or whatever]."

The downturn in your fortunes with the prospective employer may also result from a sour reference, particularly from a former employer. This is usually inadvertent because you obviously wouldn't knowingly list negative references. Yet, you must list your former employer. If you guess that your former boss will be less than enthusiastic about you, forewarn your prospective employer; give as positive a reason for a possibly negative review as you honestly can.

A reference may also innocently mention something like divorce that triggers the negative reaction. Mention, but don't emphasize, such sensitive points in your first interview. The same goes for health problems such as diabetes, heart problems, and former alcoholism. Stress, if you can legitimately do so, how you have overcome the difficulties. Don't overemphasize such troubles, but acknowledge them in the first interview. What looks even faintly like a cover-up will torpedo your hiring chances.

You may find yourself in a cross-fire with references. For instance, you were told you had to take early retirement because the company faced economic difficulties. Yet, the former employer denies this when checked because he doesn't want publicity about the downturn. Another example: You misguidedly say you wrote your boss's speeches for him. He lies and says you only "helped" him write them because his ego won't allow him to credit anyone but himself. It's his word against yours, and you will probably lose the debate. (The current trend whereby former employers won't give references beyond confirming dates of employment offers some solace.)

Sometimes, the trouble stems from a subtle lack of empathy. For reasons not always clear, you and the interviewer don't hit it off. This may arise for superficial reasons—your appearance, your manner, or the interviewer's appearance or manner. The potential employer may dislike you subliminally as a Yale graduate because the school wouldn't admit him 40 years ago.

You can do little about such neuroses when the interviewer suffers from them, but you *can* do much if you stifle them. In dealing with the potential employer, make allowances. Interviewing sessions always pose stress.

It's always wise to embark upon interviews with a coping plan if intuition or even more tangible indications signal a lack of empathy. Here are some hints: The interviewer appears bored or distracted; he (or she) contradicts you or cuts you short; he does not react to anything you say or present; he concentrates on some seemingly irrelevant or minor item in your biography. Some suggestions for coping:

1) Think of analogies from your past when you successfully dealt with difficult people. What did you do—jolly the offender into a better humor, ignore the objectionable behavior, stop and ask what the trouble was?

2) What course(s) worked best?

3) What course(s) failed, at least partly?

Coping with Mister or Madame Monster is never easy and rarely fun. Summon a vision of how the encounter would go if everything works well. This mental anticipation of success will help move you past self-doubts, uncertainty, or unforeseen difficulties. Your brighter psychology alone may improve your empathy with the other.

Don't expect a miraculous improvement. Although you must make quick decisions and take fast remedial action, advance preparation may help.

Don't smoke. If you wear a hearing aid, make no reference to it and be sure it's working. Consider changing to contact lenses if you need vision aid all the time. An applicant for a sales job turned his broken arm into an asset, not a liability, by explaining he had broken it skiing, thereby implying his energy and vigor.

Sometimes, you never will achieve empathy with another. So, forget this opportunity and go on to something else. However, dealing effectively with troublesome individuals is possible, even on short notice. Know that many people have found it so. It's like making an important speech—a heart-stopper to anticipate, but a pride-builder to accomplish.

Other Causes of Trouble

PART alone may not turn your interview off course. Some potential colleagues to whom you were introduced may blackball you. Reasons may range from fear of your competition to doubts that you can handle the job.

Dame Fortune may turn you down. A senior thought he had won a job as sales manager until the offer was suddenly withdrawn. He learned later that his ex-wife's brother had recently become vice-president of human resources for the firm.

Inpatience may harm you. You push too hard and don't impress the interviewer for that reason. Middle managers particularly need patience as never before. Changing corporate strategies, mergers and reorganizations have created a strong demand for chief executives and other top officials, but for middle managers, the pickings are slim.

Lamalie Associates Inc., a New York executive-recruiting firm that fills about 250 openings a year for client corporations, says that fewer than 40 percent are middle-management jobs. This split—more openings for top jobs and fewer for those in the middle—has been widening over the past few years as more big companies including Union Carbide, Owen's-Illinois, Exxon, Chevron, Black & Decker, Eastman Kodak, Du Pont, and General Motors have whittled their middle-management staffs by as much as 30 percent. Ford, for instance, plans to keep reducing its salaried staff right through the 1980s at a rate of about 5 percent a year. Such mergers as Wells Fargo & Company's takeover of Crocker National Corporation will mean a reduction of 70 percent in Crocker's managerial staff. Even companies that aren't cutting aren't necessarily hiring.

"There's a great deal of caution in the executive suites," says Lester Korn, chairman of the search firm Korn/Ferry International. "What's going on today," adds Herbert Northrop, a professor of industry at the University of Pennsylvania's Wharton School, "is a tremendous—and absolutely necessary—change in the world of work." He and others say the underlying reason is that of increasing competition, especially from abroad, which forces cutbacks in white-collar ranks that are relatively larger in America than elsewhere.

In 1985, Lamalie Associates got 36,000 unsolicited resumes, up from 32,000 the year before. About three-quarters of them came from middle managers. Middle managers counseled by deRecat & Associates, a San Francisco outplacement firm, took 4.5 months to find new work in 1984, 4.8 months in 1985, and 5 months in 1986. That's longer than the average, so some people find trouble with the timing and show their frustration too much. If you are such a person, work at controlling yourself better. A good way to start is by reminding yourself that such time spans are *averages*. The length of time that it takes *you* to find a job may vary all over the calendar.

Furthermore, getting fired means moving to another town or city more frequently now than as recently as 1981. Challenger, Gray & Christmas Inc., the outplacement firm, says 45 percent of all managers discharged from their jobs must now relocate to find work.

Your interview can also go awry because you focused your sales pitch on the wrong person. Normally, you concentrate on the individual who will be your boss, but what if he or she doesn't have the go/no-go decision? Moral: Always learn who has the employment decision and focus there, even if that person won't be your direct boss.

The Bread-and-Butter Letter

Finally, a careless oversight may damn you, especially if you simply fail to write a thank-you letter after the first interview. As suggested previously, within 24 hours, you ought to write to *everyone* you met during the interview, including secretaries.

Include one or two pieces of paper with your follow-up. The first is your proposal of how you intend to solve the problem discussed. With this, cite chapter and verse from your past when you solved similar or analogous problems. In doing this, you review the heart of the interview and make it clear you are more than a supplicant. You *can* do something for the potential employer.

Occasionally, a senior objects to giving too much advice and information to someone who has not yet made a commitment to you. "It's proprietary to me," he or she says. "This character might steal my solution and have some present employee put it into effect, leaving me out in the cold." Possible, but not probable. Most employers are honest, despite what you may think. Furthermore, they want on their staff an expert like you who can solve problems. All employers face more than one challenge; they'll put the second one to you as soon as you're on board and have solved the first.

If necessary, include another document with your thank-you note— your résumé. You may even wish to submit a revision, if you already gave the first, on the grounds that you have added data. Remember how we urged you not to surrender your résumé too early? Now's the time, because at last you know clearly what the employer wants. Tailor your new résumé carefully to respond to those needs. Edit it so that every bit of information as to skill, experience and biography is relevant to what the potential employer should know about your qualifications to solve the appropriate problem. Yes, other things may be interesting, but not at this moment when, in all likelihood, he focuses exclusively on that problem.

To the principal, at the very least write, "Per our discussion yesterday, I include a copy of the proposal I made to control inventories statistically for my former employer," or, "I thought you'd be interested in the attached article on inventory control from Purchasing." Tearsheets would be ideal from an article, you wrote, but a better strategy here would have been to offer it during the interview. If you have authored many articles, submit others with your thank-you note.

The follow-up letter also serves as a reminder to the people you met, reiterating your interest in the position (if so). When the job doesn't attract you, say that in your note. If that's the case or this opportunity comes to nothing, somebody you thank may recommend another. It doesn't hurt to ask for suggestions.

Seniors can get hired on the strength of a follow-up letter. It's the most overlooked step in the jobhunting process, says Richard N. Bolles in *What Color Is Your Parachute?*

How To Recover

In discussing how you can recover from any fumble, we start by reminding you of what Shakespeare wrote in *Julius Caesar*:

> *There is a tide in the affairs of men,*
> *Which, taken at the flood, leads on to fortune;*
> *Omitted, all the voyage of their life*
> *Is bound in shallows and in miseries.*

The flood in the tide of your job search may be the opportunity you face now. Although you may never know for certain, always assume that it is your apex. So, use the thank-you letter for still another purpose—to refute any negatives you think surfaced during the interview, such as

- Loose ethics or dishonesty
- A tendency to goof off

- Excessive aggressiveness
- Unassertiveness
- Tardiness or failure to keep commitments on time
- Failure to follow instructions or obey rules
- Blaming others or otherwise dodging responsibility
- Laziness or weak motivation
- An inadvertent failure to show enthusiasm for the interviewing organization or anything else
- Instability

For example, suppose you fear that your history of many jobs during your career indicates instability. You can refute that possible misconception with a statement such as this: "Although I have worked for nine different employers over 30 years, note that six of them were in the first five years of my career when I was trying to find myself." Or: "I left eight of my nine employers voluntarily for a better job. In the one instance of discharge, the cause was poor economic conditions."

Perhaps you know you sometimes give the impression that you are unenthusiastic. To counter this possibility, over-do the enthusiasm in your follow-up letter. What you consider excessive will probably come across as moderate or even normal. However, don't go so far as the newly-hired manager of a small store owned by Ira Hirschmann, the department chain executive. He visited the place and the new manager rushed up to him. "I pride myself on motivational programs through inspirational slogans," the neophyte explained. "Mine today is: 'If a thing is worth doing, it's worth doing at all.'"

If you think things went well in your first interview, but you have heard nothing within 72 hours, ask yourself questions such as these:

1) Did I clearly and fully explain my skills?

It's not enough to say, "I'm an accountant." You must add, "I'm an accountant with 30 years' experience in a wide range of accounting disciplines. I am particularly interested in statistical inventory control [or whatever]." Similarly, you court disaster if you describe your skills in pompous language, as, "cognitive schema processing" (organizing a program to learn something, such as inventory costs).

2) Did I uncover a real problem?

It is the most important problem? If not, what is more important? Watch out for interviewers who let you ramble on this subject. Part of the way into your pitch, you should have asked if you were on track.

3) Did I offer a viable solution to it?

Did you come across as the know-it-all teacher, or were you too tentative? Did you offer something already tried, found wanting, but the interviewer was too polite to say so? You can learn the answer to this last question only by asking. If you discover the solution you suggested had been unsuccessful, you should have probed briefly about why, and then tried to dredge up an alternative.

4) Did I answer all the employer's questions fully and unsatisfactorily?

A clue that you did not turn up if the interviewer repeated a question at least once in different words. You should not have dismissed this as careless repetition, but should rather have tried to answer it more carefully the second time.

5) Did I have trouble with any of the potential colleagues I met—for example, any obvious prejudice against age?

No one would likely voice prejudices flatly, but you can hear the echoes in such comments as, "We usually promote from within," or, "We pride ourselves on solving our own problems," or, "We're a young organization here." Yes, listen for the nuances, but don't borrow trouble. Some seemingly ominous statements may come because the questioner is simply inarticulate or inexperienced.

6) If I unquestionably detected prejudice, what did I do about it?

The most dangerous bias for you is against your age which you can't very well deny. Rather, emphasize your experience, the number of years you expect to continue working. Do this obliquely, to avoid argument or even a semblance of a confrontation. If these tactics don't work, go on to another job opportunity.

7) Am I sincerely interested in getting a job or just going through the motions to forestall criticism by relatives and friends?

The usual cause of going through the motions lies in financial security. Hopefully, you don't really need to work to support yourself, yet you should do something, although it need not be for pay. Hippocrates was the first to observe aging scientifically. He offered two bits of advice: Practice moderation in all things and do not give up your occupation. Some experts advise that if you must retire, do it early and often. Even if you're 65 you have, actuarially, 6,000 days left in your life. You can lead an active, fruitful life. You can try to make the rest of your days one long vacation; you can lead a living death in a nursing home or comparable place; or you can compromise between activity and rest, with rest gradually gaining dominance. For your own good and for the good of society, we urge an active, fruitful life.

8) Have I asked for the job?

Most employers will assume you don't want it, or at least have serious doubts about it, if you don't specifically ask for the job. If you want it, say so. How else can the employer know?

9) Do I *really* want this job?

You may definitely not, or you may have doubts. If so, say so, and ask if you may think things over for a few days. Usually, the employer will ask what's troubling you. State your misgivings. Know that you could jeopardize your chances of an offer when you do name your concerns. On the other hand, you could whet the employer's appetite. Know that you take a gamble here.

10) Have I called the employer back to learn my status or to give my decision?

Within about three days of your interview, you are either owed a status report or owe one to the employer. Call and get things clarified. Why hang in limbo any longer? "Delay always breeds danger," wrote Cervantes in *Don Quixote*.

11) What will I do if I learn I lost out?

You'll go on to other opportunities. Yet, try to salvage something by learning why you failed. Store the knowledge in your mental computer and use it the next time.

12) If I learn my status is uncertain, what will I do?

Ask why. It's usually because another candidate has surfaced. Proceed as previously suggested for that situation. If something else, such as uncertainty about your ability to handle the job, try to reassure the employer with additional concrete evidence of your qualifications.

You have one final way to recover when a promising interview fades: Never count on just one job possibility.

19

Why You Need More
Than One Offer

"You grow up the day you have the first real laugh—at yourself," Ethel
Barrymore said.

Let's hope such a laugh comes when you get second job offer after all
your stewing that you'd be lucky to get just one. They come easier after
the first.

A 52-year-old New Yorker, out of work three years, returned to the job
market. Besides his age, diabetes and Meniere's syndrome (an ear malady that causes dizziness and impairs hearing) handicapped his search.
Although diet and insulin controlled the diabetes and medication kept
the other in check, it took three years and four lengthy hospital stays to
achieve medical stability.

In his search, he reported his medical history when asked. It usually involved explaining his three unemployed years. For more than 12 months,
he applied for job after job in his field, business reporting for print or
electronic media. Although the interviewers gave many reasons for not
hiring him, none cited either his age or his health. He suspected, however, that the two dealt him a double blow in his efforts.

Finally, a Wall Street reporting service offered him a part-time job. He
took it despite the fact that it provided no benefits and soon demanded up
to 60 hours a week. While he had lost his health, he had not lost his skills.
Although he negotiated an hourly deal and thus was paid for all his time,
he found he lacked the stamina to keep up such a pace. He began jobhunting again, holding on to his "part-time" position temporarily and now
concentrating only on the prospects that had shown even faint interest
before.

The fact that he had stuck with one reporting service for six months as-
suaged another employer's doubts about his health and the possibility of
obsolescent skills. The employer offered a 40-hours-a-week job and
promised that overtime would be rare.

To his surprise, when he announced he was leaving, the first employer wanted to take him on full time with all benefits and to top the second offer by $5,000 a year. He did not succumb to the temptation to stay because of considerations regarding ethics and his health.

The experience taught him that the second offer comes easier when you have the first.

One obvious reason to try for more than one job offer is in case the promising interview fades. As the New Yorker's experience shows, there are at least four better ones, as follow.

A. To Stimulate Other Offers

Your first offer can serve as Pied Piper. A powerfully effective statement is the casual comment somewhere in your first interview with a second prospect that you are already considering a job proposal. If you are free to name the prospective employer, do so. The New Yorker saw no reason not to. The specifics make your comment still more persuasive. Don't reveal them, though, if you have the slightest doubt about the propriety of doing so.

A first offer also helps encourage the interviewer at a second prospect to skip, or at least hurry through, those "delicate" probes that cover the fallacies about age.

An interviewer's realization that you are in demand also arouses competitive instincts in many. The earlier offer likewise encourages the second prospect to move faster in making a decision about you. In the New Yorker's case, the first employer made the new offer within minutes of learning his erstwhile part-timer had found another job. An earlier offer also stifles questions in the back of every potential employer's mind about your possible hidden liabilities. (If the other fellow's not concerned, he reasons, why should I be?) In the New Yorker's case, the first employer hadn't found any performance negatives in his six months on the job.

Strictly speaking, the New Yorker erred in accepting the full-time offer on the spot. In normal jobhunting circumstances, it's wise not to accept unilaterally the first offer for the reason that you want at least one more (preferably two or even three). However, the New Yorker's circumstances were not normal, and he is forgiven.

B. To Have a Choice

The second good reason for ferreting out another offer is to give yourself a choice. Seniors commonly grab the first proposal that surfaces.

How do you know it's the best you can find unless you have at least one more to which to compare it?

This may turn out to be more than a choice of the same kind of job. The second (or third) offer may lie in another field, allowing you to exercise a long-dormant skill.

The New Yorker soon had another surprise awaiting him. Not quite out of the blue came a proposal to handle business reporting on an all-news radio station in New York City. Months before, he had applied for the job, unsuccessfully at that time. In his twenties, he had been in radio, but had left it because of the erratic hours. In refusing the position, he learned that the station's personnel man had kept informal track of him and knew of his jobhunting adventures. Even New York can be like a village when a narrow expertise is involved.

You need choices on which to make an informed judgment. So, relax. When you have the skills, have done your research and worked hard at making contacts, you will get more than one offer from which to pick.

C. To Facilitate a Quick Turnaround

It's wise to have another offer when you discover something wrong about the first. This is not the same as learning the potential employer has cooled toward you. Here, you become cool toward the potential employer.

When you discover something amiss with the lone offer presented to you, you're tempted to take it anyhow, shutting your eyes to the possible negative. The New Yorker could have gone that route and taken the part-time offer if he didn't have the other proposal and if he didn't know the negative—excessive overtime—about the part-time job.

How do you discover something amiss? By painful experience, as in the New Yorker's case. By research. By telltale occurrences belatedly unearthed, such as high turnover. By information from friends. This is why you're wise to consult discreetly with them before you definitely accept any offer.

A reality of the jobhunting world is this: *Some employers will take advantage of you if they know, or even suspect, that you have just one offer currently active.* Therefore, search for the secnd (or third) proposal to forestall such tactics.

D. To Better Negotiate Employment Terms

When the potential employer knows another offer sits out there, he or she will be more likely to agree to a more generous job package. This goes beyond pay and benefits. It involves reporting arrangements, the physical details of your workplace, a reserved parking space, commitments about promotion.

The key here lies in knowing what you want in areas other than compensation. Often, you don't think about them until too late. Promotion and reporting provisions usually head the list, but you may have other priorities. Sort them out when you have at least one other offer to back you up and before you make the final commitment.

Compensation, of course, is an important part of the package, but it may not be the most vital for seniors. Some people over 50 would put the general job environment first. Yet, compensation would still be high even for them and rank at the top for most other seniors.

So important is it that you should review the basics of negotiating for pay and benefits in the next section.

Comprehensive Compensation

On the simplest level, compensation negotiations amount to little more than questioning what the job pays, what benefits come with it, and saying "yes" or "no." Even here, the second (or third) offer provides a valuable benchmark. Without it, you might think the proposal too low and refuse it, only to discover too late that nobody pays more.

Your second offer also is nearly an indispensible benchmark when you enter more detailed negotiations on compensation. Your best debating point is: "X proposes $2,400 more per year than you," or, "X offers virtually the same pay, but its benefits are more generous, particularly in profit-sharing."

In the course of the negotiations, the employer may suggest you go jump in the lake, more politely phrased as, "Take the other offer." When you use these tactics, always be prepared to go with the other employer. If you don't really want the other job, despite somewhat higher total compensation, hedge your statements to the preferred employer with something like this: "Although your policy of no layoffs attracts me, X's higher compensation also tempts me. X offered me _____ per year. Can you come closer to that?"

This is the time to get specific. At this point, you may want to show the other's written offer. Always try to persuade the employer to put his numbers on paper for you. Your best argument for him to do so: "You've been very professional in this negotiation. Let's continue on this basis. I've given you my employment background and my solutions to your problem in writing. I'd appreciate your outlining the job on paper, including the compensation that goes with it."

Note also that another offer prevents you from going *too low* in your salary expectations. Occasionally, this kills negotiations because the employer belatedly discovers that you rate yourself lower than he had. Avoid the bargain basement route in pay negotiations. It may get you the job, but it will also mire you in a hole for the rest of your term with that employer.

If you're creating your own job, you face special challenges. On the one hand, you will have an easier time naming your own figure for a unique position. On the other, neither you nor the employer have as much to compare it with. Make your demands reasonable! In general, you can expect to be paid more than the person below you on the organizational chart and less than the next individual above you. Imagine the persons immediately above and below you as your bookends. If you can pinpoint the numbers for your bookends on the chart, you know approximately what your salary should be. For instance, if the one below you makes $30,000 and the one above you $36,000, your range would be $31,000 to $35,000.

Naturally, you want the highest point possible in the range, the employer the lowest. Split the difference? Perhaps, but other compromises exist—more benefits and a lower salary, or fewer benefits and a higher salary.

Here's another pay guideline that may help, especially if you're after a top job: Superior managers earn more than twice their age, multiplied by $1,000, says a survey by New York-based Johnson, Smith & Knisely Inc., executive recruiter. The survey says exceptional managers age 50 earn $212,000.

Challenger, Gray & Christmas Inc. confirms those findings and predicts that by 1990 top people age 50 and older will at least double the formula.

Your negotiations should also cover future raises and/or promotions. Over the past century, inflation has occurred in 75 percent of the years. Even if you plan to work only 12 more years, chances are inflation will take place in nine of them. You need protection against that erosion, and you shouldn't neglect promotion, despite the fact that seniors sometimes do. If you give your boss that impression, he or she may also conclude you care less about the job than you really do.

Benefits are part of compensation, 30 percent or more on average. Bargain here, too, getting the equivalent in another benefit or in more salary if you forego a benefit, such as a pension.

Before you get the second compensation offer, you need the first. How do you know what to ask for?

You can learn generally what a nonsupervisory job pays in the latest monthly issue of the U.S. Department of Labor's *Employment and Earnings*. Also, *The Occupational Outlook Handbook* will give you ball park figures for selected jobs, some of them in supervision and management.

Yet, the operative word is "generally." Regional differences occur. Usually, the north-central area of the United States pays most, closely followed by the northeast, west and south. In the northeast, employers there were paying the most to lower-level jobs in 1986 because of its exceptionally tight labor market.

Industry differences also range widely. Consult such publications as *National Business Employment Weekly* or *Career Opportunities News* and others in your library.

Next, go beyond publications by probing among employees of the organization, their friends and associates. If you draw a blank, try to learn salary information about competitors. If you don't research, you may be off a mile in your negotiations and thus a mile away from success in your job interviews.

Some cautionary notes that relate mostly to pay:

● Never ask for frosting when the cake is already baked. Although this largely involves compensation, it also involves late requests for working hours other than the organization's customary times, special-order equipment such as an amber screen for your word processor instead of the usual green, or a reserved parking place.

● Never intimate you have independent means or that salary is not important. Employers want hungry people.

● Never reveal the state of your personal finances, good or bad.

● Try not to get trapped in a salary lower than you earned in your last job. It's bad psychologically if you are. While you may be so relieved at first to find a job, *any* job, that soon pales and a corrosion sets in as you can't help continually comparing your present pay with your former higher compensation.

● Never let the seniors' "fat cat" image go unchallenged. Seniors are *not* the wealthiest group in America as is sometimes claimed. Their economic status is far more varied than that of any other age group. While some seniors have substantial resources, a surprising number do not. Anyhow, what does an age group's image, correct or incorrect, have to do with you? You are an individual, not a group.

Rebutting the Pay Arguments

Seniors commonly encounter employers' arguments against higher pay that younger people seldom face. Here are typical employer statements, with their rebuttals:

Employer: "Because you already have a pension, you don't need as high a salary as we might otherwise be willing to pay."

Your rebuttal: "My pension is paid by my former employer and has nothing to do with you. I want the salary normally paid for this position."

Employer: "You don't need a pension because you're already getting it from your former employer."

Your rebuttal: "Okay, but I want something in its place. How about a better rate on profit-sharing?"

Employer: "Because you'll be working only half-time, we'll put you on half-salary."

Your rebuttal: "I'll take the equivalent in an hourly rate." (You want this because most "half-time" jobs come to involve much more than half-time.)

Employer: "Because of your age, we can't promise any increases or promotions."

Your rebuttal: "My age has nothing to do with my getting this job. I want to be treated exactly like any other employee, including pay increases and promotions."

Employer: "Your salary will be _____ ."

Your rebuttal: "That's below what you pay for others on comparable jobs and what your competitors pay."

Employer: "You don't need a salary as high as others because your kids are educated and your house is paid for."

Your rebuttal: "That's irrelevant. I want what this job pays."

Employer: "We can't give you a salary as high as others because older people have lower productivity."

Your rebuttal: "I cannot accept that argument. My productivity will probably be higher than that of your younger employees." Never let the "low productivity" image go unchallenged. Your work performance improves as you age, according to the results of the largest U.S. research project ever done on aging and productivity. Researchers David A. Waldman and Bruce Avolio of the State University of New York at Binghamton, NY, analyzed the findings of 13 employment studies done from 1940 to 1983. Their study found that as you get older, your productivity increases moderately but steadily. The study also found that professional and blue-collar employees improve almost the same amount in terms of productivity, but the former group scores higher with the boss and peers.

A possible reason: Professionals may have more stimulating jobs and are more likely to be allowed to take on new roles as they grow older. "Too many people place a lot of importance on how aging affects performance, believing older people can't do jobs as well. Our evidence proves that's not the case," says Waldman.

Premature Pay Proposal: Phenomenon and Problem

We have touched on the phenomenon of the premature pay proposal. Now, we caution you not to use the second bid to force a premature pay bid from other prospects. The temptation to do so apparently often proves overwhelming. The trouble with prematurity is that it generates a proposal lower than otherwise in two cases out of three.

Why? We used the term, "bid," advisedly. When you prematurely throw in the dollars offered by an earlier prospect, you turn the interview into a kind of auction. Employers react in several ways, most of them bad.

They may resent getting pushed into talking money before they're ready. They don't yet know you well enough to make a valid pay judgment, and so stay low to play it safe. They decide you're overly concerned about money, and so name a figure so low they know it will jet you out of their office.

What's the right time for you to bring up the subject? Never. It's the employer's role to bring it up. Let him play his part. You may make him unhappy if you step on his lines. Occasionally, he may go dry because of incompetence, inexperience or insanity. Then, you can legitimately take the lead, but only if you have decided you want the job and guestimate that he wants you. This should rarely happen until at least the second interview, sometimes even later.

The Risks in Compensation Negotiations

Be aware that you gamble when you use a second offer to generate a better deal with another on pay and benefits. The ploy irritates some employers, perhaps to the extent that you ruin your chances. Also, when you negotiate on this basis, you stall your decision with another, perhaps fatally.

There's no advice an outsider can give you on these delicate maneuvers, except to be very, very careful. Accept the sensible risk, reject the stupid one, and know the difference.

The Second Offer in Self-employment

Are there second offers in self-employment, too?

Yes.

Here, the second offer involves choosing between two or more small-business opportunities. For example:

- Know yourself and stick with what you know. It will help you focus your search and weed out the also-rans.

- Pick something you like. You want to spend the rest of your life doing it. You want to enjoy it.

- Know that small manufacturing firms historically do better than small service outfits. Cash is more available to handle debts, and there may be undervalued assets lurking.

- Also know that new service firms outnumber new manufacturers, largely because less capitalization is needed.

- Get sufficient capitalization. Most new ventures fail because of undercapitalization.

- Know how and where you will recruit your personnel. An inadequate staff is the second most common reason for new or small-business failures.

- Look for stability. A sales roller coaster throws many small businesses off track.

- Find the failures. They usually can tell you more about the business than the successes.

- Develop a good business plan and stay with it. It's your road map to success.

If you are considering self-employment, you can't avoid investigating franchising, but look at more than one opportunity. Virtually every line of consumer business uses franchising in some form or another, especially since 1955 when McDonald's Corporation began its successes with its restaurants. Franchising has been around since 1851 when I.M. Singer & Company used the technique to set up a chain of sewing machine dealers. At the turn of the century, fledgling automakers and soft drink bottlers—notably General Motors Corporation and Coca-Cola Company—used franchising to build national distributorships.

According to Commerce Department statistics, one-third of all retail sales currently generated annually in the U.S. are through franchises. Franchise operations sold about $576 billion in goods and services and employed 5.7 million by the end of 1986.

Franchising helps companies expand quickly mainly because the franchise operator or franchisee puts up the bulk of the capital necessary to open an outlet. In return, the franchiser usually provides training, business techniques, trade secrets, promotional aids, a recognized name and a defined trade territory.

However, there are drawbacks. Although failures amounted to less than 4 percent of the more than 450,000 U.S. franchises in 1985, failure is still traumatic. Franchises also cost money—up to $360,000 to set up a McDonald's restaurant, excluding real estate costs. Other franchises can cost up to $750,000. While many small businesses thrive by following a franchise handbook and clear-cut company policies, others feel unduly constrained once the business is up and running. Finally, franchisers don't look kindly on franchisees who withhold fees or otherwise won't conform with the original agreement. To put it bluntly, litigation flourishes in the franchising business.

A Footnote on the Second Offer

Why not consider a radically different kind of second offer—installment retirement vs. a new job? Under this, you take a slice of retirement now of one year or so, instead of a new job at this time. Later, you go back to work again.

For this to work from a psychological standpoint, you need a job proposal to weigh against the alternative of piecemeal retirement. If you voluntarily leave the work force temporarily, you can:

● Take off when you still have good health.

● Pursue or investigate hobbies that might turn into a new career later.

● Try mountaineering, or whatever, which you have dreamed of attempting all your life.

● Recharge your batteries.

● Help an offspring or other relative get established with a new business.

● Please your spouse.

Of course, this route poses drawbacks. For instance, you may also:

● Not be able to afford not to work. Rebuttal: There isn't a good one unless you are willing to take a drastically lower standard of living. A speechwriter with General Electric made such a sacrifice. When last heard from, he lived in a shack in Maine.

• Not be able to find any job after a long period out of the market. Rebuttal: Many people have successfully reentered the market after being out of it for years, such as the New Yorker who found work after three years out of the labor force. John Fanning, president of Uniforce Temporary Services, Hyde Park, NY, contends that 11 million new jobs were created from 1982 through 1984 with only 4.5 million workers entering the job market. The minimum wage, he says, is "nearly obsolete." His firm surveyed 485 U.S. companies and found that 70 percent paid above minimum for entry levels.

• Not be able to find a job you like when you finish your retirement installment. Rebuttal: Reread this book.

• Lose your health before or soon after you decide to return to work. Rebuttal: People are living and working longer. Working at age 75 is growing more common. If you chose an installment on your retirement at age 55, you'll still have a long work span ahead even if you took a year or longer off.

• Displease your spouse. The GE man's wife divorced him over the issue. Rebuttal: We can offer none because this matter is so personal.

Try for good humor, even insouciance, in your search for a new career. If you project an image of desperation, you're more likely to win rejection than sympathy. That second offer does wonders, too, in dispelling desperation. Then, you will be more apt to agree with Elbert Hubbard who said, "Do not take life too seriously. You will never get out of it alive."

PART III

When You Get the Job

After you win the new job, you'll want to keep it. Or will you? A psychological phenomenon sometimes occurs with seniors soon after they begin. The new work is an anticlimax at best or a grave disappointment at worst. The last section suggests how to cope with these all-too-familiar reactions.

20

Why You Feel So Strange

Once you start the new job, you may feel like the person who lifts a box thought to weigh 25 pounds to find it weighs 50.

You can still handle it, but it's not as expected. You've worked as hard as you ever have in your life to land this position. Won't they let you relax a little?

No, because your employer has a problem. You sold yourself on the basis of solving that problem. Remember? If you're self-employed, you may have to work still harder to get your business on its feet now that you've completed the arduous analysis of what business you wish to enter.

The Dangers of Change

The typical immediate reaction to a new job is euphoria. Malaise often soon replaces this short-lived feeling, especially in management and administrative jobs where 12 percent of today's workers labor. Two out of four seniors who win new positions in these types of work leave the job within three years. Seniors leave new positions in other new situations, too, but the turnover is not so high.

Tragically, failure may result from an inability to recognize danger spots, perhaps the same shortcoming that lost the senior a job in the one before this position. Here are a few things to watch out for in the new job:

1) Undelivered promises on your side or the employer's. You may not solve that problem as well or as quickly as you or the hirer hoped. When you sell yourself as a problem-solver, don't promise the moon! Even so, employers tend to justify their hiring of seniors both to themselves and peers on the ground that they uncovered a genius. If it turns out you are not, prepare for a big letdown. The employer may also promise pay increases, promotions or added responsibilities that never materialize.

229

2) Failure to fit the job specifications. Neither you nor the hirer researched properly. You can recover by recasting the specifications better to fit you and what you want to accomplish, but you face difficulties if you have a rigid boss. Ideally, no one should be shoehorned into a job description; the opposite ought to occur. Yet, reality dictates that the former happens more often than necessary.

3) Mergers. In these days of corporate amalgamations, this risk never fades. Displacements inevitably result from mergers because there's never room for two vice-presidents of human resources. When Wells Fargo & Company acquired Crocker National Corporation on May 31, 1986, it immediately fired 1,650 Crocker people with the announcement that a total of 5,000 would be gone by 1988. Some 70 percent of Crocker's senior people were scheduled to depart.

4) Business failure. Middle managers are often the last to know and the first to go, particularly the most recently arrived seniors.

5) Scandal or even mild impropriety. Word about expense account cheats and the like travel fast—right to the boss.

6) The "rats" in most offices. Some present employees may look upon you as competition and try to undermine you with malicious gossip and even outright lies about your performance or alleged nonperformance.

7) Imbalance. Your sense of insecurity may persist. Things are different, and you find it hard to adjust. You may confuse this with job dissatisfaction, when imbalance resulting from change is what bothers you most.

So important is this that you should review the next section to learn how to cope with it.

The Psychology of Change

When the Burlington Northern Railroad was formed by merger in 1970, the Brotherhood of Railway Clerks obtained a job protection agreement. Under the pact, workers in the Chicago regional office were offered transfers to and new work in the line's St. Paul, Minnesota headquarters.

However, 41 clerical workers refused to go. In their case, the agreement specified that they nonetheless could not be fired but had to be kept on at full pay, even though there was no work for them to do. The railroad tried to be understanding and sent some of the nonworking workers home at full pay, but other employees protested, so the railroad had to require all 41 to put in a full, do-nothing day.

Did that make everyone happy? Not at all. Dissatisfaction remained among many of the 41. "Who wants to do nothing all day?" complained one woman in the group. "It's definitely more tiring sitting all day than being useful. You'd think *something* could be found for us."

Aside from the irony of the circumstance, the psychological implications are rife. In work-change situations, four considerations rule us whether we're a file clerk or a president:

1) We need a sense of the familiar.
2) We need order.
3) We fear risk.
4) We need to conform.

Let's examine each in detail.

1) The Need for the Familiar

Your new job naturally throws you into a new environment with new methods and new people. To cope better, look for methods that are the same as or similar to what you were accustomed to formerly.

In things that are different, concentrate on *aspects* of familiarity. For example, all the people you work with are new to you; yet, doesn't each have characteristics that remind you of former colleagues? Keep those similarities in mind.

You may even have the opportunity to change part of your environment to resemble what you are more accustomed to. Do this with caution, however; others may resent change as much as you. Although you proceed carefully, do so as quickly as possible. As a new senior, your license to change your new environment fades with your time on the job. Just six months into your new job, you can get away with actions that may not be possible a year later.

The railroad clerks thought they were hanging onto the familiar. Instead, they found themselves in a profoundly unfamiliar environment— doing nothing. Hence, their malaise.

2) The Need for Order

Every new job involves disorder, at least temporarily. So, set a date for yourself when you will have your new job in order. This is private. Don't publicize it because you may not make your deadline. Your objective is to achieve order at least in the part of your environment you control directly, your job.

If you don't meet your date, set another one, but make it more realistic this time.

You can also "exercise" to put yourself in better shape to cope with disorder. First, try new kinds of order; vary your morning routines, for example. Second, try disorder occasionally; skip morning routines altogether for a while. Third, be aware of your tendency toward excessive order. Fourth, think positively. This helps at any time, but it's especially useful in overcoming excessive order and in keeping from relying too much on the familiar. Don't try this suggestion with muscles clenched and mind set in determination to get out of your rut. Instead, simply be conscious that you do not wish to become stifled by excessive order or a need for the familiar. The involuntary muscles of your body and the cells of your brain will help you get out of the rut—and without herculean effort of mind or body.

The do-nothing railroad clerks certainly had order—so much that it bored them to distraction. Let their experience teach you that you can demand too much order. Hang loose, at least a little.

3) The Fear of Risk

Risk is inevitable with every new job. Authorities attest to the importance of risk. Professor Silvan Tomkins of Princeton University believes that "creativity without willingness to gamble is highly improbable." As the manager of your own job destiny, remind yourself of the rewards of risk-taking—new experiences, a new life, perhaps greater creativity.

Another aspect of risk concerns the kinds of chances you choose to take—defensive or offensive. Stated another way, you can decide to maximize your gains or minimize your losses.

Take an objective look at your new job. Did you take it as a defensive or offensive move, or a mixture of the two, with the balance on the defensive or offensive side? For example, if your new job is almost the same as your old, you went defensive to minimize your losses. If it's markedly different, you went offensive to maximize your gains. Either course may be right for you. The important point is to recognize the kind of chances you take and to live with that decision.

Trouble surfaces if you thought you took an offensive risk, but discovered it was largely defensive, and vice versa. Betty bought a restaurant franchise, thinking she took the offensive after years of working as a dining room manager for others. She soon found herself in the same predicament as before—but fighting with the franchiser instead of the restaurant owner, driven nearly mad by negligent or temperamental employees in both situations, worrying over profits as a franchisee and over budgets as a manager, and straining all her creative resources in both circumstances to attract diners. She failed as a franchisee, largely because she misunderstood the kind of risks she took.

Charlie knew he was taking a defensive risk, with a dash of the offensive, when he connected as a salesman for a small chemical company in Cleveland, Ohio by buying a minority interest in it. He had been a chemical salesman all his life, but his last employer retired him early, thinking to cut costs. Within three months, he grew so frustrated that he seriously considered selling out, but the majority owner wouldn't buy his share for a price he considered fair. The firm's only other salesman, the son of the owner, was an alcoholic who lost more customers than he found. The production foreman was a thief. Charlie's wife persuaded him not to quit but to negotiate further with the majority owner to buy the entire company, partly with an inheritance she had received and partly with money raised by mortgaging their house. Although it took Charlie nearly three months to negotiate a satisfactory price and an additional three years to turn the company around, this became the happiest and most productive period of his life. Magically, a defensive risk turned into an offensive one. He originally bought a minority piece of the business to guarantee himself a job. Yet, he stuck with it, just as he did with his jobhunt, and knew the chance he was taking.

The railway clerks also took a defensive risk. Most of them paid for it in a boredom that sapped their spirits and drained them of initiative.

Comfort with new technologies is an area in which older employers receive their lowest rating from human resource decision-makers, according to the Yankelovich, Skelly and White survey for AARP. Before we jump to any conclusions about this finding, consider this: The history of technological introductions, including office automation, has hardly been one of unbroken successes. In fact, many such "panaceas" have proved disappointing. Thus, the perceived lack of comfort with technology on the part of the 50-plus employee may be partially rooted in a healthy skepticism based on previous experiences.

Management might be best advised to bring seniors on board in situations of technological change as a defense in minimizing risk, so as to use their experience to anticipate potential trouble spots.

4) The Compulsion To Conform

Most of us don't think we're conformists. The following list of symptoms will help you decide one way or the other:

- You make decisions largely on the basis of the opinions of others.
- You base your feelings of self-respect and self-worth largely on what others think of you.
- You do routine things—dressing, eating and so on—in the same way and the same order every day.
- You believe that to fit in and belong to a group you must imitate the members and conform to their mindsets.
- You prefer passive observation to participation.

If an objective appraisal is agreement with three or more of the five foregoing statements, you are a conformist. If you never realized or didn't fully understand that before, you now have a clue about why you're unhappy on the new job. Conformity inhibits you.

One type of conformist is the consensus conformist who rationalizes his conformity as a democratic step, never fighting outwardly the wisdom or power of the people who he thinks compel him to conform. They may not actually wish him to conform, but he does it anyhow out of habit or character.

A second type, the expedient conformist, believes he has the right answer but goes along with the group even when he thinks it's wrong because he "doesn't want to rock the boat."

A third type, the passive conformist, lacks self-confidence and accepts group opinion.

Tragically, all conformists, no matter what their type, sense what they are doing and dislike themselves for doing it. Recognize that conformity is an endemic disease of our time. Always be on guard against it. Do something out of character once in a while.

On the other hand, also recognize that all conformity is not bad. The new employer's methods may have much to recommend them. Analyze what's good and accept it, and try to discard what's bad. How? Carefully and tactfully. We all need approval. Your ability to recognize symptoms that indicate an excessive need for acceptance constitutes the best means of avoiding the pitfalls of a tendency toward too much conformity.

The Mind and Change

Let's look at the human mind and try to understand what goes on there during a profound change, such as a move to a new job. A better understanding may help us adjust more successfully to the demands of a different position.

The human mind is not tangible. It's a function, not an entity. It's analogous to the speed of a car. The mind is the function of learning. It's a combination of reason, wile, reflection, intelligence, intellect, perceptual and conceptual thinking, association of ideas, foresight, curiosity, purposefulness, self-control, conscience, sense of humor, creativity and appreciation.

The physical evolution of our species has stood at an approximate standstill for 500,000 years, but not the mind's evolution. We have the written story of humankind—history—for only 7,000 years, about 1 percent of the human story. That 1 percent indicates the extent of the evolution of the mind. In other words, most of the mind's evolution has taken place in only 1 percent of our species' existence. In that period has come most of the change in humankind's condition, driven largely by its mind.

"The human brain is capable of seemingly unlimited expansion," writes John Roddam, "and . . . if expansion takes place in a direction which offers opportunities of yet further development, then mental evolution is quickened."

As one or a few minds make new discoveries and initiate changes, other quick minds accept the changes, and eventually most minds climb to a new plateau. Guttenberg's invention of movable type for printing was such a change, Einstein's theory of relativity another, and the development of the computer still another.

All these changes increased the tempo of mental evolution on a breathtaking scale. Most changes may not have such scope, but they can quicken the psychological pace to a degree commensurate with their scale. That's why a change in jobs can so stimulate a person.

With no or little change, a race, a nation, a company, or a person will atrophy. Australian aborigines, Mandarin China, numerous American companies, and countless individuals have suffered that (psychological) fate. A senior may legitimately dislike his new job, but he had better not dislike it simply because it's a change.

We can draw the following conclusions about the individual's psychological reaction to change:

1) The prospect of change upsets most people until they know it doesn't threaten their status or well-being.

2) Positive change stimulates most people.

3) A lack of change dulls most people.

4) A lack of change enrages some people, to the extent of revolt.

5) Change tends to have a Pied Piper effect; other changes follow good changes, explaining the actions of people who retire early and often, who go from one new business to another, or who seek new jobs for the sake of the new experience.

6) It is more comfortable to prepare for and accept change, such as a new job, than to wait until it is forced upon us.

7) Man has the intelligence to cope with change, such as new work. Animals have to await, unconsciously, their adaptation to their changed environment in the course of an evolution spread over numberless generations.

8) Man can adapt to change, such as new work, through continuous learning and patience.

9) Change, as in a new job, does not necessarily make the values of the old job obsolete, just its values pertaining to you.

10) The long-term effects of a change in your job are invariably more important for you than in the short term, but you are not likely to consider the future in appraising the effects of a job change. Try looking harder at the long-term results.

The Metric Analogy

Seniors who have trouble with a new job may be compared with people who have trouble with the metric system. Both the new position and metric measurement are unfamiliar. Both seem difficult to understand, at least at first. The necessity of both comes under question.

Yet, we can't return to the old comfortable ways because:

● The old job is gone to us forever. The metric system has rapidly supplanted others throughout the world. Even England no longer officially uses the English system of measurement.

● The new job can open new vistas for us. The metric system can open new vistas for us in science and technology.

● The new job can provide greater financial ease and convenience for us, if we let it. The metric system is easier and more convenient as a measurement method, if we just learn it.

It's disquieting to discover that only two nations in the world have not wholeheartedly adopted the metric system—the United States and Uganda.

So, Courage

"I think we are in constant danger . . . from losing our nerve," says Dr. Herbert A. Simon, Nobel Laureate and professor of computer science and psychology at Carnegie-Mellon University's Graduate School of Industrial Administration. He explains, "When Columbus came to this continent, he could come in hope of fulfilling his own goals—and in ignorance of the plague and syphilis that he was bringing the Indians. We don't have that ignorance anymore. We know a lot about the germs we are bringing with us, and we tend to become overawed by the responsibility for these waves of consequences of any action we take."

Despite the negatives of plague and syphilis, can anyone question that Columbus should have forsaken his voyages of discovery? Of course not, if only because he could not. Similarly, you can find renewed courage for the adventure of your new job when you:

● Analyze the extent to which your new job is producing changes within your purview.

● Recognize that you make most of the decisions about your job.

● Realize that your new position is no threat; it's the way you handle or mishandle it that poses the threat. You can keep your courage up by reminding yourself often that the risks of your new job may pay off handsomely. Charlie sold his chemical company for triple what he paid for it when he became 72.

● Avoid endless post-mortems on your decision to take a new job because they waste your time and psychological energy.

● Resist magnifying your problems with the job; you may be doing little more than trying to magnify your own importance.

● Don't let your possible failure with the job become a self-fulfilling prophecy; it's so easy to do!

● Keep abreast of the current events happening to your employer that don't directly affect you or your job now, but may in the future.

● Learn the job's role within the framework of your employer's activities; learn its history; contemplate its future; thus develop an intuition about it.

● Give your intuition full play by increasing your experience with the job; intuition and experience then become partners working toward simplifying, expanding and otherwise remolding your position, thus leading to greater comfort with it.

● Be realistic about your work, but idealistic if possible, too. Keep reminding yourself of its helping, healing, informing, or comforting characteristics, for example.

A miraculous thing happens with courage. The more you use it, the stronger it gets. As Shakespeare commented in *King John,* "For courage mounteth with occasion."

21

When You Must Go Through It Again

First, a Chicago retailer had a vice-president of personnel, then a vice-president of human resources. Now, Carson Pirie Scott & Company has a vice-president of customer satisfaction through people involvement.

Okay, we'll even accept the retailer's claim that the job titles describe differently focused positions. We'll acknowledge that a department store is peculiarly dependent upon customer satisfaction through people involvement. Yet, we hope the monicker doesn't catch on. Imagine the displaced holder of such a title giving it with a straight face in a job interview.

Lorin Maazel, 57, was offered a million-dollar annual contract as "music director" of the Pittsburgh Symphony. The deal almost fell through, not because of disagreement over money, but over his title. Maazel wanted to be named "principal conductor."

Who knows what motives prompt someone to refuse a job or fire an employee? Louis XIV is said to have recalled an ambassador because he discovered him to be less than graceful as a dancer.

Keep On Smiling

We're not trying to make light of someone's dilemma or even the tragedy in still another job change. If we don't smile, we might cry. The sad truth is that one-fifth of all seniors who take new jobs pick the wrong ones. Within a year, they have to start jobhunting again.

If you are in this boat and have already read this book, then read it again. Analyze your talents. Decide what you want to do and where you want to do it. Research for the career opportunities that match your abilities. Hunt for problems you can solve either for others or yourself. Investigate that opportunity more thoroughly this time than last. Above all, find at least two opportunities so you can comparison shop.

You're sadder but wiser now. Use that wisdom to play up your maturity, experience and contacts. By now, you have unmistakable evidence that the right new job won't materialize overnight. Take a year if you have to (and can afford to) before you accept your next position.

What caused your latest job loss? If you aren't sure, ask your employer. The reasons for discharge often remain ambiguous, at least to the severance sufferer. Your erstwhile boss should level with you when you emphasize the importance of the answer, and you *must* know to minimize the chances of a repetition next time. If you were self-employed and your venture turned sour, analyze why. If you quit, wait a while to ask yourself if you were justified.

"History repeats itself because nobody listens," says Laurence J. Peters. This time, listen!

Take a More Radical Turn

You may conclude from more careful listening this time that you have taken the wrong kind of jobs—you don't belong in management but rather in a "doing" job, or vice versa; you should work for yourself rather than for others, or vice versa; you should work for a small company rather than a large one or vice versa.

You may conclude from more careful listening that you should take advantage of a long neglected skill or turn a hobby into a business or learn something completely new.

Perhaps you took that radical turn in the work that just ended. Maybe you should return to what you formerly did. The sea change resulting from your most recent voyage may better accommodate you to the more familiar shore.

Where else can you look or what should you avoid? Here are suggestions:

- Stay clear of those fields where your sex has the most difficult time competing. *Working Women* advises females to stay clear of insurance, investment banking and architecture as bad careers for women because they are male-dominated. Women make up only 11 percent of all architect professionals; of these, just 27 percent are in upper management. The insurance industry is a slightly better bet; about 30 percent of its officers and managers are women. While women can earn more in investment banking than other industries, only seven of 600 partners and managing directors are women, the magazine reports. On the other hand, men face strong competition from women in selling residential real estate, in the editing and publishing fields, and from Marion the Librarian.

• Study anew your activities in trying to help others. Alexander Graham Bell's wife was deaf. In seeking to ease her disability, he tried to invent a hearing aid. He didn't develop a practical device, but he did invent "the talking wire" that became the telephone.

• Reexamine your subsidiary activities. Clarence B. Randall was an excellent executive of Inland Steel Company for many years. As a sideline, he began writing and exclaimed, "Creating a book is like an adventure into the unknown!" In *A Creed for Free Enterprise*, he revealed a hitherto unexpected visionary side in such passages as: "This is a magnificent time in which to live . . . Vast ideas are on the march . . . We must hold aloft the symbol of our faith that the driving power and infinite ingenuity of private initiative makes people more happy than planning by the cloistered few."

• Learn from your dreams, especially from repeated dreams. F.A. von Kekule, who predicted the molecular structure of organic compounds as the result of repeated "visions," advises, "Let us learn to dream, gentlemen."

• Gain new insight from your experiences. World War II gave Winston Churchill new insights into himself, as he admitted in historical writings that won him a Nobel Prize. Noah Webster compiled his dictionaries because his experiences told him during the early days of this republic that the fragile United States needed some unifying force. It had no king, no national religion, no standing army to hold it together, but it did have a common language. Hence, his series of dictionaries to make sure that English survived as the language of America. (German, Dutch, French and Spanish threatened that supremacy in some areas.)

• Stay flexible. Robert Fulton, inaccurately credited as the inventor of the steamboat, actually developed it from the designs of others. He gave up a career as an itinerant artist for invention when he realized he lacked outstanding artistic ability. He discovered he had a greater challenge in selling the inventions than in developing them. So, he became a superb salesman and perhaps the first and most successful public relations man in America by selling the safety of the steamboat. (Its soldered boiler tended to blow up.)

Flexibility includes the ability to keep up with our society's increasing transience. Seniors, particularly, may have difficulty here to their detriment in the job market. Inflexibility poses even more serious challenges than discomfort on a new job. It can lead to severance.

Dealing with Transience

For a society that has seen the silk stocking virtually disappear, the propeller-driven aircraft become almost as rare as the steam locomotive, and the personal computer threatening to grow as ubiquitous as the typewriter, we should be used to transience. Still, it's a shock— or "future shock" as Alvin Toffler phrased it for a book that has itself suffered from transience even though it was published as recently as 1970. It seems like yesterday, right?

Other examples of the new transience in our society:

- Some 7,000 new products found their way onto supermarket shelves in 1966, but most don't exist today.
- Paved streets and roads have been built in the United States at a rate of 200 miles a day every day for the last 35 years.
- Some 36.6 million Americans move their homes each year. This is as though the combined populations of Turkey and Lebanon moved within a year.
- In 70 major American cities, including New York, the average residence in one place is just four years.

This transience finds expression in rapidly changing clothing styles, even for men. The phenomenon of fads—skateboards, super balls, etc., etc.—is symbolic of transience. Temporary buildings, the trend toward renting cars and many other items, temporary help agencies—all indicate transience and change. A recent survey of 1,000 business executives revealed that one-third of them occupied jobs that hadn't existed before.

The job turnover rate today is particularly high among engineers and scientists because this is where great changes are taking place. The "half-life" of an engineer may be about 10 years—that is, about half of what he or she learned in school will be obsolete within a decade.

The British prime ministership has changed hands 13 percent faster since 1922 than between 1721 and 1922. Celebrities seem to pass through more quickly, also. Whatever happened to Twiggy, Jackie Kennedy, Spiro Agnew, Billy Carter? Evidence is persuasive that even today's symphony orchestras play the music of Mozart and other classical composers at a faster tempo than in former times. Of the 450,000 "usable" words in English today, Shakespeare would be able to understand only about 250,000, estimates Stuart Berg Flexner, senior editor of the *Random House Dictionary of the English Language*. He believes most of the language turnover has occurred in the last half-century.

The late Charles de Gaulle stated, "The world is undergoing a transformation to which no change that has yet occurred can be compared either in scope or in rapidity."

The late Dr. Robert Oppenheimer, when he was director of Princeton's Institute for Advanced Study, expressed the break with former eras this way: "This world of ours is a new world, in which the unity of knowledge, the nature of human communities, the order of society, the order of ideas, the very notions of society and culture have changed, and will not return to what they have been in the past. What is new is not new because it has never been there before, but because it has changed in quality. One thing that is new is the prevalence of newness, the changing scale and scope of change itself, so that the world alters as we walk in it, so that the years of man's life measure not some small growth or rearrangement or moderation of what he learned in childhood, but a great upheaval."

How Are You Handling Change?

As a senior who faces jobhunting again, a reasonable conclusion is that you haven't dealt with change too successfully. You may challenge such a judgment. If you do, ask yourself how you cope with change.

Most of us don't do anything about it. We "sleep" through it—and thus lose many jobs. The sleepers "manage" change by trying to ignore it, by refusing to acknowledge it, or by actually not realizing the scope and speed of it. The most common sleeper protests that things really aren't changing as much as they seem. "There's always been and always will be a generation gap," they often say, for example. Of course there has, but the nature of today's gap is unique because today's youth feel in their bones, as some of today's seniors do not, the nature of the changes now occurring.

A second common reaction to change is, "It's inevitable." Inevitablists tend to the liassez faire school. Nothing can be done; it's God's will. They might agree with the little old lady who refused to fly in a Boeing 747. "If God wanted me to fly in *that*," she said, "He wouldn't have provided the 707." Inevitablists tend to look on attempts to control change as unwarranted incursions into personal freedom. Like the sleepers, they do little or nothing about change.

A third common approach is hand-wringing. Isn't all this change awful? What's the world coming to? Hand-wringers tend to favor strategies that attempt to stop or slow the clock. Many want tighter government controls. They want higher tariffs or higher taxes, all in the name of protecting the status quo, although they wouldn't call it that. They term it protecting jobs in the steel industry or helping the poor, despite the fact that steel import quotas have not curbed imports and higher welfare outlays have not reduced the number of the poor. They fail to see that fundamental changes probably can't be stopped for long.

We espouse the fourth approach—to try to control change within the limits of our purview and jurisdiction. We call it the let's-do-it approach. We accept change as inevitable, just as the inevitablists do, but we differ in that we believe something can be done to cope and control this increasingly important aspect of twentieth century life.

We let's-do-it people favor a pragmatic approach to change. We say, let's try to predict what is most likely to occur in our job in the immediate future. We appraise what effect(s) it will have on our own operation. We decide what result is most desirable. Finally, we try to devise ways and means of maximizing the chances that the most desirable alternative will indeed come about.

Now, how does managing change work in real life?

Case Study: Sam, Age 62

Sam finally won a job as weekend disk jockey with a radio station on Long Island in New York. It was far smaller than any operation he had been accustomed to in the Big Apple, but it was a start back up from the depths into which alcoholism had driven him.

He worked alone, operating as his own engineer in the station's small concrete-block building which housed semiautomated broadcasting equipment, but no men's room. Management had "thoughtfully" arranged with a gas station across the street to share its facilities when necessary.

For Sam, the gas station was necessary. Although he rationed himself to only one 12-ounce can of beer every 30 minutes, his need for relief grew acute after four hours. One night, he set his equipment to run for 12 minutes without his supervision and dashed across the street, He returned in eight, to discover himself locked out. He had left his key to the building in his jacket hanging inside.

The gas station attendant had no key to the station. In a panic, Sam would have called the station owner, but neither he nor the attendant had the owner's phone number. In desperation, Sam called the police emergency number. A squad car arrived 10 minutes after the owner, who had been alerted by the strange sounds emitting from his radio at home.

Sam had not really overcome his alcoholism and lost still another job.

Case Study: Olive, Age 55

Olive returned to the workforce after 15 years when her children no longer needed close supervision. She took a six-week course in word processing at the local community college, and so answered "yes" in good conscience on the job application form that she was competent in that skill. Word processing was almost unheard-of when she last worked as a secretary.

However, she had learned her word processing on an IBM PC at the college. Her new employer had a Digital Equipment Corporation system. She quit rather than endure the embarrassment and burden of learning a new system.

Olive had not really prepared for technological change. Neither she nor Sam had truly analyzed their circumstances, weighed alternatives, or predicted how they should make change help them to a new future.

Case Study: Al, Age 59

Al lasted just five months as an expediter with Volkswagen in western Pennsylvania. The stress drove him to distraction. His wife and doctor urged him to quit before he suffered a heart attack. As an expediter with a specialty steel producer, which went out of business, he thought he knew all about stress. That was nothing compared to what he experienced with the auto company.

Even in his economically depressed area, he found another job within 10 months, in inventory control with a Pittsburgh printer. He learned of the opening through his contacts, and checked it out through friends and business associates. He particularly checked out the stress factor, largely during his interviews with principals when he estimated the working environment in which he would find himself. Fortunately, he knew a lot about the printer already because it produced promotional materials for Volkswagen.

Nevertheless, before he began his new printing job, he had to stifle misgivings. This time, however, his research prepared him well. He stepped into the work as though he had been doing it for years, which is the reaction that every new job should ideally impart. The stress proved, or at least seemed, less.

The Factor of Fear

Al coped more successfully the second time with his feelings of anticlimax that had troubled him with the automaker. He had been particularly disturbed because such sensations gradually evolved into fears—a fear of failure and a fear that he suffered some psychological malady.

Change is not the only factor that impinges on job severance. Mergers, business failures, and office politics can also affect us. Yet, we can control one factor that also often enters the job picture as a Siamese twin of change. It's fear.

Case Study: Ted, Age 58

Ted performed well as a salesman of business forms and supplies, but fears dogged him. He often felt he should try for the administrative side of marketing, but had never asked for such a move. With good reason, he believed his employer valued him too highly on the line to give him a chance to achieve that ambition. At other times, he felt he lacked talent for anything but "peddling." Despite the fact that he knew he was superb as a salesman, he repeatedly fell into such depressive bouts that one finally forced him to resign.

Is Ted mentally disturbed? Perhaps, but so are a lot of us. One in eight Americans will suffer a bout of depression serious enough to warrant psychiatric help during his or her lifetime. A particularly vulnerable age is during the senior years.

According to the National Institute of Mental Health, 125,000 Americans are hospitalized each year with depression, while another 200,000 are treated on psychiatrists' couches or in physicians' offices. The suicide rate among seniors is climbing, after an earlier decline. From 1948 to 1981, improvements in medical care and pension programs helped reduce the suicide rate of the elderly to 17.1 per 100,000 people from 28.1. Now, the rate is rising again, climbing to 18.3 in 1982 and 19.2 in 1983. Indications are that the rate has continued to rise. White men are most at risk, largely because of money problems and feelings of uselessness.

Depression has been diagnosed by physicians at least since Hippocrates. The disorder has afflicted many notable figures—Winston

Churchill, Abraham Lincoln, Vincent van Gogh, and numerous others. Studies of those who patronize free psychiatric clinics indicate that depression knows no boundaries set by talent or economics. It hits anyone.

Depression's irony lies in the fact that it drives some victims to prodigious effort and achievement. When Ted suffered periodic attacks, usually caused by a new selling rival whom he feared would supplant him as the top salesman, he would frequently accomplish his best performances. Yet, these manic periods also left him tired and apathetic about his family and other responsibilities.

Finally, his family persuaded him to see a psychiatrist. The doctor gave him this advice: "Get your former employer or someone else to give you a trial in marketing administration. At the worst, they can say no. Then, you can try for a job elsewhere. You must answer this question: Can I make it as a manager? If you know you can, fine. If you learn you cannot, you know you can still be an excellent salesman. You have to learn at last what you can do. When you make that discovery, then you can accept your limitations."

Ted's former employer had no administrative opening, so he went to a competitor who was delighted to take him on. The result? Ted handled marketing management to the new employer's satisfaction, but the job bored him. His new employer was even more delighted to send him back on the road where he never again suffered bouts with depression.

Unknowingly, both Ted and Al heeded Madame Marie Curie's advice, "Nothing in life is to be feared. It is only to be understood." Ted finally understood where his true vocation lay. Al understood what had happened to him at Volkswagen.

22

You Can Flourish After 50

A mother heard the alarm clock in her son's bedroom. When breakfast was ready and there was still no sign of him, she went to his room.

"Come on," she scolded. "You have to go to school."

"I'm not going, and I'll give you two reasons: I hate school, and I hate the teachers."

"I'll give *you* two reasons you're going to school: You're 51 years old, and you're the principal."

That story may be apocryphal, but it illustrates our point: You can fall into the slough of despondency in your senior years, or you or someone can boot you out of it. Hopefully, you'll do it to yourself, with a little help from demographics.

When Seniors Will Rule

Throughout most of history, seniors have controlled the family and the land. Beginning with the start of the nineteenth century, though, youth has enjoyed a gradual ascendency, largely because of demographics. Nevertheless, between now and the end of the century, the baby boom will be preparing us for the reign of the old. By the year 2000, one person in eight will be at least 65 years of age. This group is growing at a rate twice the growth rate of the population as a whole. With this turnabout will come what will amount to the restoration of the power and position of the elderly in society.

The ancient Sardinians pushed their elders off cliffs when they were no longer useful. We do not destroy the elderly; we ignore them. The media, especially television, habitually portray seniors as eccentric, stubborn, nonsexual and even silly. The height of disrespect comes with such statements as, "Never trust anyone over 30." Such nonsensical attitudes reached their apogee in the 1960s when youth probably had its last fling.

Demographics now favor the seniors, but gradually. Let's hope we handle our ascendency with better sense.

New hope, energy and enthusiasm can come for seniors in many ways, including the right new job. You don't even have to work for pay. If you can afford it, voluntary positions may be rewarding. So can part-time activity, job-sharing and flextime. Some 29 percent of employers surveyed by the Administrative Management Society now offer flextime, up from 22 percent in 1981 and 15 percent in 1977. Job-sharing is also more common, but the gain is not as dramatic as for flextime. The 40-hour, five-day week remains the norm.

The only essential is this: To do something that you believe is worthwhile and gets you out of yourself.

New Breed of Volunteers

An effort in Minneapolis to place retired professionals in challenging volunteer positions is so successful that some agencies have more people than they need.

"We have to restrict the number of volunteers," says Mary Wiser, coordinator of volunteer services at Courage Center for the physically disabled.

This is the result of corporate efforts to help retiring employees find high-level volunteer jobs that make use of their skills and experience.

In 1977, the Junior League of Minneapolis created the project VIE (French for "life") to encourage retirees to do volunteer work. Two years later, Honeywell Inc. asked for the group's help in setting up its own program for retiring Honeywell employees. Out of the cooperative effort came the corporate retiree volunteer program.

Elmer Frykman, a retired Honeywell field engineer and volunteer manager of the company's retiree program since its inception, describes how it works. "Before people retire, we invite them to attend a seminar. We introduce the program . . . Then we wait three to six months before we contact them again."

If a new retiree is interested, he's scheduled for a two-hour interview during which he reveals interests, skills and talents. A researcher then goes to work matching the volunteer with an appropriate position at one of the area's many agencies that keep the program informed of its needs.

Since Honeywell initiated its program, 21 other companies have either followed its lead or plan to. Representatives from the various groups meet once a month under the sponsorship of VIE to share ideas.

At Honeywell—the oldest and largest of the programs—retiring union workers, office workers and administrators sign up in equal numbers. In 1986, six retired vice-presidents were participating.

"Normally, a retired executive vice-president isn't going to go down and volunteer at the local YMCA," says Harlan Cleveland, VIE advisory board member and dean of the Hubert H. Humphrey Institute of Public Affairs. "There's a difference in culture, particularly for men who've held high positions. Volunteering, to them, is something their wives do. But if the company says, 'the Blue Cross needs someone to go in as an executive officer, they need help,' it gives volunteering a respectability."

Retired corporate volunteers enjoy their work for many of the same reasons other volunteers do—they feel useful. Finding their work through their old employers offers an additional benefit—the chance to maintain relationships with former coworkers.

Florida even has a "volunteer service credit" program whereby a record is kept of the services rendered the elderly by other seniors who are then entitled to certain free volunteer services should *they* become in need.

Where Do You Fit?

Whether you work for pay or the fun of it, you should know where you fit.

Signal, a multisponsor business service which measures and tracks work values, attitudes, needs and expectations within the labor force, has summarized the five groups comprising the labor force today. Each group has a unique set of work-related characteristics. You're probably familiar with three of them because they represent long-standing, "traditional" values:

1) The Uncommitted
2) The Job-Oriented
3) The Work-Oriented

The remaining two groups, in contrast, reflect a much greater degree of social values that have emerged since World War II. Signal calls these:

4) The Fulfillment Seekers
5) The Money Seekers

The Uncommitted (also known as Adversaries) have "turned off" value attitudes, resulting in strong adversary roles vis-à-vis management. Their key objective is maximum earnings in return for minimal commitment.

This group consists basically of blue-collar males with strong union representation.

The most downscale, nonwhite, blue-collar group is the Job-Oriented Worker. Here the job is the thing. This group of workers has the highest union membership, is the most ritualistic and least innovative of all the worker groups. These people are most concerned about job security, yet are not advancement-motivated and have a relatively weak commitment to their work. Their earnings objectives fall largely in line with their commitment level. Having a job (almost any job) is *the* most important thing.

The third of the familiar work value groups, The Work-Oriented, are also known as Horatio Algers. You may belong here because this group consists of the oldest and best-educated workers. It contains the largest proportion of professionals, managers and supervisors and thus is the most interested in improving and sustaining work and career skills. These people are the most strongly committed to their jobs, and are the least motivated to maximize earnings via unappealing trade-offs. Although Horatio Algers are not particularly interested in increased responsibility and authority for pay reasons, they do respond to work-related incentives. They are much more committed to their careers than to their employers and thus often have worked for several different bosses during their adult lives.

You may find yourself more at home with the Fulfillment Seekers, the first of the two new emerging value groups. This group is relatively upscale, the least tolerant of traditional formal job structures, the most innovative, and the least ritualistic. These workers respond best to challenging work. They are most interested in advancement, but maximum earnings are not a major objective. They feel that money is not a substitute for fulfillment. They keep a positive attitude, develop the inspirational side of their lives, and use their time constructively. Unfortunately, evidence shows only a moderate level of job satisfaction for this group, so employers may mistakenly dismiss them as mere job-hoppers.

The fifth group, the Money Seekers (or the Full, Rich Lifers), leads the others in its proportions of women, whites, white-collar and sales people. They have a relatively low union membership and only a moderate level of job commitment. Their primary objective is increased responsibility that will maximize their income. Money is important primarily for lifestyle reasons. Therefore, there's a tendency to "hold back" until they achieve the objectives of a fine and well-furnished home, good clothes, one or more expensive cars, considerable restaurant dining, and expensive vacations.

Why should you care to what group you belong? Because employers increasingly care. Remember that Signal is supported by many employers, and so its findings and conclusions are percolating well beyond the supporting members. Employers look primarily for participants in the third and fourth groups.

If you decide you qualify for either, fine. If you decide otherwise, either try to modify your proclivities or downplay them in job interviews.

More importantly, you have one of the greatest opportunities that ever existed to restructure your life more along lines that you believe will be more appropriate for you. You are moving from a producing economy through a service economy into an information economy. You are also leaving behind the culture wherein an organization is introverted and focuses on internal activities; you are moving into a much more open culture that focuses on the environment, seeks out opportunities, and actively tries to shape the environment. In any event, you have no choice but to look forward. You cannot look at your life through a rearview mirror. Why concentrate on the Great Depression? The year 2000 is much nearer than the 1930s.

Ten Principles To Guide You

Here are standards to follow in pursuing your new career to the year 2000 or beyond:

- Get into something that challenges you, so that you feel useful, productive, fulfilled and successful.
- Set goals and timetables; do not drift, because people who don't know where they're going will end up nowhere.
- Evaluate your performance regularly; if you don't trust your own objectivity, enlist that of your spouse or of someone else whom you trust.
- Reward yourself for good performance with a good dinner, a long weekend away, or even an extra vacation for noteworthy accomplishments. *Everyone* needs positive feedback.
- Punish yourself for poor or mediocre performance— withhold that celebration.
- Take corrective action when things go wrong and evaluate future performances even more carefully.
- Be open with people and encourage them to express their ideas and opinions on your new career.

- Act without delay on ideas and suggestions that have merit and let the contributors know you have done so.
- Expect excellence from yourself, nothing less.
- Keep trying.

Winston Churchill, not renowned for brevity, once gave a speech of only five words. To a class of airmen who had just completed their training, he said, "Never . . . never . . . never give up."

The Top Four Priorities of Employers

Employers have four key concerns, according to the Yankelovich, Skelly and White study for AARP—productivity, cost, technology, and competitiveness. Ignore these at your peril in your jobhunting.

You have a leg up on the productivity issues—attendance, commitment to quality and solid performance—because employers generally rate seniors high on these. Seniors rate almost as well on costs, but sharply lower in technology and competitiveness.

For example, 32 percent of the respondents saw new technology as vital for their operations, but only 10 percent of them rated older workers as excellent or very good in adapting to it. The issue of adaptation to technology suggests a broader set of issues related to what YSW calls competitiveness, criteria such as flexibility, initiative, aggressiveness, the ability to learn new skills quickly, and creativity.

Unlike productivity and cost, the issues of technology and competitiveness constitute an area of vulnerability for seniors, particularly among larger employers. Regardless of their accuracy, these negative perceptions stand in the way of the older worker.

So, you must concentrate on turning those negatives into positives during the course of your interviews with prospective employers. If you can honestly do so, cite examples of how you have incorporated new technological developments, showed flexibility, taken the initiative, learned new skills quickly, and applied creativity to your work. These can include your use of computers, your adaptation of new methods, and your initiative in finding new uses for a product or new ways of doing things.

The Good News

The concept of "fairness" remains one of the fundamental values in America, although its meaning shifts with time. What does it mean for the senior in today's climate?

On the one hand, it means systematic unfair treatment of the older worker—technological displacement with a disproportionate impact on seniors, forced retirement, or denial of training or promotion opportunities. Although these practices are illegal, they nevertheless happen.

On the other hand, a new consensus of reciprocity is developing in which the organization rewards those employees, regardless of age, whose contributions most advance its objectives. "The development of a framework for reciprocity between American business and the older worker would seem to be a critical prerequisite for ensuring continued employment options for the older employee," says YSW.

"Such a framework must take into account four important areas of changing attitudes brought to light by the survey . . . continuation of employment, utilization of special skills, entitlements and self reliance."

The respondents to the YSW survey recognize that the recent trend toward lower labor participation for the 50-plus individual may be waning, and that the bloom may be off the rose of early retirement in the minds of many. Eighty-one percent agree that most of today's older employees would prefer to continue working as long as possible. Nevertheless, almost two-thirds of all workers retire before age 65. The average male in the decade of the 1980s is spending 20 percent of his lifetime in retirement, vs. only 3 percent at the turn of the century.

Respondents also see a decline in the belief in entitlements—special treatment for longer service employees—which flowered in the 1960s and 1970s. In today's climate, employees must be judged according to their continuing ability to contribute to the organization's goals; in other words, in their self-reliance to keep their abilities honed and up-to-date.

"If older employees should not automatically receive favored treatment," continues YSW, "there is wide recognition they do have the ability to make a unique contribution. Overwhelmingly, the [respondents] agreed that elder workers have special skills for tackling new problems. By implication, therefore, a framework for reciprocity should provide opportunities for the skills and abilities of older employees to be utilized."

Another important finding emerging from the YSW survey data is that, from the respondents' point of view, seniors "hold the keys to their own destinies. Older workers are believed to be their own most effective advocates by far, as well as their own most potent obstacles."

YSW adds, "The generally positive attitudes toward older workers held by (respondents), the vigorous generation now reaching 50-plus status, and expected acute labor shortages all point to the desirability of fully utilizing the older worker. We believe that with cooperation and effort, the attainment of this goal is within the reach of American business and its older employees."

The Essence of Jobhunting

To jobhunt successfully after 50, three things are essential. First, be acutely aware of problems. Second, never give up in looking for answers to those problems. Third, improve and use the gifts you have and forget the skills you lack.

Millions of people go through their working lives as square pegs in round holes. Some never realize they are in the wrong jobs. Others lack the discipline to make changes even though they may be aware of the misapplication of their skills. Still others, perhaps the most fortunate, are fired and are forced to jobhunt. One particularly perceptive boss fired this author twice. Whether the severance is called early retirement, "leaving to pursue private interests," or some other euphemistic phrase, the discharge is usually traumatic. It need not be the end of the world, though. Indeed, it can become the beginning of a new world for you.

Consider an analogy. Forest Rangers, Boy Scouts and other outdoor people give these four rules for survival if you get lost in the wilderness:

- Stay calm. Panic accounts for 90 percent of the problem.
- Stay in one place. Don't go off in all directions. You will get nowhere.
- Keep dry and warm.
- Have the will to live.

These four rules can also be applied to survival in the "wilderness" of jobhunting:

- *Stay calm.* Panic will avail you nothing. The experience can benefit you.
- *Appraise the situation with hard thought.* Where and how do you want to spend the rest of your working life?
- *Hang on to your fundamental principles and convictions* no matter what goes on around you. Such principles and convictions—honesty, compassion, the need for self-development and others—never change.
- *Have the will to survive.* Listless resignation to unemployment will corrode you. Seek to control your working situation. Don't let joblessness control you.

When you follow such prescriptions, you can flourish to an extent you may have never before experienced in your life.

BIBLIOGRAPHY

"Abolishing Mandatory Retirement," U.S. House of Representatives Select Committee on Aging, Washington: U.S. Government Printing Office, 1981.

Achenbaum, W. Andrew, et al., *The Aging Society,* New York: *Daedalus,* Journal of American Academy of Arts and Sciences, Winter 1986.

The Age Discrimination Study, U.S. Commission on Civil Rights, Washington: U.S. Government Printing Office, 1977-79.

Aging in the Eighties, study for National Council on the Aging by Louis Harris & Associates, 1981.

Alewine, T.C., "Performance Appraisals & Performance Standards," *Personnel Journal,* March 1982.

Alternatives To Retirement, hearings before the Subcommittee on Retirement Income and Employment of Select Committee on Aging, Washington: U.S. Government Printing Office, 1977.

American Attitudes Toward Pensions and Retirement, Study of, New York: Johnson & Higgins, 1979.

Ansberry, Clare, "Broken Promises: Retirees Learn To Live Without Pension Benefits," *Wall Street Journal,* New York: Dow Jones Co., Aug. 29, 1986.

Barron, M., *The Aging American,* New York: Crowell, 1961.

Becker, Gary S., "What Really Hurts the Job Market for Older Workers," *Business Week,* New York: McGraw-Hill, Inc., Oct. 16, 1986.

Bennett, Amanda, "Laid-Off Managers of Big Firms Increasingly Move to Small Ones . . . And Then Often Consult For Their Ex-Employers," *Wall Street Journal,* New York: Dow Jones & Co., July 25, 1986.

——, "Middle Managers Face Job Squeeze As Cutbacks and Caution Spread," *Wall Street Journal,* New York: Dow Jones & Co., April 25, 1986.

—— and Sease, Douglas R., "To Reduce Their Costs, Big Companies Lay Off White-Collar Workers," *Wall Street Journal,* New York: Dow Jones & Co., May 22, 1986.

Boll, Carl R., *Executive Jobs Unlimited,* New York: Macmillan, 1979.

Bolles, Richard N., *The Three Boxes of Life,* Berkeley: Ten Speed Press, 1978.

——, *What Color Is Your Parachute?,* Berkeley: Ten Speed Press, 1986.

Branson, Robert M., *Coping with Difficult People,* Garden City, N.Y.: Anchor/Doubleday, 1981.

Buckley, Joseph C., *The Retirement Handbook*, New York: Harper & Row, 1977.

Butler, Robert N., *Why Survive? Being Old in America*, New York: Harper & Row, 1976.

Cagan, Maxwell S., *Medianetics, Dynamic Living in Your Middle Years*, Los Angeles: Douglas-West Publishers, 1975.

Coleman, Vernon, *Everything You Want To Know About Aging*, London: Gordon & Cremonisi, 1976.

Comfort, Alex, *A Good Age*, New York: Simon & Schuster, 1976.

Cook, D.D., "Older Workers: A Resource We'll Need," *Industry Week*, July 7, 1980.

Cowley, Malcolm, *The View from 80*, New York: Viking/Penguin, 1982.

Davis, Thomas F., *Toward a National Policy on Older Workers*, study for Federal Council on the Aging, 1980.

De Beauvoir, Simone, *The Coming of Age*, New York: G.P. Putnam, 1972.

Deferred Retirement: Los Angeles Case Study, Los Angeles: Andrus Gerontology Center, University of Southern California, 1981.

Deuterman, W.V., "Voluntary Part-Time Workers," *Monthly Labor Review*, 1978, 101 (6), 3-10.

Dobrzynski, Judith H. and Berger, Joan, "The Biggest Restructuring in History Winds Down, What Did It Mean?" *Business Week*, New York: McGraw-Hill, Inc., Jan.12, 1987.

Drucker, Peter, *The Changing World of the Executive*, New York: Harper & Row, 1984.

————, *The Unseen Revolution: How Pension Fund Socialism Came to the U.S.*, New York: Harper & Row, 1976.

The Economics of Aging, a National Journal conference proceeding, Washington: Government Research Corp., 1979.

Employment Security in a Free Economy, a Work in America Institute policy study, New York: Pergamon Press, 1984.

Fanning, Deirdre, "Employer Beware," *Forbes*, New York: Forbes Inc., May 18, 1987.

Fischer, David H., *Growing Old in America*, New York: Oxford University Press, 1977.

Foner, Anne and Schwab, Karen, *Aging and Retirement*, Monterey, CA: Brooks-Cole, 1981.

Fromme, Allan, *Life After Work*, Glenview, IL: Scott, Foresman and American Association of Retired Persons, 1984.

Galante, Steven P., "Corporate Executives Quitting To Buy Rust Belt Businesses," *Wall Street Journal*, New York: Dow Jones & Co., April 28, 1986.

George, Linda K., *Role Transitions in Later Life*, Durham, N.C.: Duke University Medical Center, 1982.

Gottschalk, Jr., Earl C., "After years of Decline, Suicide Rate Is Rising Among Elderly in U.S.," *Wall Street Journal*, New York: Down Jones & Co., July 29, 1986.

Greco, Ben, *How To Get the Job That's Right for You,* Homewood, IL: Dow Jones-Irwin, 1980.

Hallowell, Christopher, *Growing Old, Staying Young,* New York: William Morrow, 1985.

Harris, Diana K. and Cole, William E., *Sociology in Aging,* New York: Garland, 1985.

Harris, I., *The Myth and Reality of Aging in America,* Washington: National Council on the Aging, 1975.

Hess, Beth B. and Markson, Elizabeth W., *Aging Statistics,* New York: Macmillan, 1980.

Humple, Carol S. and Lyons, Morgan, *Management and The Older Work Force,* New York: American Management Associations' Publications Division, 1983.

Hymowitz, Carol, and Schellhardt, Timothy D., "After the Ax: Formula Aims To Predict Length of a Fired Manager's Job Search," *Wall Street Journal,* New York: Dow Jones & Co., Oct. 20, 1986.

Incentives for Hiring Older Workers, Los Angeles: Andrus Gerontology Center, University of Southern California, 1983.

Jacobson, Beverly, *Young Programs for Older Workers,* New York: Van Nostrand Reinhold, 1980.

Jorgensen, James, *The Graying of America: Retirement and Why You Can't Afford It,* New York: McGraw-Hill, 1981.

Jud, R., *The Retirement Decision: How American Managers View Their Prospects,* New York: Amacom, 1981.

Kieffer, Jarold A., ed., *Older Americans: An Untapped Resource,* report on proceedings of the White House Conference on Aging, New York: Academy of Educational Development, 1979.

Kieschnick, W.F., "Aging in America: A Business View," paper presented at the annual meeting of the Western Gerontological Society, San Diego, March 1-3, 1982.

Levin, Jack and William C., *Ageism: Prejudice and Discrimination Against the Elderly,* Boston: Wadsworth Publishing, 1979.

Lowen, Walter, *How and When to Change Your Job Successfully,* New York: Simon & Schuster, 1954.

Magnusson, Paul, "U.S. Gaining Jobs Despite Deficit," *Detroit Free Press,* Detroit: Detroit FP Co., April 27, 1987.

"Mandatory Retirement," Select Committee on Aging, Washington: U.S. Government Printing Office, 1977.

McKay, Jim, "Along with 30-year Careers, Corporate Loyalty is Waning," *Pittsburgh Post-Gazette,* Pittsburgh: PG Publishing Co., March 24, 1987.

Melloan, George, "Temps Now Take a Turn at Executive Jobs," *Wall Street Journal,* New York: Dow Jones & Co., May 19, 1987.

Miller, J.M., *Innovation in Working Patterns,* Washington: Communications Workers of America and German Marshall Fund of the U.S., 1978.

Morgan, John C., *Becoming Old—An Introduction to Social Gerontology*, New York: Springer Publications, 1979.

Morganthaler, Eric, "Although the Scarcities Are Fewer, Some Jobs Still Are in Short Supply," *Wall Street Journal*, New York: Dow Jones & Co., October 7, 1986.

Myers, Albert and Andersen, Christopher P., *Success Over Sixty*, New York: Summit Books, 1984.

Nollen, S.D., *Alternative Work Schedules, Parts 2 and 3*, New York: American Management Associations, 1978.

Odell, Charles E. and Louise M., *You and the Senior Boom*, Hicksville, N.Y.: Exposition Press, 1980.

"The Older American Worker," report of the Secretary of Labor to Congress, Washington: U.S. Government Printing Office, 1965.

Olmstead, B., *Working Less But Enjoying It More, New Ways To Work*, Palo Alto: Stanford University, 1978.

Patton, A., "The Coming Promotion Slowdown," *Harvard Business Review*, March-April 1981.

Pearson, Durk and Shaw, Sandy, *Life Extension*, New York: Warner Books, 1982.

———, *Life Extension Companion*, New York: Warner Books, 1983.

Pellegrini, Mike, "Older Workers Find More Jobs," *Pittsburgh Post-Gazette*, Pittsburgh: PG Publishing Co., Feb. 11, 1986.

Piper, Alan and Bronte, Lydia, eds., *Our Aging Society—Paradox and Promise*, New York: Norton, 1986.

Purcell, D.E., "Labor Supply: The Challenge of the 1980s and 1990s," testimony before the U.S. House of Representatives Select Committee on Aging, Oct. 28, 1982.

Ragan, Pauline K., ed., *Work and Retirement*, Los Angeles: Andrus Gerontology Center, University of Southern California, 1980.

Reibstein, Larry, "Many Hurdles, Old and New, Keep Black Managers Out of Top Jobs," *Wall Street Journal*, New York: Dow Jones & Co., July 10, 1986.

———, "After Takeover: More Managers Run, or Are Pushed, Out the Door," *Wall Street Journal*, New York: Dow Jones & Co., Nov. 15, 1985.

———, "More Companies Use Free-Lancers To Avoid Cost, Trauma of Layoffs," *Wall Street Journal*, New York: Dow Jones & Co., April 18, 1986.

Rich, Bennett M. and Baum, Martha, *The Aging: A Guide to Public Policy*, Pittsburgh: University of Pittsburgh, 1984.

Rix, Sara E., ed., *The Future of Older Workers in America*, White Plains, N.Y.: Work in America Institute, 1984.

Robbins, Paula I., *Successful Midlife Career Change*, New York: Amacom, 1978.

Robinson, P.K., "Soon We'll Need the Older Worker," *Los Angeles Times*, April 6, 1982.

Rones, P.L., "Older Men—The Choice Between Work and Retirement," Washington: Bureau of National Affairs, November 1978.

Rosenbloom, M., "Jobs for Older Workers in U.S. Industry," Washington: Department of Commerce, September 1977.

Schul, J.H., *Economics of Mandatory Retirement*, New York: Industrial Gerontology, 1974.

Schwartz, Joseph, *Don't Ever Retire, But Do It Early and Often*, Rockville Centre, N.Y.: Farnsworth Publishing Co., 1979.

Semerad, Roger D., "2000: Labor Shortage Looms," *Industry Week*, Cleveland: Penton Publishing Co., Feb. 9, 1987.

Sheppard, H.L., *R&D Strategy on Employment-Related Problems of Older Workers*, Washington: American Institutes for Research, 1978.

———, *Toward an Industrial Gerontology*, New York: Schenkman Pub., 1970.

——— and Rix, Sara E., *The Graying of Working America*, New York: Free Press, 1976.

Siconolfi, Michael, "Recruiters Alert To 'Flag' Traits of Job Seekers," *Wall Street Journal*, New York, Dow Jones & Co., Dec. 26, 1986.

Skinner, B.F., *Behaviorism*, New York: Vintage Books, 1976.

Smith, Bert Kruger, *Aging in America*, Boston: Beacon Press, 1973.

Snelling, Robert O., Jr., *The Opportunity Explosion*, New York: Macmillan, 1969.

Stoddard, Gerard, "Surveying the Executive Recruitment Jungle," *Wall Street Journal*, New York, Dow Jones & Co., May 4, 1987.

Tibbits, Clark and Donahue, Wilma, eds. *Aging in Today's Society*, Englewood Cliffs, N.J.: Prentice-Hall, 1960.

Toffler, Alvin, *Future Shock*, New York: Random House, 1970.

———, *The Third Wave*, New York: Random House, 1980.

Ture, N.B., *The Future of Private Pension Plans*, Washington: American Institute for Public Policy Research, 1976.

Walker, James W. and Lazer, Harriet L., *The End of Mandatory Retirement*, New York: Wiley, 1978.

Wallfesh, H.M., *The Effects of Extending Mandatory Retirement*, New York: Amacom, 1978.

Weaver, Peter, *Strategies for the Second Half of Your Life*, New York: Franklin Watts, 1980.

Willing, Jules, Z., *The Lively Mind*, New York: William Morrow, 1982.

———, *The Reality of Retirement*, New York: William Morrow, 1982.

Woods, Michael, "America's Centenarian Population Could Mushroom Past 1 Million by 2050," *Pittsburgh Post-Gazette*, Pittsburgh: PG Publishing Co., February 16, 1986.

Summary of Aids for Getting a Job After 50